英語教師のための
Intonation in Context 読本

伊達 民和　著

校閲　Bill Rockenbach・牧 晋也

朗読　Bill Rockenbach・Warren Wilson

大阪教育図書

目　　次

序　論

　英語教育において、イントネーションは全く stepchild であると言わざるを
得ない。大学の英語教職課程においても、イントネーションの指導に割かれる
時間数と労力が圧倒的に少ない。そのための授業時間が足りない。

　元高校の英語教師（15 年）であった経験から言えば、授業中にモデル朗読
するときに最も気を遣うのはイントネーションである。どの教師も前もって教
科書準拠の voice actor/actress の音声を聴いて練習していく。ところが、モデ
ル音声の中に、「不可解な」イントネーションが聞かれることがよくある。例
えば、叙述文（statement）の冒頭、中ほど、末尾の位置で上昇調または下降
上昇で発音されている。それは、談話の状況や文脈を反映したイントネーショ
ンである。明らかに、そこには何らかの intonational meanings が込められて
いる。率直に言って、大部分の教師には、どのような intonational meanings
であるのかが理解できないだろう。嘆かわしいことに、頼みの綱となるべき指
導書にはいつも解説が欠落している。イントネーションについて、ALT に尋ね
るのは愚の骨頂である。そもそもほとんど無意識で発しているイントネーショ
ンについて、彼らは日本人が理解できる言語で説明することはできない（感想
は述べてくれることはあるが）。教師は、仕方なく――自信なく――、授業での
モデル朗読ではネーテイブスピーカーの物まねするしかない。また、前著の第
2 章の冒頭で述べたように、英語会話能力と朗読力は、全く別の話である。英
語が流暢な人であっても、朗読するとき、intonation in context への配慮が足ら
ないことがよく見受けられる。これは、GDM 英語教授法研究会が主催する「英
語発音ワークショップ」から得た知見である。

　以上の状況を念頭において本書では、intonation in context を解説している。ま
た、私の解説を裏付ける専門的な知見も豊富に原文のままで紹介している。なお、

本書は、前著『教室の
音声学読本――英語の
イントネーションの理
解に向けて』（2019）の
続編である。出版年の
12 月 に Asahi Weekly
誌で紹介された。

書籍
「教室の音声学読本」
（提供：大阪教育図書）

　副題は「英語のイントネーションの理解に向けて」とあ
るように、日本でも珍しい、英語のイントネーションについ
ての専門書。概略から日常的に使うフレーズまで幅広く
取り上げている。教材 CD 1 枚付き。著者は、プール学院
大学で教授を務めた伊達民和さん。3 人にプレゼント。

※ 応募方法を参照し、「音声学」係まで。当選者の発表は、賞品の発送をもってかえさせていただき
ます。

　本書の出版に際し、Paul Tench から読者に向けて文章が寄せられた。Tench からは、過去 20 年以上にも亘って、主として SUPRAS（a closed international e-mail list of phoneticians）を通して多くの教示を得てきた。その一端を原文のまま本書の各所で紹介している。

The teaching of intonation in English lessons is really very important. Intonation accompanies everything we say in whatever language we speak or learn; you cannot even greet people without intonation! You can be quite formal and say "Good morning" with a falling tone, or you can sound more interested in the other person's feelings by saying it with a rising tone. Similarly, you can say "Good bye" with the usual rising tone, because you are being friendly, but if you say it with a falling tone, it would sound quite rude, because it sounds as if you want them to go immediately!

Intonation can be taught right from the beginning of a language course; and at first it is best learnt by imitating a good teacher or native speaker of the language. But different meanings of intonation can also be taught early on, like the different ways of greeting and saying farewell. Because intonation with its different forms and meanings can be described, it can therefore also be taught and learnt, and a syllabus can be constructed for a whole language learning programme.

English relies a good deal on intonation to communicate a host of different meanings. Falling and rising tones, and also falling-rising tones, and high falls and low falls and so on "say" a lot. Furthermore, where a tone comes in a message "says" what the focus of the message is and what a speaker thinks you know – this is called tonicity, and it can vary quite considerably. Also, a speaker can divide up their message in different ways in organizing the sequence of units of intonation – this is called tonality; here is a very telling example:

　| he didn't \go | because he \loved her!

(*the reason why he didn't go is given*)

|he didn't go because he ∨ <u>loved</u> her |

(*there was another reason why he did go!*)

So, learners should do their best to acquire good intonation as well as grammar, vocabulary and the pronunciation of words.

Wishing you every success with your new book.

yours sincerely,

Paul

注：英語イントネーションに関する著書：*The Roles of Intonation in English Discourse* (1990) & *The Intonation Systems of English* (1996)

英語イントネーションに関する論文や書物を読んでいると、*system* という用語をよく目にする。この場合、system とは、「体系」というよりも、「選択肢」（a limited number of choices, a fixed number of options）のことである。例えば、名詞には、単数形か複数形かの options があり、動詞には、様々な時制の options がある。イントネーションにも、幾つかの options がある。O'Connor & Arnold, *Intonation of Colloquial English* には、1. Intonation is significant; 2. Intonation is systematic; 3. Intonation is characteristic. とある。また、Tench の著書には *The Intonation Systems of English* がある。Wells の *Sounds Interesting*（2014:106）には、以下のような記述がある。

A student from Argentina wanted to know how to account for the word 'system' in the expression 'the English intonation system'. 'I know Brazil talks about the system of English intonation,' she wrote, 'but why is it called a system?'

Intonation is systematic, or a system, in the technical sense of having a finite set of either/or options (e.g. a syllable either is, or is not, prominent).

イントネーションは、特定の（固有の）意味を伝えるというよりも、むしろ文脈とか場面によっては、かなり違った意味合いを伝える。しかし、ある意味を伝えるには絶対に下降調を用いなければならないことがある。同じように、上昇調でなければならないこともある。従って、どのイントネーションを使ってもよいのではなく、文脈がどのイントネーションを使うべきかを決定する。

授業でイントネーションを教える場合に、文の種類とイントネーションとの

間に一定の関係があれば便利であるが、実際には確実と言える関係は存在しない。しかし、イントネーションに関して最も標準的なパタンがあることは認められている。それを英語教育の現場で教えることには意味がある。

　Crystal（1969）の収集したデータによると、音調の割合（%）は、下降調（51.2）、上昇調（20.8）、下降上昇調（8.5）、下降調＋上昇調（7.7）、上昇下降調（5.2）、平坦調（4.9）、上昇調＋下降調（1.7）の順になっている。

　　　注：データとは Crystal, D. *Prosodic Systems and Intonation in English*（1969:
　　　　 225）

　厳密に言えば、下降調には、高下降調と低下降調がある。同様にして、高上昇調と低上昇調がある。高下降調は、声域の高い位置から低い位置まで下降する幅が広い。低下降調は、声域の中間、または、それよりも少し低い位置から下降が始まる。このような差異は、通例、感情移入の程度の違いであって、大まかに言うと、高下降調は、より強い感情（more involved）を伝えるのに対して、低下降調は無関心、そっけなさ、冷静さ、不満や怒りなどを伝える。高上昇調の場合、声域の比較的高い位置に核強勢があり、そこを起点として上昇が始まる。低上昇調は、声域の比較的低い位置に核強勢があり、そこから中間あたりまで上昇する。

　高いイントネーションと低いイントネーションとの間には用法と意味の区別があることを重視する研究者もいれば、そうでもない研究者もいる。例えば、本書で度々引用する Ladd は、両者の区別を全くしていない。高イントネーションと低イントネーションには共通した意味があるからである。Wells は、次のように言う。"In this chapter we do not distinguish between them, but treat them all as just falls. There is also something in common in all the various kinds of non-falling tone…"（*English Intonation* 2006: 15）

　本書では、一部を除いて、高低の違いを論じていない。また、音声学の教本には、核強勢のみならず、前頭部（prehead）や頭部（head）を考慮に入れ、細かく分類している記述があるが、教育的には、核強勢の配置に関する知識だけで十分である。

　イントネーションの働きの1つは、話者の心的態度を表現することである。大部分の日本人の認識には、下降調と上昇調の2つしか存在していないように思える。とかく、日本人はどんな文であれ、それがピリオドで終わっておれば下降調で言う。時には、下降上昇調とか下降調＋上昇調で言うほうが適切で

あるという認識がない。それというのも、日本語には、下降上昇調は存在しないからである。郡 史郎『日本語のイントネーション』（2020: 135）によれば、末尾のイントネーションには 6 種類あり、それらは、疑問型上昇調、強調型上昇調、平坦調、上昇下降調、急下降調、無イントネーションである。留意するべきは、下降上昇調が含まれていないことである。下降上昇調は、英語の授業でも教わることはないだろう。平叙文（statement）や疑問詞疑問文をいつも下降調で言っていると、聞き手に誤解されることもある。日本人が聞き手の場合、相手が statement を上昇調、または、下降上昇調で発したとき、その真意を十分に汲みとれない。

　本書の「課題」の中で取り上げたイントネーションの型は、私がこれまで映画や TV ドラマの中で何度も耳にし、研究書に照らし合わせて確認し、まとめたものである。そのためには、ネーテイブスピーカーの「生の声」も参考にした。文献にある用例を参考にするだけでは物足りない。幸い、私は、SUPRAS に所属しており、その都度、一斉配信して会員にコメントを求めてきた。彼らの「生の声」は非常に貴重であった。特定のイントネーションについて、いろいろな示唆に富むコメントが返信されてきた。また、SUPRAS 以外にも、Paul Tench や Rebecca Dauer, John Wells, Jack Windsor Lewis 諸氏から個人的に度々教示を受けた。

　英語イントネーションを調べるには、いろいろな方法があるだろうが、私は、もっぱら映画と TV sit-coms、また、Oxford University Press (OUP) や Cambridge University Press (CUP) から出ているリスニング教材をコーパスとしてきた。かつて、SUPRAS の初代 "house keeper" で 2001 年以来の友人でもある Judy Gilbert（*Clear Speech*, CUP の著者）から激励のメールをもらったことがある。

> Your use of movies as a "corpus" is very interesting to me. I consider movies an important reflection of culture. Also, more recent movies have used more realistic language. So your project is quite original and should be very useful for serious students of English.　(2001. 9. 21)

　　Clear Speech（4th Edition）の *Acknowledgments*（謝辞）には私の名前がある。

　私は、旧作・新作の sit-coms——*I Love Lucy, Bewitched, Family Ties, Full House* など——が好きである。何と言っても、登場人物の発音が聞き取り易く下品な俗語がない。映画とは違って、各エピソードが 30 分以内なので時間

的、心身的に負担にならない。有難いことに、往年の作品であっても、新たに字幕が付けられているのでメモする手間が省けて助かる。最近、*Downton Abbey* を全 40 episodes と映画版を観たが、字幕がないと貴族の館で働く使用人（downstairs staff）の話す Yorkshire 訛りがほとんど聴き取れなかっただろう。特有の語彙に加えて母音の発音が General British（GB）とはかなり違う。但し、butler と house keeper の英語は GB である。私は、気になる英語——イントネーション——を聞いたら、中断してメモをとる。こんなことを頻繁に行っている。

　これから映画や sit-coms を利用して英語イントネーションを学ぼうとする人たちに助言するとすれば、セリフをただ聴く（listen to）だけでは、英語イントネーションの何に着目していいのかは分からない。まず、イントネーションについてしっかりした基本的知識がないと着目点が分からない。要は、listen to ではなく、listen for を目標にするべきである。スタート地点は、核音調である。

　今日、英語イントネーションを研究する人の間では、無料で手軽に入手できる音声分析ソフトを利用するのが当たり前になっているようである。学会では、そのようなソフトを使った研究発表が増えてきている。特に比較的若い研究者にそのような傾向が見られ、質疑応答では、出席者から疑義が発せられることも珍しくない。音声分析ソフトは日進月歩で進歩しているが、それから得たデータを信じ込むと危険である。音声ソフトには、いろいろと特徴・癖があり、それを理解した上で適切な使い方をしないと信頼できる結果を得ることができない。特に難儀なことは、聴覚印象に基づくイントネーションと音声ソフトによる physical evidence とがしばしば食い違うことである。そんな場合、有能な人間の耳による分析のほうが信頼できると言われている（Wells, 2006: 248-9）。音声分析ソフトによる physical evidence がどうであれ、実際の音声を聞くのは、生身の人間の耳である。それが音調分析に重要な役割を果たすべきである。

　音声分析ソフトに頼る方法は安易とは言わないが、英語イントネーションを学んだり研究するには、まず、自分の耳を鍛えることを最優先にするべきである。それだけでは危ういので、研究者の場合は、聴取した資料をできるかぎり文献と照合する必要がある。また、生身のネーテイブスピーカーのコメントを参考するのも有意義である。とにかく、実践に勝る研究方法はない。Practice makes perfect.

　私たちは、非・ネーテイブスピーカーであるので、然るべき先行研究を凌駕することは望めず、「後追い研究」にならざるを得ない。それでも、教育的目的には、私たちのイントネーション研究の成果は十分に意義あるものであろう。それが、私の基本的な研究姿勢である。

　ところで、本書の英語のイントネーションの表記法として、イギリス英語で用いられているものを使用することに疑問を抱く読者がいるかもしれない。また、前著と本書は、イギリス英語のイントネーションに関するものであると思っている読者もいるかもしれない。しかし、本書はイギリス英語のみに関するものではない。音声コーパスは英米豪などの英語である。

　英語のイントネーションの分析には、3 領域——①発話をどのように音調単位に分割するか、②音調単位の中のどの語に核強勢を置くか、③どの音調を使うか——を対象にする。その際、①と②とは、英米語に共通であると言われている。詳細は、J.C. ウェルズ著、長瀬慶來監訳『英語のイントネーション』（研究社 pp. 408-410）を参照。③については、英米語に共通なものとそうでないものもある。講演の中で、Wells は、ESL に関する限り、核強勢とその音調だけを重視するべきであって、核より前の tone は英米語では違いがあっても、特に考慮する必要はないとのことであった。

　　Prenuclear patterns (and therefore heads) are one of the less important phenomena in the intonation of English (they don't seem to encode much meaning), and I therefore relegated the whole matter away from the core chapters of my book to chapter 5, "Beyond the three Ts". (Blog: 2012.10.29)

また、Jack W. Lewis は、blog の中で次のように言う。

　　Incidentally, I think the topic of the differences between British and American tone usages is a negligible one for EFL students.

　本書の出版に際しては、Bill Rockenbach 教授と牧晋也さんに校閲をお願いした。お二人は、私の監修による『実践的な英語の学びかた・教えかた：通訳修業、GDM 教授法、イントネーションの観点から』（2021）の出版でも大変お世話になった。Rockenbach 教授は、Iowa 州立大学卒・Cornell 大学大学院修了後に来日して以来、英語教育を天職とされ、多くの教科書や参考書の出版に関わっておられ、日本における英語教育事情を熟知されている。その意味で、

本書の内容の校閲者として最適任である。

Books and books could be, and indeed have been, written about intonation. Even with a slight shift in word stress, a small change in pitch contour, there may be a very large change in the message sent by the speaker and received by the listener!

How to master English intonation? Well, I think that one thing is clear: It can't be done overnight, and, in fact, I think that we all spend our entire lives listening to other people's intonations and honing our own to most accurately express what we are feeling and exactly what we want to convey. But intonation can be learned, and the secret is, I think, starting with certain very basic intonation patterns that are appropriate for use with basic sentence (i.e., grammar) patterns in basic situations. Toward that end, I would wholeheartedly recommend one of the excellent books on that subject which have been written by Mr. Date!

I wish you good luck and all the best in your language learning!

Bill

牧さんには、原稿の推敲の段階からゲラの校正に至るまで深い専門的知見と洞察力でもって的確な助言を頂いた。牧さんは、東京外国語大学大学院で英語音声学を専攻された。また、『英語イントネーション論』の著者渡辺和幸教授からも直接に薫陶を受けられた。そのこともあって、英語イントネーションについて深い造詣をもっておられる。

また、上野舞斗さんにもゲラの校正でお世話になった。上野さんは、和歌山大学大学院で英語音声教育史と英語音声学を専攻し、現在、日本英語教育史学会理事及び日本実践英語音声学会評議員をされている。また、長瀬慶來教授古希記念出版『英語音声学・音韻論』（2022）の編集委員会の一員として優れた技量を発揮され、代表の私を支えてくださった。

最後になるが、私が所属する芦屋聖マルコ教会（英国国教会系）の Warren Wilson 司祭には、再び、資料朗読のご協力をしていただいた。

この４名の方々に衷心より感謝の念を捧げたい。

第一章　英語イントネーション概論

　音楽にリズムやメロディーがあるように、話し言葉にもリズムやメロディーがある。リズムは音の強弱の相互作用によって作られ、メロディーは音の高低によって作られる。イントネーションとは、話し言葉のメロディー、即ち、話すときの声の高さの上昇や下降のことである。イントネーションはどの言語にも存在し、コミュニケーションにおいて非常に重要な役割を果している。イントネーションの多くは、全ての言語に共通しユニバーサルなものであるが、同時に、各言語に固有の特徴も備えている。換言すれば、その言語らしさを出しているのもイントネーションである。

1.　英語の話者は、話すときに3つの決定を瞬時に行っている。①発話をいかに分割するか、換言すれば、どのように音調単位に分割するか、②音調単位の中のどの語を最も強調して言うか、換言すれば、どの語に核強勢を置くか、③どの音調を使うか、換言すれば、下降調、上昇調、下降上昇調、その他の音調の中でどれを核音調として使うかである。

　短い文は、通例、1つの<u>音調単位</u>（tone unit）に相当する。音調単位とは、1つの音調——下降、上昇、下降上昇など——で言われる発話のことである。下図は、下降調の音調単位 を示している。

[So what's the news?]　　Track 1

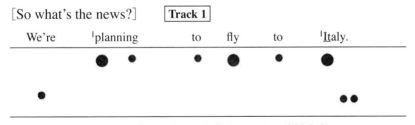

Wells, J. C. *English Intonation* (2006: 9)

音調単位の中で情報上重要である語は、強勢（stress）を受ける。また、音調単位には、文アクセント（accent）があり、強勢と区別される。文アクセントは、声の高さ（pitch）の変化を伴う強勢のことである。例えば、*Italy* という語には、最初の音節 *It-* に強勢があると辞書に表記されているが、このままでは、この強勢は文アクセントとは言えない。ピッチの変化があって初めて文アクセントと言える。上図を見ると、*plan-* と *It-* に文アクセントがあることが分かる。ピッチは、*We're* から *plan-* にかけて上昇し、*Italy* で

は下降している。一方、*fly* は、直前と直後の音節とピッチの高さが同じであるから文アクセントを受けない。強勢は、文アクセントをもたらす潜在的要素である。　　注：英語では、短母音 /ɪ/ で終わる音節（語）はない。

2. イントネーションの型を選択する際に話し手が行う決定のうち最も重要なことは、核（nucleus）をどこに置くかである。核は、音調単位の中でもっとも目立った（prominent）音節のことで、通例、音調単位中の最後の文アクセントに置かれる。上図では、*It*(*aly*) に核強勢が来る。

　概して言えば、文中に起こるピッチ変化の１つ１つが言語的に重要なのではなく、特定の１つのピッチ変化だけが重要である。それは最後の文アクセント（換言すれば、核）に起こるピッチ変化である。核では、単に「大きな声」よりも、むしろ「急激な高低変化」と「長さ」のほうが重要である。

　核強勢は、話し手が聞き手の注意を最も引き付けたい部分の中核となるものである。厳密に言うと、核強勢を受ける語は、新情報を伝える部分（領域）の最後の文アクセントのある語である。以下の３例では、文脈はお互いに違うけれども、核強勢は末尾の語 *races* に来る。　 Track 2

NEW

(What's on today?) We're going to the RÀCes.
Predication is 'new':

NEW

(What are we doing today?) We're going to the RÀCes.
Final adverbial is 'new':

NEW

(Where are we going today?) We're going to the RÀCes.

Greenbaum, S & Quirk, R. *A Student's Grammar of the English Language* (1990: 398)

　核強勢を起点として始まる際立った声の高さの変動は、核音調（nuclear tone）と呼ばれる。核音調には、下降調（fall）、上昇調（rise）、下降上昇調（fall-rise）、上昇下降調（rise-fall）、平板調 (level) などがある。核音調には、いろいろな表記法があるが、本書では、下記の方法を使うことにする。

fall	rise	fall-rise
↘	↗	↘↗

A driving instructor.

なお、下降調は、声がいきなり下降方向に転じるのではなく、多くの場合、核音節（nuclear syllable）の直前に、声がそこに向けていったん上昇し、それ以降に急激な下降に転じる。例えば、左図ではピッチが下降する直前に *A* から *dri-* に向けて上昇している。詳細は、課題 6 を参照。

・下降調：「完結」、「断定」の心的態度を表す。情報を事務的に伝える叙述文、疑問詞疑問文、命令文、感嘆文で用いられる。
・上昇調：「不確実」、「未完結」、「非断定」の心的態度を表す。yes-no 疑問文や文の途中で使われる。また、柔らかな命令文、激励的な助言、依頼、勧誘、挨拶にも用いられる。
・下降上昇調：「不確実」、「未完結」、「非断定」の心的態度を表したり、言外の含みを持たせたりする。また、警告や対比にも用いられる。

　実際には、下降上昇調は、上昇調の一種であると見なされ、意味と用法の点で共通点が多い。むしろ、下降上昇調のほうが、より強調的である。注意するべきは、これらの 3 つの音調は、特定の種類の文に固有のものとして定まっているのではいということである。実際の発話におけるさまざまな状況に応じて、また、話し手の意図や心情に応じて、音調の型が決まる。従って、必ずしも平叙文は下降調で、yes-no 疑問文は上昇調で、命令文は下降調で、疑問詞疑問文は下降調で発せられるとは限らない。

3. 英語のイントネーションの標準的な型は、核強勢が文末の内容語（content word）に来ることである。内容語とは、名詞、動詞、形容詞、副詞、疑問詞、指示代名詞などで、通例、文アクセントを受け強調して発音される。内容語に対して、機能語（function word）がある。機能語（冠詞、代名詞、（単音節の）前置詞、助動詞、be 動詞、接続詞、関係代名詞、（目的語用法の）相互代名詞と不定代名詞）は、通例、文アクセントを受けることが少なく、弱く短く発音される。
　　また、「時の副詞（句）」、「場所の副詞（句）」、「程度の副詞（句）」は、音調単位の末尾にあるとき、通例、文アクセントを受けない。詳細は伊達（2019）の課題 6，7，8 を参照。

4. 音調単位とは、1つの核音調で言われる文や句のことである。通例、1つの音調単位には1〜2の文アクセントがある。文中に、それを超える数の文アクセントがある場合には、2つ、またはそれを超える数の音調単位に分割される。以下の文は、2つの音調単位で言われている。

'I WENT to a REStaurant / that had FAbulous PAsta.　**Track 4-1**

但し、casual & faster speech では、この文は1つの音調単位で言われるだろう。また、意味単位や文法単位も音調単位の分割に関与する。例えば、短い単文であっても、重要な情報項目が2つあると見なされるときは、2つの音調単位に分かれる。

Harriet　What's your sister doing at the moment, Jo?　**Track 4-2**
Jo　She's studying Arabic at university.
Alan　Any news this morning, Sarah?
Sarah　Yes, there's been a bank robbery in Sheffield.

Thompson, I. *Intonation Practice* (1981: 49 - 50)

また、名詞（句）主語は、しばしば独自の音調単位を構成する。特に初出の場合、それが顕著である。以下では、音調単位の区切りを記号（I）で示す。

Various examples of tone units:　**Track 4-3**
a. There was a big earthquake I in Chile. (2 tone units)
b. A heavy snow I generally comes early I in October. (3)
c. Her parents are here I from out of town. (2)
d. What I want I is a chance to try. (2)
　What I want is I a chance to try. (2)
e. Which do you like better, I tea I or coffee. (3)
f. She said it was wrong, I but he said I it was right. (3)
g. *Hamlet* is a tragedy of a man I who cannot make up his mind. (2)
h. March I comes in like a lion I and goes out like a lamb. (3)
i. John Wayne always was (will be) I my favorite Hollywood star. (2)
　John Wayne I always was I and will be I my favorite Hollywood star. (4)

　　注：上記2文の音声は、John Wayne is ... という前提を踏まえている。

音調単位の構造は、通例、次のような部分からなる。

・前頭部（prehead）：音調単位の初めから最初の文アクセントの直前までの弱音節の部分。この部分は弱く短く、通常、低いピッチで発音される。但し、時々、前頭部が高いピッチで始まるときがあり、それは高前頭部（high prehead）と呼ばれる。課題 39 及びその「参考」欄（pp. 126 と 130）を参照。

・頭部（head）：最初の強勢音節から核音節の直前までの部分。独自のピッチ変化（pitch change）を伴うことが多い。

・核（nucleus）：音調単位中で最も強調して発音される文アクセント

・尾部（tail）：核強勢の後に続く全ての音節。

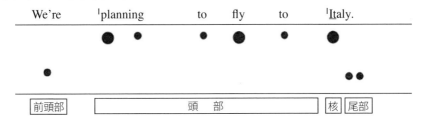

なお、音調単位内の最初の文アクセントは、オンセット（**onset** 頭部開始点）と呼ばれる。上記の例文について言えば、*plan-* がオンセットになる。オンセットは、通例、高いピッチになる。核は全ての音調単位に必ず 1 つ存在するが、前頭部、頭部、尾部は存在しないこともある。

【Listening Practice】 **Track 4-4**

これまでは、核強勢が音調単位の最後の内容語に来る default pattern を示してきたが、以下の文では、「異例な」ケースが混じっている。解説文 3（p. 11）を手掛かりにして、どの語に核強勢が置かれているかを指摘しよう。

1. Good bye. Thank you for a delicious dinner.
2. I usually get up around six o'clock.
3. What're you looking at?
4. What're you looking up?
5. After graduation, what do you want to be?
6. During the game I fell and hurt myself.
7. Hearing the story, he couldn't help himself and burst out crying.
8. Sorry I made such a fool of myself the other night. I must have been drunk.
9. The players are rivals but respect each other.

10. They're in constant contact with one another.

11. Have you done the homework yet?

12. Hello? Is anyone home?

13. He was with someone then.

14. She's busy at work, so she can't be here today.

15. Ken's such fun to be with.

16. Keiko is a tour guide, so she travels a lot.

17. He's not himself recently.

18. I was very tired, so I slept most of the day.

19. I can't keep it quiet any longer. I've just got to tell somebody.

20. Watch what you have for dinner. You are what you eat, you know.

21. She thought to herself, "Something's wrong with me recently."

22. What you need now is self-confidence. You should trust yourself.

23. Put it on the table, not beside it.

24. She had a worried look on her face.

25. [What's your job?] I haven't got a job. I'm between jobs.

Answer keys は、巻末 p. 215-6 にある。

5. イントネーションの主な機能

ここでは、3 で述べた文アクセントの有無に関する規則から逸脱する例外的ケースを検討する。これから以降では、記号を用いて、文アクセント、核強勢、音調を表すことにする。文アクセントは、当該語の強勢音節の直前に記号（ˈ）を付記し、核強勢は、当該語の強勢音節に下線（＿）を付記する。

(i) 聞き手の注意を引きつけたい箇所を伝える。　Track 5-1

a. ˈPut it ˈunder the ↘desk, ｜ ˈnot ↘on the desk.

b. He comˈmutes ˈto and ˈfrom school by ↘bus.

c. A: It's ↘cold.

B: It's ↘not ↗cold. *or* It's ↘not cold. (not on CD)

A: It ↘is cold. ↘Terribly cold.

d. To ↗be ｜ or ↘not to be, ｜ ˈthat is the ↘question.

or To ↘↗be ｜ or ↘↗not to be, ｜ ˈthat is the ↘question.

e. ↘So, ｜ my ˈfellow A ↘↗mericans, ｜ ˈask ↘not ｜ what your ˈcountry

14

can ˈdo for ↘you. ｜ ˈAsk what ↘you can do ｜ for your ↘country.

(ii) 意味を区別する。　Track 5-2

 a. ① Would you ˈlike ↗tea ｜ or ↘coffee?　(*Which one?*)

  ② Would you ˈlike ˈtea or ↗coffee?　(*Any drink?*)

 b. ① We are ex↘pecting him, ｜ ↘aren't we?

   (*I'm almost sure, but want to make sure.*)

  ② We are ex↘pecting him, ｜ ↗aren't we?

   (*I'm not sure, so please tell me.*)

 c. ① She ˈdressed and ˈfed the ↘baby.

  ② She ↘↗dressed ｜ and ˈfed the ↘baby.

   (*She dressed herself and fed the baby.*)

 d. ① A: I traveled to Wales recently.

   B: ↘Where?　(*Where in Wales?*)

   A: Bangor.

  ② A: I traveled to Wales recently.

   B: ↗Where?　(*asking for a repetition*)

   A: To Wales.

 e. ① He ↘asked himself.　(*He put the question to himself.*)

  ② He ˈasked him↘self.　(*He did the asking himself.*)

 f. ① ˈWhat's your ↘name?　(*matter-of- fact*)

  ② ˈWhat's your ↗name?　(*more polite/friendly*)

  ③ ↗What's your name?　(= *I didn't catch it.*)

(iii) 言外の意味をほのめかす（imply）。　Track 5-3

 a. ˈThat ˈmay be ↘↗true.　(*But it may not be true.*)

 b. I'll ˈdo it if I ↘↗can.　(*But it may be impossible.*)

 c. The ↘↗boys are here.　(*But I don't know where the girls are.*)

 d. I ex↘↗pect he'll come.　(*But I can't say for certain.*)

 e. I ↘↗think so.　(*But I'm not quite sure.*)

 f. I'm ˈawfully ↘↗sorry.　(*But it couldn't be avoided.*)

 g. I ˈcan't ˈdo it to↘↗day.　(*But I may be able to tomorrow.*)

(iv) 自分の感情・態度を加味する。　Track 5-4

 a. ˈGood ↘↗bye. ˈTake ↘↗care.　(*friendly or reassuring*)

b. You ˈmustn't ↘↗worry.　(*ditto* 同上)

c. There's ˈno ↘↗rush. ˈTake your ↘↗time.　(*ditto*)

d. A: Sorry to be late.

　 B: ˈThat's ˈall↗right.　(*ditto*)

e. A: There's only instant coffee, no coffee coffee.　(*no genuine coffee*)

　 B: Well, ˈthat's ˈbetter than ↘↗nothing.　(*ditto*)

f. A: I'm sorry to be so late. ˈDo for ↘↗give me.　(*pleading* 懇願)

　 B: ˈBetter ˈlate than ↘↗never.　(*reassuring*)

g. Oh, ˈplease ˈstay a little ↗longer.　(*pleading*)

h. [There's such a draught.] ˈShut the ↗door.　(*request*)

注 : 下降上昇調は、上昇調よりも more emphatic な気持ちを表す。

但し、心的態度や感情の表出には、声の高さ、顔の表情、しぐさ、文脈も関与するので、核音調だけが決定要因ではない。

6. 語用論的理由により、文アクセントが抑制される

音調単位では、通例、新（初出）情報は文アクセントを受け、旧／既知情報は文アクセントを受ない。これを別の観点 ── 語用論 ── から見てみよう。語用論とは、言語表現とそれを用いる使用者や文脈との関係を研究する分野である。　 Track 6

a. A: Shall we go there on foot?

　 B: Yes, let's. I ↘love walking.

b. A: Would you like some bacon?

　 B: No, thanks. I ↘don't like pork.

c. A: What's your job?

　 B: I ˈhaven't ↘got a job. I'm be↘tween jobs.

d. A: Can I offer you a piece of cake?

　 B: Sorry, I ˈdon't ↘like sweets.

e. A: What's new?

　 B: We're ˈhaving a ↘barbecue at our place.

f. A: What's going on this Friday night?

　 B: There's a ↘party at my place.

g. A: I donated the prize money to the child support center.

　　　B: ˈGood for ↘you. I'm proud of you.

　h.　A: What's it like being a nurse?

　　　B: Nursing is a good job for me. I ˈlike ↘helping people.

　i.　A: I'm going to a picnic.

　　　B: Oh, really? ˈWho's going to ↘be there? Is ↗Jane going to be there?

　　　A: ↘No, she ↘isn't going to be there. She says she's busy this weekend.

7.　名詞優先主義

初出の名詞は、文中のどこにあっても、他の内容語に優先して核強勢を受ける。それ以降の述部は尾部（tail）となり核音調の終結部を引き継ぐだけである。もし尾部に内容語があれば、それは文アクセントをもたず、ピッチ変化を伴わない強勢（リズム強勢）をもつだけである。以下は、種々の文構造における名詞優先の例である。

(i)　叙述文（ただし、out-of-the-blue statement の場合）　Track 7-1

　a.　↘Autumn came. The ↘leaves started to fall.

　b.　The ↘snow | generally comes ˈearly in Oc↘tober.

　c.　Ow! My ↘back's killing me!

　　　My ↘feet're killing me!

　d.　The ↘room's drafty. You've ˈleft the ↘door ajar.

　e.　Excuse me, but you've ˈspelled my ↘name wrong.

　f.　OK. I'll ˈkeep my ↘eyes open.

　g.　I need luck with this exam. ˈPlease ˈkeep your ↘fingers crossed for me.

　h.　She was ˈon the ↘↗beach, | ˈwatching the ↘sun go down.

　i.　[What're you doing here?] I'm ˈwaiting for the ↘store to open.

　j.　I ˈneed to ˈhave my ↘hair cut | and my ↘face shaved.

　k.　I can't go skiing this next weekend; my ↘boots want mending.

　l.　It's freezing cold in here; the ↘windows must have been left open.

(ii)　疑問詞疑問文と感嘆文　Track 7-2

　a.　ˈWhat ↘language do you speak?

　b.　ˈWhat's the ↘weather like in your area?

　c.　ˈWhat an ˈawful ↘month we're having!

　d.　ˈWhat a ˈnice ↘couple they make!

   e. So ˈhow did the ↘test go?

   f. ˈPlease be ˈcareful what ↘company you keep. （交友関係には気をつけて）

   g. ˈWhat a ˈlovely ↘hat she is wearing!

(iii) 関係詞節   Track 7-3

   a. Wow! ˈLook at the ˈcool ↘car he's driving! It's a Porsche!

   b. Johnny, ˈwhere's the ↘dictionary I lent you a while ago?

   c. Hello, Violet. You look good. ˈThat's ˈsome ↘dress you have on!

（素敵なドレスだね）

8. 出来事文（event sentence）   Track 8

上記の7で述べた名詞優先の核強勢配置と同じであるが、特に第1文型（S+V）によって、「状態の変化」（change of state）、特に、出現、不慮の出来事、不運、失踪の内容を伝える。初出の名詞主語が核強勢を受け、動詞の強勢は抑制される。つまり、名詞主語が主情報、動詞は副次情報となる。

   Kye sentences:

Be careful! There's a truck coming!   There's a stranger at the door.

~~My~~ watch has stopped.
~~The~~ train's coming.
~~The~~ sun's come out.
The kettle's boiling.   Thompson (1981: 49)

(i) 第1文型（S+V）

   a. Sorry to be late. My ↘car broke down.

   b. Ow, my ↘back hurts!

   c. Oh, no! The ↘store's burning!

   d. Brrr...there's a ˈcold ↘front approaching. （寒冷前線）

      or there's a ↘cold front approaching.

   e. Look! ˈThis ↘door is falling off. It's so loose!

   f. Hang on! An ↘ambulance's on the way. (*coming*)

   g. Look! The ↘house is on fire! (*burning*)

   h. Hey, ˈthere's a mos↘quito on your arm!

      There's a ↘bruise on your head.

    i. Then a ↘waiter came along | with a ↘coffee. (2 tone units)

    j. A: What's the news?

        B: My ↘parents are here | from ˈNew ↘York. (2 tone units)

    k. ［story の冒頭］It was very cold, and it rained a lot that night.

        ↘Susan came home, | ˈtired and ↘hungry. (2 tone units)

（ii）第 2 文型（S+V+C）の出来事文もある。異常事態、不慮の事故など突発的なことを伝える。

    a. A: Hey, your ↘eyes are red!

        B: Yeah, I'm suffering from a pollen allergy.

    b. Jimmy, your ↘bed's messy.

    c. I must get home early. My ↘daughter's sick.

    d. Oh, no! My ↘wallet's missing!

    e. Uh-oh. The ↘battery's dead.

    f. Oh, shoot! The ↘coffee machine's out of order.　(*not working*)

    g. Oh dear, the ↘printer's jammed. I can't make copies of this.

9.　複合音調　　Track 9

　　英語には、複合音調と呼ばれる 2 つの核音調を含む文がある。それは、下降調＋(低)上昇調から成る。下降調は新情報の末尾に起こり、(低) 上昇調は旧・既知情報に起こる。後者の場合、話者が、そこに<u>多少の重要度（some degree of importance）</u>を付加している。複合音調の文は核が 2 つあるので、2 つの音調単位から成ると考えることができる。

    a. A: Here's some chocolate, Susan.

        B:Great! I ↘like | ↗chocolate.

          参考：I ↘like chocolate.　(*possible: matter-of-fact*)

    b. A: Shall we go there on foot?

        B: Yes, let's. I ↘like | ↗walking.

          参考：I ↘like walking.　(*possible: matter-of-fact*)

    c. A: Do you like our city?

        B: Yes. I ↘like it | ↗here.

          参考：I ↘like it here.　(*possible: matter-of-fact*)

    d. A: I'm from Tokyo.

B: Are you? My ↘parents | were born in ↗Tokyo.

e. A: That's Jane standing at the bus stop over there.

B: Oh, I ↘know | ↗her. She's in my biology class.

f. A: Uh-oh. It's starting to rain!

B: I ↘thought | it would ↗rain.

g. A: Hello, David. Did you have a hard day at work?

B: Yeah, a bit. Ooh! The ↘soup | smells ↗good!

h. A: What sort of wine shall we have?

B: A ↘Riesling | would be ↗nice.

i. A: I've got a free day tomorrow. I want to go somewhere I've never been.

B: ↘Cambridge | is the place to ↗go.

j. A: It's started raining.

B: Mmm… They ↘promised | ↗rain.

A: Well, | they were ↘right | ↘this time.

B: I ↘hoped | they would ↗be.

複合音調の詳細は、課題 4, 14, 24, 39 と 40 で論じている。

10. まとめ

　これまで、音調の種類によって、それらと結びつく意味や話者の態度がそれぞれ異なる代表的な例を紹介してきた。音調は、特定の（固有の）意味を伝えるというよりも、むしろ文脈とか場面によっては、かなり性格の違った意味合いを伝える。文脈が、どの音調を使うべきかを決定する。

　しかし、上記でのべた内容とは逆行する default tone/intonation という概念が存在する。default（デフォルト）は、辞書では「不履行」とあるが、言語学では、意図的に変化を加える前に存在する「ノーマルな」状態のことで、一般に「neutral（中立的）」、「unmarked（無標の）」という訳語になっている。例えば、A fall is the default tone for statements（平叙文）とか、Yes-no questions are by default pronounced with a rise. などと言う。このような一般化には一理あるが、必ずしも真ではない。文タイプと音調の選択の間に単純で予測可能な関係があるとは言えないケースがある。しかし、教育的な（pedagogical）目的で——少なくとも英語音声学の初心者向け教本では——

default、または、それと同等の概念を用いると便利である。

　最後に、本書で提示している例文の intonational meanings は、文献でもよく言及されているものであるが、文脈によっては、他の解釈もあり得る。

課題 1　強勢と文アクセント

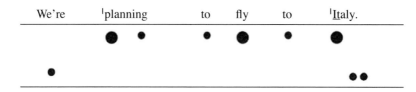

　図では、*planning*, *fly*, *Italy* に強勢が置かれている。しかし、文アクセントは、*planning* と *Italy* のみに置かれている。以下でも、中間の *don't* と *cup* は独自のピッチ変化を伴わないので文アクセントを受けない。

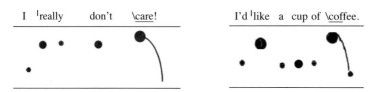

　次の対話中の最後の文 *It's really not that cold.* では、強勢のある語が 4 連続しているので、一見すると発音が難しく思えるが、not は文アクセントが置かれないので軽く言えばよい。

Alice: It's COLD.

Betty: It's NOT COLD.

Alice: It IS COLD.

Betty: COME ON... It's REALly NOT THAT COLD.

Celce-Murcia, Brinton & Goodwin (2010: 236)

　音調単位は、通例、1 つまたは 2 つの文アクセントから成る。後者の場合、文の音調曲線は、以下のどちらかになる傾向がある。

hat pattern　　　　　　bridge pattern

　図から分かるように、各パタン中の左端と右端の高い部分は、それぞれオンセットと核強勢を示している。左図 hat pattern では、中間部はオンセットの強勢音節と同じ pitch を保持しており、一方、右図 bridge pattern では、中間部は step down し「中だるみ」になっている。*It's REALly not THAT cold.* を参照。

Cruttenden の解説を見てみよう。

When there is only one accent preceding the nucleus, a high-pitched accent (without a fall）and following falling nuclear tone produces what is known as the '**hat pattern**'. (1997: 160)

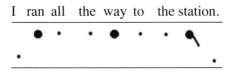

The primary stress/accent is on *sta-*, the prominence being mainly produced by the fall in pitch initiated on *sta-* and completed on *-tion*; a secondary stress/accent occurs on *ran*, the prominence being provided by the step-up in pitch from *I* to *ran*; and a tertiary stress occurs on *way*. (ibid.: 18)

次に Bolinger の解説を見てみよう。

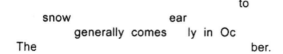

Here the first accent is on *snow* and the last is on *-to-*, which stand as the pillars of the *bridge*. The roadbed is heaved up somewhat on the syllable *ear-*, … (1972a: 23)　　　　　　　　　　　　bold letters は伊達が追加

以下も、どちらかのパタンで言われる。最初の文アクセントはオンセットである。

a.　ˈEdinburgh is the capital of ˈScotland.

b.　I ˈreally don't ˈlike it.

c.　It's the ˈfirst thing we did in the ˈclass.

d.　I ˈknow what ˈstreet it's on.

e.　I'd ˈlike a cup of ˈcoffee.

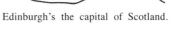

Edinburgh's the capital of Scotland.
Ladd (2008: 107)

なお、機能語——特に前置詞——が、音調単位全体の stress timing のリズムを確保するために文アクセントを受けるケースもめずらしくない。

f.　He's ˈ*at* the door of the ↘house.

g.　It is ˈ*in* the ↘box.

h.　He's ˈ*on* his way ˈback to the ↘city.

また、詩の朗読でも、同様のことが起こる。

i.　The ˈboy stood ˈ*on* the ˈburning ↘deck.

j.　Shall ˈI comˈpare thee ˈ*to* a ˈsummer ↘day?

k.　If ˈmusic ˈ*be* the ˈfood of ↘↗love, ˈplay ↘on.

　　　注：Shakespeare, *Twelfth Night*

参考：(i) Bob's lost his keys. を 1 つの音調単位で発音するときの強勢配置の options を考えてみよう。核強勢が置かれる最有力候補は、***keys*** であり下降調で言われる。***Bob's*** は、オンセットとして文アクセントを受け、平坦な高いピッチで言われる。次に、***lost*** には幾つかの options —— a range of choices —— が考えられる。これは、発話の速さと関係がある。① [at a faster and natural tempo] ***lost*** は強勢を受けない。文全体は、two-beat rhythm で発音される（三連規則）。② [at a slower tempo] ***lost*** は強勢を受ける。その場合、文全体は、three-beat rhythm になる。③ [at a slow, more deliberate tempo] ***lost*** は<u>文アクセント</u>を受ける。これは、異例な emotionally-colored speech であり、insistence または emphasis の心的態度が表出されている。

(ii) [What did you do?] I bought a large piece of pizza. における強勢配置を考えてみよう。ここでは、faster and natural tempo の発音のみを考えることにする。言うまでもなく、***pizza*** に核強勢が来て、***bought*** はオンセットである。***large piece*** には 2 つの options があり、large ˈpiece または ˈlarge piece となる。文全体に 3 連規則が適用され、どちらかの強勢が抑制される。このように、文頭（sentence-initial position）と文末（sentence-final position）の語の強勢は一定しているが、文中（sentence-medial position）の語群——この場合は、名詞句——の強勢配置は一定ではない。

以下の例でも、オンセットと核の位置は安定している。

ˈA ˈB ˈC ˈ<u>D</u> → ˈA B ˈC ˈ<u>D</u> *or* ˈA ˈB C ˈ<u>D</u> → ˈA B C ˈ<u>D</u>
ˈthree ˈsix ˈfive ˈ<u>seven</u> → ˈthree six five ˈ<u>seven</u>
ˈA ˈB ˈC ˈD ˈ<u>E</u> → ˈA B ˈC D ˈ<u>E</u> → ˈA B C D ˈ<u>E</u>　　　Wells (2006: 229)

(iii) 尾部（tail）は、文アクセントを受けないが、強勢（リズム強勢／ beat（拍））を受けることがある。例えば、

　　［生徒のいたずらについて］

　　A: ˈWho put the ˈdrawing pin on the ˈteacher's ↘chair?

　　B: It was ↘<u>Bob</u> who put the pin on the chair.　注：画鋲

尾部は低いピッチになるが、*put*, *pin*, *chair* には rhythmic beat がある。

即ち、尾部中の beats は、stresses without accent である。

課題2　**Great progress is made daily.**

　標題の文では、強勢をもつ語が4つある。音調単位では韻律が関係するのでそれら全てが文アクセントになるわけではない。

| Gréat | prógress | is máde | dáily |

Prator & Robinett (1972: 27)

この図は、学習者に誤解を与えるだろう。文脈を考えない機械的な言い方をするとき以外は、この文は1つの音調単位で言わないだろう。

　　? ˈGreat ˈprogress is ˈmade ↘daily.　(Not likely)

なぜならば、初出の名詞（句）主語は、独自の音調単位を形成するからである。また、成句 *make progress* では、各要素が semantic unity を構成し、There is a degree of expectedness/predictability between *make* and *progress*. そして *progress* のほうが major information であり、*make* は minor information である。従って、

　　ˈGreat ↘progress ｜ is made ↘daily.

ところで、Tench（1996: 64）は以下の類似例を示している。

　　When a clause ends in a common intransitive verb of motion or happening,
　　the verb − though it is the final lexical item − does not take the tonic…

　　　　注：lexical item 内容語に相当；tonic 核強勢に相当

　　An accident has happened

　　A question was raised

　　Discussion took place

以下の文でも、述語は予測可能（predictable）と見なされる。

　　a.　A ˈgreat dis ↘covery was made.

　　b.　A ↘promise was made.

　　c.　Listen! The ↘phone is ringing.

　　d.　The ↘kettle's boiling.

なお、述語の予測性の観点から核強勢配置を考えるほかに、「概論」7で述べ

25

た「名詞優先主義」を考慮する方法もある。

    e. He didn't do it. His ↘courage failed him.

    f. I didn't do it. My ↘conscience hurt me.

    g. ↘Fate brought us together.

    h. If a war happens, |all ↘hell will break loose.　（大混乱が起こるだろう）

    i. When he was running a marathon, his ↘legs gave out.　（動かなくなった）

    j. Oh, my! The ↘room is in a mess.　（散らかっている）

    k. Hang in there. ↘Help is on the way.　（がんばれ！救援がこっちに向かっている）

    l. Congratulations! Now a cele↘bration's in order.　（望ましい）

    m. ［日焼けして］Ouch! It feels like my ↘skin's on fire!　（皮膚がヒリヒリする）

    n. A: Did anything happen while I was out?

        B: The ↘doctor called.

ところで、The doctor called. における核強勢配置について 3 通りの考え方がある。

  ① Nouns are innately more accentable than verbs.

    （名詞は、本来的に動詞よりも文アクセントを受け易い）

  ② It's a special pattern for event sentences.

    （この強勢パタンは、出来事文に特有なものである）

  ③ 'Call' is what doctors typically do and is therefore said to be 'culturally given' or predictable.（call は医者の業務の 1 つであり、予測可能な情報である）

    （以上は、adapted from Cruttenden (1984: 67)）

    注 1：culturally given とは、文化的に（日常的に）既知内容であること。

    注 2：出来事文は、突如の appearance/presence などに関わる文であるが、なぜ The doctor called. を出来事文と呼べるのか。それは、「電話をかける」行為が主語（agent）の presence を示唆するからである。つまり、電話によって突如、場面に登場する。以下は、Bolinger (1986: 105) の説明である。

      My móther's coming. / My móther just phoned.

      These actions are rather highly predictable as causes of the focus of interest on the agent (what counts is the agent's *presence*)…

課題 3 **Large cars waste gas.**

　標題の文を適切なイントネーションで発音するには何に留意するべきだろうか。下図は、学習者の誤解を招くだろう。

LARGE　　CARS　　WASTE　　GAS

Woods (1992: 5)

学習者は、図を見て次のように考えるであろう。「*large, cars, waste, gas* に強勢（文アクセント）が置かれ、最後の *gas* に核強勢が来る」。しかし、それは、半分正しく、半分間違っている。これら 4 語全てに文アクセントを置いて、1 つの音調単位で言うことは通常ない。そんなことをすれば、文全体が機械的で不自然に聞こえる。1 つの音調単位は、通例、1 ～ 2 つの文アクセントから成り立つ（ただし、稀に 3 つもある）。そして、名詞（句）の主語は、通例、独自の音調単位を形成する。従って、この文は、2 つの音調単位に分割される。

- large cars が<u>初出</u>の場合、下降調で言われる。

　 ˈLarge ↘cars ｜ ˈwaste ↘gas.

- large cars が<u>既知</u>の場合、非下降調で言われる。

　 ˈLarge ↗cars ｜ ˈwaste ↘gas.

　 ˈLarge ↘↗cars ｜ ˈwaste ↘gas. となる。

　　参考：文の冒頭または中位では下降上昇調は、上昇よりも強調的である。

　　　　　At the beginning or in the middle of a sentence, the fall-rise tone is a more

　　　　　forceful alternative to the rising tone, expressing the assertion of one point,

　　　　　together with the implication that another point is to follow:

　　　　　Most ↘↗young people ｜ take plenty of ↘exercise.

　　　　　He's not a re ↘↗laxed lecturer ｜ but he's a ↘driving lecturer.

　　　　Leech & Svartvik (1994: 25)

他の例を紹介しておこう。

① 名詞主語が<u>初出</u>の場合、

　 a.　A: What happened?

B: Her ↘husband ｜ was in an ↘accident.

```
        hús                   ác
  Her
                  was in an
          band                    cidₑnt.
```
Bolinger (1986: 165)

b. Then ↘suddenly ｜ a ↘noise ｜ ｜broke the ↘night.

```
        súddenly    nói
  Then            a    se  bróke the ní
                                       ght.
```
(ibid.: 166)

c. A: What happened?

B: Your ↘brother ｜ broke his ↘leg.

```
         bró              lé
  Your
          ther broke his   g.
```
(ibid.: 182)

d. An ｜old ↘friend came to visit me last night. （注：event sentence）

```
       óld  frí
  An        eⁿd
                came to visit me last night.
```
(ibid.: 289)

② 名詞主語が既知の場合

a. A: What have your family been doing recently?

B: My ↗parents ｜ have been to ↘China.

or My ↘↗parents ｜ have been to ↘China.

b. ↗March ｜ comes ｜in like a ↗｜lion ｜ and goes ｜out like a ↘lamb.

or ↘↗March ｜ comes ｜in like a ↗｜lion ｜ and goes ｜out like a ↘lamb.

注：イギリスの気候を表す名言

以下も Bolinger からである。

c. A: What happened to my brother?

B: Your ↘↗brother ｜ broke his ↘leg.

```
         bró              lé
  Your
          theʳ broke his
                          g.
```
(ibid.: 182)

In answer to *Tell me more about the alligator* one might have any one of
the following:

課題 3　Large cars waste gas.

```
              álligator        cáught              húnt
(1)  The                got              by the
                                                       ers.

              álligator        cáught              húnt
(2)  The                got              by the
                                                       ers.

(3)  The                cáught              húnt
              álligator got         by the
                                                       ers.

                            cáught        húnt
(6)  The alligator was            by the              (ibid.: 368)
                                                       ers.
```

念のため、私の解説を加えると、以下のようになる。

(1) The ｜alligator got ｜caught by the ↘hunters.　(in faster speech)

(2) The ↗alligator ｜ got ｜caught by the ↘hunters.

(3) ‾The ↗alligator ｜ got ｜caught by the ↘hunters.
　　　(*The* は高前頭部 high prehead)

(6) The alligator was ｜caught by the ↘hunters.　(in fast speech)

参考：イントネーションの分析と表記法には 2 つの大きな流れがある。1 つは、イギ
　　　リスの伝統的な表記法で、下降調、上昇調、下降上昇調などの tones を基にイ
　　　ントネーションを表記する。本書はこのような表記法を踏まえている。他は、
　　　イントネーションの変動をピッチレベルで示す方式で、Pike や Fries をはじめ
　　　アメリカ構造言語学の流れを汲む表記法である。アメリカ方式では、4 段階
　　　のピッチを認め、ピッチレベルがイントネーションに有意義であると考える。
　　　Pike はピッチを高い順に 1,2,3,4 と表記するが、Trager-Smith などの多くの研
　　　究者は低い順に 1,2,3,4 と表記する（課題 43 参照）。日本の英語教育は、後者を
　　　踏襲している。なお、本書で度々引用する Bolinger と Ladd は、ピッチレベル
　　　ではなく発話全体の音調曲線の形状を重要視している。課題 13 を参照。

```
                    do                              finish
What are you                                Did he
                 ing
```

課題4 **Proclaiming tone vs. referring tone**

　談話（discourse）において、話し手が留意することは、聞き手に対する配慮である。通常、話し手は、相手が全く知らないことを述べるのではなく、聞き手がある程度の予備知識をもっていることを前提として、または、両者の間に共通の認識があることを前提にして、それに新しい事柄、情報を付け加える。その際に、イントネーションが重要な働きを果たす。その1つは、音調単位の中の新情報の内容と既知情報の内容とを区別することである。

　一般に、情報の単位は音調単位という形で具現化され、核強勢は情報の焦点があるところを示す。典型的な情報単位は、新情報と既知情報である。＊Brazil（1994）は、新情報を伝達する音調を proclaiming tone、また既知情報を伝達する音調を referring tone と称し、前者は下降調をとり、後者は下降上昇調または上昇調をとると言っている。なお、それぞれ宣言音調と言及音調と訳されている。　　　　　　　　　　　　＊詳細は課題44を参照。

It is Saturday and Mandy and Paul are talking about what they should do.

Notice how Paul uses a RISING tone (↗) for the subject they are already talking about and a FALLING tone (↘) to give new information.

Hewings (1993: 65)

　本来、predictable または redundant（余剰）な内容は、既知情報と見なされ文アクセントを受けない。しかし、話者が、そのような内容に、ある程度の卓立（prominence）－ a degree of accenting －を与えるときは、別個の音調単位として上昇調で言う。Wells（2006: 111）によれば、

> Alternatively, the speaker can preserve a degree of accenting on the repeated item or idea, while relegating it to secondary (minor) status by placing it in a separate intonation phrase, typically with a rising tone.

具体例を見ていこう。

a.　A: How about going to the concert this Saturday?

B: Oh, I'd love to. But do you think there'll be any tickets left?

A: *I've ↘ got ｜ ↗ tickets*.

これは、相手を安心させる言い方である。単に切符をもっているというのなら、I've ↘ got tickets. となる。

　以下の例文では、上昇部は、一見すると新情報に見えるが predictable/ redundant であるので既知情報と見なされている。

b.　A: When are you going to New York?

　　B: *I'm ↗ flying ｜ at ˈten o'↘ clock*.

　　　　参考：I'm ˈflying at ˈten o'↘ clock.　(at faster tempo)

c.　A: When did you first meet Tony?

　　B: Oh, *I've ↗ known him ｜ for ↘ years*.

　　　　参考：Oh, I've ˈknown him for ↘ years.　(at faster tempo)

d.　A: What do you think of Picasso?

　　B: *I don't ↘ care ｜ for ˈmodern ↗ paintings*.

e.　A: I don't know how John is going to keep in shape, working such long hours at the office.

　　B: *He's ˈtaken up ↘ swimming ｜ to ˈkeep ↗ fit*.

f.　A: Excuse me. I'm looking for the Peking Restaurant.

　　B: Oh, sure. *I ↘ know ｜ ˈwhere it ↗ is*.

g.　[*The Adventures of Tom Sawyer*]

　　Aunt Polly: What have you been doing, Tom?

　　Tom: Nothing.

　　Aunt Polly: Nothing? Look at your hands. And look at your mouth.

　　　　　　　It's jam! ↘ *That's* ｜ ˈwhat it ↗ *is*.

h.　A: I have always preferred wild flowers to pretty ones from a florist.

　　B: *I sus ↘ pected ｜ as ↗ much*.　(= I suspected so.)

i.　A: The police couldn't find any sign of a break-in.　（不法侵入）

　　B: *I ↘ thought ｜ as ↗ much*.　(= I thought so.)

j.　A: I got a divorce because my wife was having an affair with a man.

　　B: God, that must've been really demoralizing.　（破滅的な）

　　A: Well, *I ˈthink I ˈtook it rather ↘ well ｜ under the ↗ circumstances*.

　　（このような事情であったが、何とかうまく対処した）

31

反復の例もある。

k. A: I see the castle.

B: No, that's the cathedral. (Pointing) ↘*There's* | *the* ↗*castle*.

l. A: What's up? （何が起ったの）

B: A discovery. ↘*That's* | *what's* ↗*up*.

　既に述べたように、既知内容は、通例、焦点を受けない（out of focus）けれども、話者が、何らかの理由で、ある程度の卓立を与えることがある。その解説となる記述を紹介しよう。

> Given information is usually out of focus, unless it is being specifically highlighted or contrasted. But, … a speaker may wish to give an item of given information "some prominence as essential information"; for example:　　　　　　　　注：given は「既出の」という意味である
>
> 　　A: Did you see any of the new plays while you were in London?
>
> 　　B: No, | *we don't often* ↘*go* | *to the* ↗*theatre*.

where ***theatre*** is implied as a result of the mention, by A, of ***plays*** and is therefore given, but B chooses to give it some prominence. B could, naturally, have chosen not to, by saying:

> 　　No, | *we don't often* ↘*go to the* °*theatre*.　　　Tench (1990: 225)
>
> 　　　注：例文中のリング状の記号 (°) は、リズム強勢 / beat（拍）を意味する。
>
> 　　　　　課題 1 の「参考」欄（iii）を参照。

「ロンドンにいた間、何か新しい演劇を観ましたか」が発せられたとき、「劇場」という概念は既に speaker と hearer には共有されており、その語を強調する（highlight）必要がない。それでも、話者が、「劇場」に少し卓立を付加したいと思うと、それを上昇調で言う。勿論、反復の「劇場」を重要視しない選択肢もある。複合音調では、下降調が主たる音調であり、上昇調は付随的なステータスにすぎない。他の解説文を紹介しよう。

A: They'll have no place to hide.

B1: |*Of* ↘*course they'll have no place to hide*.

　　　The repeated *they'll have no place to hide* constitutes only an intonational tail without an accent (usually at a low pitch level)

　　　or

B2: |*Yes, in* ↘*deed* | *they'll have no place to* ↗ *hide*.

The final rise pitch movement would be perceived by native-English speakers not as an independent accentual rise.

(adapted from Lewis' paper "Accentuation: 'global' versus analytical stresses")

最後に、芝生のところに立っている看板英語 Do not walk on the grass. のイントネーションを考えてみよう。これは、禁止を意味するので下降調で発せられる。

A written notice standing in a lawn reading

DO NOT WALK ON THE GRASS

is a true prohibition, preventing the action before it starts. Prohibitions are spoken with falls.　　　　　Knowles (1987: 192)

では、看板に気付かないで芝生に侵入している人に、どのように注意を促すだろうか。proclaiming tone の ˈDon't walk on the ↘grass. は neutral pattern に思えるかもしれないが、場面を考慮していない。侵入者（trespasser）は既に芝生に入っているので、芝生は 'given'（既知）information である。従って、referring tone の ˈDon't walk on the ↗grass. が妥当である。

ところで、この場合の上昇調は、friendliness/politeness を表す指標でもある。念のために Lewis に確かめた。彼は、Blog218 (2009.10.1) の中で答えてくださった。

Intonation of "Don't walk on the grass."

Tami Date has asked for comments on these intonation choices which I make on the understanding that the paralinguistic features such as loudness, voice quality, tempo and pitch range employed are relatively neutral…The alternative ˈDon't ˈwalk on the ˌgrass is more patient and/or friendly and it would be favoured by many speakers because a final Rise is generally used to avoid the effect of giving an order… The neutral one does have a slight danger of being taken as patronizing…With a high fall, as ˈDon't ˈwalk on the ˎgrass or more urgently two falls ˎDon't ˈwalk on the ˎgrass, the remark seems likely to suggest something like "You ought to know better" or "I've told you not to already."　　　（もっと分別があるべきだ）

注：patronizing 上から目線の；high fall（高下降調）は、声域の高い位置から低い位置まで下降する幅が広い。

33

課題 5　新情報の強勢 vs. 対比の強勢

　核強勢は、話し手が聞き手の注意を最も引き付けたい部分の中核となるものであるが、文脈によっては、核強勢の卓立の度合いに差がある。

a.　① A: Is Colin happy in his job?

　　　 B: No. *He's* ' *going to* ↘*move*.

　　② A: What's Colin going to do?

　　　 B: *He's going to* ↘*move*.

　　③ A: Did you say Colin had moved?

　　　 B: No. *he's* ↘*going to move*.　　　　(adapted from Bradford (1988: 8-9))

①と②の B では、共に *move* に核強勢が置かれているが、音声資料を聴くと、② B 中の *move* のピッチ変化のほうが① B よりも幾分目立って聞こえる。つまり、ピッチの下降がもっと急激であると感じられる。ついでに言うと、② B 中の *going* は反復語であるので、① B 中の初出の *going* よりもピッチが低い。そのために、② B 中の *move* のピッチの上昇が、より高く聞こえる。

以下は、対比の有無が明確な例である。

b.　① A: How was the job?

　　　 B: *It was* ↘*easy*.

　　② A: Was the job hard?

　　　 B: No, *it was* ↘*easy*.

言うまでもなく、双方とも *easy* に核強勢が来る。前者は、「通常の」核強勢であり、後者は、*hard* との対比強勢である。対比強勢では、核のピッチがより高く始まり、下降に転じるのがもっと顕著であるので、卓立度がより高く聞こえる。類例を挙げよう。

c.　① A: You're looking depressed. What's the matter?

　　　 B: *My* ↘*head aches*.

　　② A: I suppose your back aches.

　　　 B: You're wrong. *My* ↘*head aches*.

以下の模式図で対比強勢のピッチを確かめてみよう。

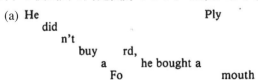

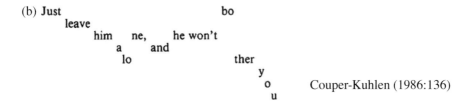

Couper-Kuhlen (1986:136)

(a) では *Ford* と *Plymouth* は、それぞれ上昇調と下降調で言われる。(b) の *alone* と *bother* においても同じである。しかし、*Ford* との対比である *Ply–* のピッチは、急激に高くなって、その後、下降に転じている（高下降調）。一方、*bo–* のピッチは、非対比の強勢であり、ピッチ変化はそれほど急激ではない。

　ちなみに、対比強勢の例ではないが、以下のケースでも seen と him の強勢の度合いに違いがある。

d.　① A: John Cleese is a very funny actor.　　注：イギリスの喜劇俳優

　　　B: Oh, yes. *I've* ↘ *seen* ｜ ↗ *him*.

　　② A: Have you seen my father yet?

　　　B: *I've* ↘↗ *seen him*, but I haven't had time to talk to him.

　　(adapted from Roach (2009: 141))

　　①の *him*/hɪm/ は②の *him*/ɪm/ よりも more prominent である。

　　　　注：両例ともに、ほぼ同じ音調曲線になる。I've↘seen↗him

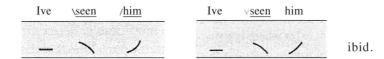

ibid.

e.　① We have been talking about their customs, dress, ceremonials, marriage, etc. Now I'd like to know about another aspect of their culure.

　　　ǀ *What did they* ↘ *eat?*

　　② They were forbidden pork, beef, cereal grains, and fruits?! ǀ *What did they* ↘ *eat?!*　('How was it possible for them to eat?!' There is a focus of interest on *eat*.)

　　　(adapted from Bolinger (1986: 95))

　　後者の疑問文は、驚きの要素を含むので、*eat* は more prominent である。

　最後に、上昇調でのピッチの違いを見てみよう。話者の心的態度の違いが読みとれる。

1) A: What did you usually have for breakfast?

   B: Cornflakes, <u>a cup of tea</u>, and some buttered toast.

2) A: <u>A cup of tea?</u>

   B: No, thanks. I've just had one.

3) A: Would you like <u>a cup of tea</u>?

   B: <u>A cup of tea?</u> Me? You must be mad! You know very well I don't like tea.

All three underlined instances of the expression "a cup of tea" will be spoken with a rising intonation. To explain the difference between the third example and the others we should need to bring into our analysis some such semantic feature as "surprise".   Hirst (1977: 52)

なお、最後の例は、驚きを表し<u>高</u>上昇調で言われる。

参考：上記 d ①の I've ↘<u>seen</u> | ↗<u>him</u>. では、なぜ、*him* に上昇調の文アクセントが置かれるのか。まず、I've ↘<u>seen</u> him. は、*him* に興味がなく、素っ気なく言い切る（cutting the topic short）印象を与えかねない。換言すれば、not interested in pursuing the topic any further という「話題の打ち切り」の態度（an air of finality）を伝えるかもしれない。一方、*him* に（低）上昇調の文アクセントを置くと、John Cleese に興味があり会話を続行しようとする気持ちの表れになる。言ってみれば、"I'm willing to talk about him more." の含意がある。関連内容が課題 23 にある。Lewis にコメントを求めると PhonetiBlog に取り上げられた。

The latest questions Tami Date has come up with show him quoting from Peter Roach's *English Phonetics and Phonology*…

ᶦOh ↘<u>yes</u> | I've ↘<u>seen</u> ↗<u>him</u>   əʊ ˋjes. aɪv ˋsiːn ˌhɪm   （Lewis 式表記法）

This response might be said in conversation on hearing someone's name; *him* has much greater prominence than in the parallel and is not possible in a weak form. It may be here very possible that the speaker could have a (slight) preference for avoiding the finality of a fall. A fall could tend to rather be felt as cutting short the topic from lack of interest or worse. (Blog 287: 2010.7.16)

注：parallel（並行するもの）とは、弱形の *him*/ɪm/ のことである。

課題 6　下降調の認識

　Bolinger は、あるグループを対象に行ったピッチ識別の実験結果（一部）を報告している。

　　Many people have difficulty abstracting the ups and downs of pitch from the flow of speech. In fact, informal tests show that when groups of listeners are given a sentence like

```
Does she    ways act that way?
        al
```

practically everyone can tell that the syllable of *al-* "stands out," but many will say the pitch goes up instead of down. (There are other ways besides pitch － extra "loudness" for example － to make a syllable stand out…)　　　　　　　　　　　　　　Bolinger (1986: 4)

上記の内容を敷衍すれば、音調単位の中で、どの語――厳密には、どの音節――が目立っているか（stand out, prominent）は聞き取れるけれども、その語（音節）のピッチが上昇しているのか、下降しているのかを聞き分けられない人が多くいる。

　音声学の教本には下降調、上昇調、下降上昇調、上昇下降調のことが述べられているが、私の経験では、耳の訓練をしていない人には、下降調ですら聞き取れない。数年前、日本実践英語音声学会（会場：県立広島大学）で研究発表大会が開催された。私は、講演に代えて発音ワークショップを行った。イントネーションの概要を説明したあと、質問の時間を少しとると、女子学生が挙手した。

　　「講義中では、*He is hungry. Me, too.* では、*hungry* と *too* はどちらも下降調で言われるということですが、私には、どうしても上昇調に聞こえます。」会場には、それに頷く人たちがいるのが見えた。彼女の感想は尤もなことである。下降調の特徴を知らない人には、確かにそのように聞こえるだろう。なぜならば、下降調では声がいきなり下降すると誤解しているからである。

　以下は、まさに上記の学生の誤解を指摘している。

There is very often a **step up** in pitch as we reach the beginning of the nuclear fall. Do not let this mislead you into thinking that the tone is rising.

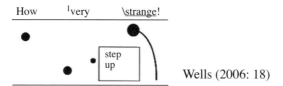

Wells (2006: 18)

同様にして、What happens when you take penicillin? では、ピッチが無強勢の -i- から核音調のある -cil- に移行するときに jump up（step up）し、その後、下降している。下降調は、多くの場合、実質的には rise-fall である。

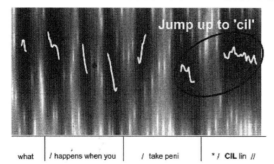

Halliday & Greaves (2008: 82)

このように、下降調は、声がいきなり下降方向に転じるのではなく、多くの場合、核音節（tonic syllable）の直前に、声がそこに向けていったん上昇し、それ以降に急激な下降に転じる。

　最後に、yesterday と progress（名詞）の下降調の音調曲線を紹介しておこう。

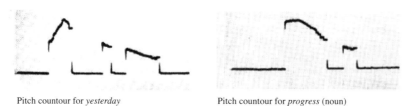

Pitch countour for *yesterday*　　　Pitch countour for *progress* (noun)

Knowles (1987: 98&99)

38

課題 7　下降上昇調（1）

　下降上昇調は、下降調と上昇調の組み合わせであるが、下降で、「確信」、「主張」、「断言」などを伝えると共に上昇で「未完結」、「保留」、「警告」、「対比」などの含みのある心的態度を伝える働きをする。この音調は、いろいろな attitudinal meanings を含むので多くの研究者が言及し議論してきた。

　下降上昇調は、日本語には存在しない音調であるが、英語では、いろいろな目的のために用いられる。

　　Learners should note that the fall-rise (especially on a single word) is rare in most languages but very frequent in English for a range of attitudinal meanings on declaratives and for subjects with their own intonational phrase. Fall-rise is also frequent on sentence adverbials in initial position, although low rise is the usual tone in final position…　　Cruttenden (2014: 301)

　さて、下降上昇調では、声の高さが比較的高いところで始まった後、下方に向かい、次に上方に戻る。以下の 3 例では、下降上昇調の動きは、単音節の語（例：voice, now, yes）内で完結する。

　　・She has a lovely ↘↗voice, (but can't dance well.)
　　・I'm busy ↘↗now, (but I'll be free some other time.)
　　・(Do you eat fish?) ↘↗Yes, (but not very often.)

しかし、複音節の un↘↗fortunately の場合、下降は強勢音節 -for- 内で起こり、それから低いピッチになり最後に上昇する。右下図は、-fortunately の部分を簡略化したものである。

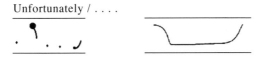

なお、無強勢の -ly のピッチが上昇しているが、これは独自のピッチ変化ではなく、単に尾部の一部である。

　　There is an accent…on **-fort**. A rise in pitch then occurs on **-ly** which is an unstressed syllable in the word and hence not potentially accented. The **-ly** is therefore not taken as an accent but merely as part of the realization of the tune following the accent on **-fort**.

　　　　Cruttenden (1997: 43)　　　　bold letters は伊達が追加。

また、At ↘↗<u>ten</u> o'clock | … や ↘↗I don't believe it. も同じような音調曲線になる。本書では、便宜的に、Un↘fortunate↗ly | …; At↘<u>ten</u> o'↗clock | …; ↘I don't believe↗it. と表記する。

　学習者には、下降上昇調が特に文頭に来るときは、大きな戸惑いがあるようである。

(i) 対比

a.　A: How are your parents?

　　B: *My ↘↗<u>mother's</u> | ↘<u>fine</u>.* But my father is in hospital.

　　　(My ↘moth↗er's | ↘<u>fine</u>.)

b.　A: What a wretched summer!

　　B: *↘↗<u>August</u> | is a ↘<u>terrible</u> month.*

c.　A: What was the meal like?

　　B: *The ↘↗<u>soup</u> | was ↘<u>terrible</u>.*

d.　A: How do you like English phonetics?

　　B: *Well, ↘↗<u>that sort of linguistics</u> | is ⌐quite be↘<u>yond</u> me.*

　　　(↘that sort of linguis↗tics)

e.　A: Sorry to interrupt, folks. Would you all like a cup of coffee?

　　B: *↘↗<u>I'd like one</u>.* How about you, Peter?

　　　(↘I'd like ↗one)

f.　A: Where's everybody?

　　B: *The ↘↗<u>boys</u> are here.* But I don't know where the girls are.

　　　(The ↘boys are ↗here)

g.　[全米ライフル協会のスローガン]

　　　↘↗<u>Guns</u> *don't kill people.* ↘<u>People</u> kill people.

　　　(↘Guns don't kill peo↗ple)

h.　A: Aren't these apples sour?

　　B: *↘↗<u>Some</u> of them are all right.*

　　　(↘Some of them are all ↗right)

i 　A: I think you should quit smoking.

　　B: Ha! *↘↗<u>You</u> should talk.* You used to be a heavy smoker yourself.

　　　(↘You should ↗talk)

ここで i は、なぜ *you* が対比強勢を受けるのかについて説明が必要だろう。

you は他の誰と対比されているのか。その contrastive (alternative) subject は誰なのか。それは、*everybody, all people* であろう。そこで、SUPRAS にコメントを求めた。*English Pronunciation In Use* (Intermediate) の著者 Mark Hancock からコメントがあった。要点の部分だけを紹介すると、

> The subject is being contrasted with 'of all people'. This expresses some surprise that you are the most unlikely one out of all the opposite candidates. So: You, of all people, should talk. (Of all the people who could criticize my smoking, it turns out to be you, an ex-smoker yourself!) 　　　　　　　　　　　　　　　　(2010.9. 15)

敷衍すると「私の喫煙癖を批判しそうな人たち（candidates）のなかで、君は最もありえない存在だ（お前が言うな）」ということである。

j.　A: I don't like her because she's always complaining.

　　B: ↘↗*You're a fine one to talk*. You often criticize this and that yourself.

　　　（↘You're a fine one to ↗talk）

(ii) 部分否定

a.　↘↗All the men didn't go.

　　（↘All the men didn't ↗go）　　　　All

　　　Ladd (1980: 146)　　　　the men didn't g°　　(fall-rise)

b.　↘↗All cats don't like water.

　　（↘All cats don't like wa↗ter）

c.　|Not ↘↗all that glitters is gold.　（外見に誤魔化されるな）

　　（Not ↘all that glitters is ↗gold）

参考として、文頭以外に下降上昇調が来る例を挙げておこう。

d.　A: Do you see anyone you haven't met?

　　B: *I* |*haven't met* ↘↗*one of them*. (= There is one I haven't met.)

e.　A: *I don't* |*dine outdoors with* ↘↗*anybody*.

　　B: Am I just anybody?

　　A: [Grinning] What do you think, preppie?　［映画 *Love Story* より］

f.　*Do* ↗*mingo* | *won't* |*sing* ↘↗*anywhere*. He insists on good acoustics.

　　注：José Plácido Domingo オペラ歌手（音響効果のいい演奏会場を要求する）

課題 8　下降上昇調（2）

　日常会話においては、単に事実を伝える文であるように思えても、イントネーションによっては聞き手に何らかの言外の意味を伝えることがある。例えば、「どこで学位を取得しましたか」と尋ねられて、「Cornell 大学です」と答えるとき、その言い方によって話者の心的態度が表出される。

A: Where did you get your degree?

B:　　　　Cor\nell　　　vs.　　Cor\nell　　　　　Ladd (1980: 111)

左の上昇調は hesitant な態度——"Have you heard of it?" or "Is it good enough?"——を伝え、右の下降上昇調は self-assured（「どんなもんだ」）の態度が読みとれる。ほかに、

　　It's ↘cold in here. (just an observation)

　　It's ↘↗cold in here. (an implicit request for the window to be closed)

以下では、下降上昇調の「含蓄」機能を伝える文をいろいろ紹介したい。先ず、文献からの例から始めよう。Knowles（1987: 191）は、次のように言う。

　　The person who enters the kitchen and exclaims

　　　　Those ∨ CAKES smell nice. (*Those ↘cakes smell ↗nice*)

　　is not reporting an olfactory response, but is almost certainly hinting "I'd like one." The **fall-rise** in these examples does not carry any 'meaning' of its own, but guides the addressee to the intended interpretation: he or she is expected to take some kind of action in response to the information given.　　　注：olfactory 嗅覚の

　次の 2 例は、Thompson（1981: 22）からである。ここでも発言に hinting または、tentative suggestion の意図が窺える。

　　・[David gets home from a long business trip.]

　　Harriet: Hello, David. I'll take your coat.

　　David: Thanks, Harriet. Whew!

　　Harriet: Are you tired?

　　David: Mmm…a bit. Ooh! *The ↘↗soup smells good!*

　　　　　　　　(The ↘soup smells ↗good)

Harriet: Are you hungry?

・Alan: Where can I get some orange juice?

Jo: Are you thirsty?

Alan: *That* ↘↗*omelette looks good*!

Jo: Are you hungry?

ある時、SUPRAS に公開メールを送ったら、Tench から以下の返信があった。

> You're right: those sentences/statements with the tone [↘↗] are more than descriptions of the state of the soup, etc. The tone [↘↗] tells you that. It tells you that something else is implied, and that the speaker expects the hearer to be able to interpret the unspoken message. I would have thought that in this case, Harriet has interpreted correctly, by enquiring about David's hunger! (2007.2.22)

以下では、いろいろな類似的なケースを紹介する。

a.　A: ↘↗*This looks like a nice restaurant.*

　　　　（実際には、↘This looks like a nice restau↗rant）

　　B: Yeah. Let's go in.

b.　A: Let's see the menu. Mmm, ↘↗*this looks good.* Macaroni and chicken. And only 500 yen. Quite cheap.

　　B: Let's have it then.

c.　A: [At a liquor shop] ↘↗*This looks like a nice wine.*

　　B: Shall we buy a bottle?

以下の例も、Tench の解説 "The tone [↘↗] tells you that something else is implied, and that the speaker expects the hearer to be able to interpret the unspoken message." に合致するだろう。

d.　A: I'm thinking of buying the nice coat that I checked out at the shop the other day.

　　B: ↘↗*Pay day's a long way off.* (↘Pay day's a long way ↗off)

　　　(The hidden message: *Are you sure you can afford it?*)

e.　A: When will Tom be back?

　　B: ↘↗*I don't know.*

(The hidden message: *Why not ask Tom or somebody else?*)

f. ↘↗ *Teacher's coming*! (↘Teacher's co↗ming)

(The hidden message: [警告] *Look out*.)

g. Ssh! *The* ↘↗ *teacher's listening*!

(The hidden message: [警告] *You'd better watch what you say*.)

h. *The* ↘↗ *door's open*. (*The* ↘*door's o*↗*pen*)

(The hidden message: [警告] *You'd better go and shut it*.)

参考：The ˈdoor's ↗open. (The hidden message: So *you can walk straight in*.)

i. A: Hullo, everyone.

B: ↘↗ *You're late*.

(The hidden message: *What took you so long?*)

j. Johnny, *your* ↘↗ *toast's getting cold*.

(The hidden message: *Hurry up*.)

k. A: Where's the remote?

B: *On the* ↘↗ *coffee table*.

(The hidden message: *On the usual place/ where it belongs*.)

l. A: That's John's painting.

B: ↘↗ *Whose painting*?

(The hidden message: *John's? Surely not!*)

m. A: How do you like my new color scheme?

B: ˈ*Not* ↘↗ *bad*.

(The hidden message: [mild approval] *It's OK, so-so*.)

n. A: Too bad you didn't do better.

B: *I* ↘↗ *tried*!

(The hidden message: *So what more can you expect?*)

o. A: Can you forgive them?

B: *They* ˈ*gave their a* ↘↗ *pology*.

(The hidden message: *What more can you ask?*)

課題 9　**Yes-no 疑問文**

　音声学の専門書や教本には、yes-no 疑問文は、上昇調のみならず下降調のイントネーションで言われると書いてある。しかし、教室では、伝統的に上昇調が教えられてきた。なぜならば、それのほうが無難だからである。

> Traditional teaching of prosody certainly has some value. For example, if you're aspiring to work in tourism, it's important to know a proper way to say *Would you like some more tea?* This is not a trivial matter, since appropriate prosody here can make or break your career. Teachers usually recommend the use of the classic final rise of "International English" for this purpose. This is universally safe. 　　　　Ward (2019: 72)

しかし、ネーテイブスピーカーは、以下のような all-new yes-no question において、optionally に下降調を使うことがある。

a.　David Merril! Come in, come in. I'm glad you came down here.
　　I'm really glad. *Can I* ⌐*get you a* ↘*drink?*

b.　[Into the phone] Good afternoon. International Artists Agency…
　　No, I'm sorry he's not available. *May I* ⌐*take a* ↘*message?*

c.　A: You want a beer?
　　B: No.
　　A: *You're* ↘*sure?*

d.　[A minister announcing from the pulpit:]
　　Shall we all ↘↗*join together* ⌐ *in* ⌐*singing* ⌐*Hymn No.* ⌐*fifty-*↘*seven?*

　しかし、必ずと言っていいほど下降調になるケースがある。この場合は、同じ質問が繰り返される。従って、質問が執拗な（insistent）印象を与える。

> The insistent yes-no fall is also regularly used when a speaker repeats a question because the other person didn't hear it properly.
>
> 　　Wells (2006: 46)

e.　A: Has Mr. ↗Paddington been in?
　　B: Sorry?
　　A: *Has Mr.* ↘*Paddington been in?*

f.　A: Sit down. Do you ⌐play ↗chess?
　　B: Pardon?

A: I said, *do you* ⌐*play* ↘ *chess*?

B: Why, yes.

g. A: Do you ↗like me?

B: You're cute.

A: I know that. *But do you* ↘ *like me?*

h. [*On Golden Pond*. 少年 A が高齢の老人 B に尋ねる]

A: Hey, Norman. Are you af⌐raid of ↗dying?

B: What?

A: *Are you af⌐raid to* ↘ *die?*

B: What the hell kind of question is that?

A: I was just wondering, that's all.

i. A: Do you ⌐speak ↗French?

B: No.

A: *Do you* ⌐*speak* ↘ *German then?*

j. A: Can you ↗eat it?

B: No.

A: Well, *can you* ↘ *drink it then?*

文献からは

```
A:          finiˢʰ
     Did he

B. Well, he's over at the grad school office right now, and...

A: Ye              fin
     ah, but did he    ish                    Ladd (1980: 105)
```

時には、苛立ち、強要、威嚇を表すときにも下降調になる。

k. [父親が、child molester について小学生の娘に問い詰める]

Did he touch you? What're you laughing about? Why are you smiling? I'm asking you a question. *Did he* ↘ *touch you?*

l. Did you put it where I told you to, down the lavatory? Did you? Answer me! ↘ *Did you?*

更に言えば、答えが明白な修辞的な yes-no questions も下降調になる。

m. Then the Lord said to Cain, "Where is your brother Abel?" "I don't know," he replied. "⌐Am I my ⌐brother's ↘keeper?" − 聖書「創世記」

注：A saying from the Bible's story of <u>Cain and Abel</u>. After Cain had murdered his brother Abel, God asked him where his brother was. Cain answered, "I know not; am I my brother's keeper?"

参考 1：General British English の yes-no 疑問文では、上昇調と下降上昇調（左図）が広まっている。General American では高上昇調（右図）が一般的である。

Lindsey (2019: 104)　　　　　　　　　詳細は、伊達 (2019) の課題 4 参照。

参考 2：上昇調の場合、核強勢を起点とするピッチの上昇は、文の最後まで徐々に継続していくとされている。しかし、尾部が長いとき、必ずしもそうとはならず、途中で平板調になり、最後で上昇することがある。

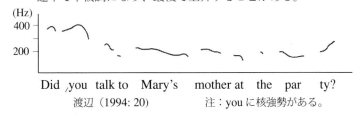

渡辺（1994: 20）　　　　　　注：you に核強勢がある。

When the tail is a long one, the ascending sequence of syllables of a high rise may be interrupted by a middle level plateau before a final upward kick, e.g.

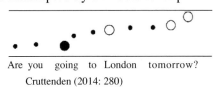

Cruttenden (2014: 280)

参考 3：日本語の yes-no 疑問文でも上昇調になるが、英語のパタンとは大きく異なる。英語では上昇イントネーションが句全体に及ぶ。日本語では最後の音節だけをヒョイと高くして発音する。

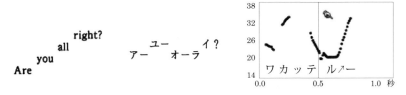

「わかってる？」でも、「る」だけを高く言う。英語学習者は、この日本語の癖に用心しなければならない。右上図は、郡（2020: 138）からである。

課題 10 **Topic vs. comment**

　英語に限らず、たいがいの言語では、情報上で最も重要な項目は文尾に置かれ、そこに「落ち」（punch line）がある。これは、end focus（末尾焦点）とか end weight（末尾重点）と呼ばれる。しかし、英語は、ほぼ語順が定まっていて柔軟性を欠くので、情報的に副次的な語や句、節を文末に配置せざるを得ないことがある。その際、イントネーションが、主情報（major/primary information）と副次的情報（minor/secondary information）との区別をする。主情報——通例、新情報——は下降調で、副次的情報——通例、既知情報、付加的情報——は上昇調または下降上昇調で発せられる。

> [P]erhaps we might say that the basic meaning of a falling tone is something like 'major information' or 'primary information'. Correspondingly, the shared general meaning of non-falling tones is something like 'incomplete information', 'minor information', 'secondary information'. We use falls and non-falls together to indicate the structuring of our message, showing what is primary (by a fall) and what is secondary (by a non-falling tone).
>
> Wells (2006: 72)

　叙述文は、通例、topic（主題）と comment（評言）に分かれる。そして、topic とは、既に文脈にある内容のことで、上昇調または下降上昇調で言われる。一方、comment とは、topic についての新たに発せられる見解のことで、下降調で言われる。一般に、文では topic は主語であり、comment が後続するパターンが多い。

> The 'topic' is in many cases the subject of the sentence, but is more generally the point of departure, something the speaker intends to comment on.　　　Knowles (1987: 169)

a.　|John ↗Wells | is a |world-famous phone ↘tician.
　　(= Talking of John Wells, he is a world-famous phonetician.)

b.　Your ↗laundry | will be |ready to ↘morrow.

c.　［エスカレーター付近の掲示］
　　↗Dogs | must be ↘carried.
　　犬を連れた人に向けた掲示であるので、犬は topic である。

d.　［電車内でのアナウンス］

　　↗Passengers ｜ should ⌐take their ⌐litter ↘home with them.

しかし、時には comment が先行し、topic が後続することもある。例えば、

e.　A: I heard that someone in your family has been to England.

　　B: My ⌐youngest ↘son ｜ has ⌐been to ↗England.

f.　A: I'm going to Sheffield.　　（イギリス中部の工業都市）

　　B: Really? My ↘mother ｜ ⌐came from ↗Sheffield.

g.　[Someone mentions Manchester. After a bit of silence, another speaker says]

　　　　　　　kíd bró

　My

　　　　　　　　ther lived in　　chester•••'

　　　　　　　　　　　　Mán　　　　　　　come to think of it.

　　　　　　Bolinger (1986: 332)

　　　注：*come to think of it*（そう言えば）は、文末では低上昇になる。課題 53 参照。

h.　A: What do you think of Jack?

　　B1: I ↘like ｜ ↗him.

　　B2: ↗Him ｜ I ↘like.

　最後に、topic と comment の視点から以下の比較対照の例を見比べてみよう。Ladd (2008: 68) からである。

　　Question: What about Anna? Who did she come with?

　　Answer: Anna came with Manny.

　　Question: What about Manny? Who came with him?

　　Answer: Anna came with Manny.

　　最初の文と他の文での *Manny* は、それぞれ新情報と既知情報であるので音調が異なっている。後者では、Manny は下降上昇調になっているが、上昇調よりも more emphatic である。

　　なお、faster speech ならば、↘Anna came with Manny. となるだろうが、その場合、Manny は尾部の一部として低いピッチの終結部を受け継ぐ。

課題 11　異例な付加疑問文

(i) 付加疑問文（tag または tag question）は、平叙文（statement）や疑問文の末尾に付加され、先行する主文に従属する。話者が純粋に情報を求めているならば、付加疑問部は上昇調になり、一方、下降調の場合は、speaker と hearer 両者に明らかなことに言及があり、純粋の疑問文というよりも、むしろ感嘆文と類似している。多くの教本には、「下降調を用いた場合は、話し手は聞き手の同意を求めている」とあるが、わざわざ返答の必要もないことが多い。

> The tag with a rising tone invites verification, expecting the hearer to decide the truth of the proposition in the statement. The tag with the falling tone, on the other hand, invites confirmation of the statement, and has the force of an exclamation rather than a genuine question. The truth of the statement may be self-evident, and therefore no response is expected.
>
> *I wasn't born yesterday, was I?*　（私は、そんなに世間知らずではないからね）
>
> Greenbaum & Quirk (1990: 235)

以下の付加疑問文——上昇調——でも hearer からの返答を求めていない。それは、checking question と呼ばれ、「そうか〜なんだね」という意味である。このタイプの文は、しばしば **so** または **oh** が文頭に来て、かなり明白な事柄や、既に言及された事柄についてのコメントにすぎない。

a.　A: Uncle, this is Myra. Myra, this is my uncle Duke.

　　B: *So* |*this is* ↘*Myra,* | ↗*is it?*　How do you do?

b.　A: Guess who I had a letter from this morning.

　　B: *Oh,* | *so he's* |*still* ↘*writing to you,* | ↗*is he?*

c.　A: *So* |*Alison's teaching* |*Economic Ge*↘*ography,* | ↗*is she?*

　　B: No, she's only studying it.

しかし、文脈次第では、疑念や皮肉を暗示することもある。

d.　*So he* |*thinks he can* |*easily* ↘*beat me at the game,* | ↗*does he?*

　　Well, he's got another think coming.　（大間違いだ）

e.　*So you* |*think you'll* |*ace the* ↘*test,* | ↗*do you?*　（テストで優をとる）

　　Well, good luck then.

f.　*So* ↘*Jane thinks* | *she's the* |*prettiest girl in the* ↘*town,* | ↗*does she?*

I'd say she's a big frog in a small pond.

g. *So you* ⌐*call* ⌐*that hard* ↘*work*, | ↗*do you?*

(ii) 昔、高校の教科書にあった異例な付加疑問文を紹介しよう。

Woman: [As she gets on a bus] Excuse me. Could you tell me whether this bus goes to Walnut Heights?

Driver: ① *It* ⌐*says "Walnut Heights" on the* ↘*front of the bus,* | ↗*doesn't it?* Then it goes to Walnut Heights.

Woman: How long does it take?

Driver: Look, lady. I'm in a hurry. Just get on the bus and I'll call out when we get there.

Man: [Behind the woman and also getting on the bus]
Driver, I think you could have spoken to her in a little more friendly manner.

Driver: ② *Oh, you* ↘*do*, | ↗*do you?*

両方の付加疑問文は上昇調で発せられる。①は、相手の同意や確認を求めているのではない。むしろ、不満を口に出している（grumble）。driver の本音は、"Yes, of course. Are you too careless to know that?" であろう。この場合の tag は、低上昇調である。

参考：He's ↘ passed, /hasn't he? (low rise: non-committal, grumbling)

Tench (1996: 127)

また、②は、「それがどうした」──"So what?" or "I don't care about your opinion."──という挑発的な意味である。ここでも tag は低上昇調である。

a. A: I was angry with you then.
   B: *Oh, you* ↘*were*, | ↗*were you?*

b. A: She thinks you're too lazy to do it.
   B: *Oh, she* ↘*does*, | ↗*does she?*

c. A: You're a mass of prejudices, aren't you? You're so much thought and so little feeling.
   B: *Oh, I* ↘*am*, | ↗*am I?*

これらの例文は、低い音域（low pitch range）やきしみ声（creaky voice）を伴う。声帯の振動数が低いので低い声になる。

なお、対話中の *Driver, I think you could have spoken to her in a little more friendly manner.* のイントネーションについては、課題41を参照。

参考：低い音域 low pitch range は不機嫌や皮肉を表すことが多く、high pitch は強い
感情表現や感情移入（involvement）を表出する。

　　・Speakers can use the pitch of their voice to send a variety of messages
　　　because it helps express intentions. Everyone has his or her own normal pitch
　　　range. In ordinary speech, we usually keep within the lower part of our pitch
　　　change, but if we want to express stronger feelings or involvement, one of
　　　the signals we can use is extra pitch height.

　　　　Rogerson & Gilbert (1990: 64)

　　・We can usually tell whether a speaker is angry or loving by listening to the
　　　tune without even hearing the words. The pitch of the voice carries much of
　　　the emotional content of speech. Ladefoged (2001: 17)

以下の2図は共に words を発しない発話の音調曲線（pitch contour）であ
る。左図は high pitch での、そして右図は low pitch での発話である。前者は
contented を、後者は *upset or angry* を表している。

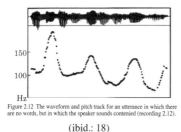

Figure 2.12 The waveform and pitch track for an utterance in which there are no words, but in which the speaker sounds contenied (recording 2.12). 　　 Figure 2.13 The waveform and pitch track for an utterance in which there are no words, but in which the speaker sounds upset or angry (recording 2.13).

(ibid.: 18)

　以下の対話中の下線部は、低いピッチで発せられ negative feeling を表すだろう。

① ［雨漏りがする家で］

　　Husband: Don't worry about a little rain, Helga. Remember, April showers bring
　　　　　　May flowers.

　　Wife: Great. With these dirt floors, I'll have fresh flowers growing in my kitchen.

② A: I knew I'd seen you.

　　B: Which of my movies have you seen?

　　A: I don't remember. I saw one once. I don't go to the movies much. If you've
　　　seen one, you've seen them all.（映画はどれも似たり寄ったりだ）

　　B: (Stung) Oh, thank you.

課題 12 「時の副詞」

(i)「時の副詞」（today, tomorrow, yesterday, now, then など）は、音調単位の最後にあり、その前に新情報を担う語があるとき、通例、文アクセントを受けない。その理由は、恐らく、これらの副詞が、主情報に付随する二次的情報と見なされるからである。文末の「場所の副詞」も同じである。

　日本語では、「時の副詞」は文頭に来るのが普通である。そのために、「昨日、〜した」とか「明日、〜するつもり」を英語で言ったり書いたりするとき、文頭に「時の副詞」を置く学習者が多い。文頭に置く場合と文尾に置く場合とに違いがあることに注意を払わない。

　英語のネーテイブスピーカーには、両者の意味のニュアンスは違う。「時の副詞」を<u>文尾</u>に置くのは default pattern である。それに対して、それを<u>文頭</u>に置くのは、「わけあり」である。日本文学研究者・翻訳家のアラン・ターニー（1988: 177-8）は、次のように言う。

> 英米人が語順を操作するときは、意味を変えたい場合だ。ふつうは文章の尻尾にある言葉を、アタマにもってくれば、意味は全然違ってくる。次の二つの文に、意味の差を感じられるかどうか。
>
> 　(i) I went to the cinema yesterday.
> 　(ii) Yesterday I went to the cinema.
>
> 前者は、ごく普通の言い回しで、「きのう映画を観に行ったよ」。後者は、「きのうは特別なことがあったんだ。きのう、しばらくぶりに映画を観に行ってね」だ。（中略）回数からいうと、後者はめったに使われない。

また、マーク・ピーターセン（2013: 199-201）は、次のように助言している。

> 日本人の書いた英文を見ると、「この頃」や「最近は」が日本語の文頭に来るときは、英語でも迷わず、"These days,..." を文頭に置くというお決まりの傾向が実に強い。
>
> 　these days という表現は、英語では特に「常に文頭に置くべき」表現ではない。【中略】それでは「この頃」「最近」と言いたいときは、どうすればいいのだろうか。多くの場合、these days よりも、recently や lately, today, at present, now などを使ったほうが「大人の文章」になる。【中略】なお、さらに洗練された文にしたい場合、［これらを］文頭ではなく、文

中や文尾に置くことも考えておくといい。

(ii) 冒頭には文末の「時 / 場所の副詞」は主情報に付随する<u>二次的情報</u>と見なされるとある。なぜそのように見なされるのか。その理由は、「時 / 場所の副詞」の「遍在性」(ubiquity/omnipresence) にある。この語の辞書定義では、"seeming to be everywhere or in several places at the same time; very common"--- *Oxford Advanced Learner's Dictionary*

これらの副詞は、文中に頻繁に登場するので、わざわざ強調するのは余計 (superfluity) なことである。Bolinger (1986: 380) の解説が明解である。

> [T]ime and place adverbials are the ones most often deaccented when they occur at the end of the sentence:
>
> > Anything happen while I was gone?　— Well, Henry got a new job a couple of days ago, but nothing much else has happened around here since you left.
>
> This simply reflects the ubiquity of the *here* and *now* or the *there* and *then*, and the relative superfluity of emphazing either.

ところで時間のみならず、人生や精神も日常生活において遍在する概念である。

> *Time*, *life*, and *spirit* are always with us, and though each of these terms may be accented, none needs to be… The omnipresence of time embraces all the common names of temporal periods —*hour*, *day*, *month*, *year*—in prepositional phrases and noun phrases used adverbially…
>
> > Bolinger (1987: 69)

「場所の副詞」の遍在性について解説を見てみよう。

> Locatives, like names, are often deaccented to suggest to the hearer that the location is familiar, close at hand, 'in the context' somehow, to signal that no real 'news' is involved in the specification of the location.
>
> > Ladd (1980: 91)

上記の locatives (「場所の副詞」) と location を、「時の副詞」に置き換えてみよう。両者の遍在性が推測できる。

課題 13　反駁の intonation

(i)　英語では、相手の言ったことに反駁（contradiction）または不満を表す典型的なイントネーションがある。大まかに言えば、冒頭でピッチが高く始まり下降に転じ、それから低いピッチになり、最後に（低）上昇するというパタンである。

a.　A: How are you going to stand up against an enemy as formidable
　　　　as that?　（君は、あんな恐ろしい敵にどうやって立ち向うのか）
　　　B: I'm not a coward. I wouldn't run.

　　　　I'm　　　　　　　　　I
　　　　　not a　　　　　　wouldn't　n.
　　　　　　coward.　　　　　　　　ru

b.　［暴力沙汰を咎められて］

　　　　I　　　　　　　　　I'm
　　　　didn't hit him!　　　not to blame!

c.　A: Aren't you afraid that John will get violent?
　　　B: John wouldn't hurt anybody.

　　　　John
　　　　　wouldn't hurt anybody!

　　　　　(adapted from Bolinger (1986: 191 & 271))

　さて、これらの音調曲線において、冒頭の下降のピッチの動きは、どのように解釈すればよいのか。それは下降調の核なのか、あるいは高下降の頭部なのか、その判断が難しい。本書では、便宜的に冒頭の高い部分を（下降調の）核強勢として表記することにする。

　　　↘I'm ｜ not a ↗coward.　　　↘I ｜ wouldn't ↗run.
　　　↘I ｜ didn't hit ↗him.　　　↘I'm ｜ not to ↗blame.

　なお、下降調の表記↘は、ピッチがいきなり下降するのではなく、直前にピッチが上昇して（step up）してから下降に転じる。実質的には rise-fall-rise

というピッチ変化がある。

> CONTRADICTION…can be seen in terms of its separate pitch movements. What makes it especially interesting is that it is not a single contour but a family of three contours with an overall similar shape that produces a similar meaning… The overall shape is rise-fall-rise… (ibid.: 246)

ところで、このような定型化した音調曲線は、contradiction だけでなく mild/polite disagreement/correction を伝える場合にも使われる。

d. ［TV show *All in the Family*、妊娠中の Gloria は夫の浮気を疑っている］

　　Gloria: Why wouldn't he be running around, Ma? Look at me --- I'm fat and ugly.

　　Mother: (solicitously) Aw, Gloria, you're not ugly. (canned laughter)

```
                    you're
    Aw, Gloria,           not
                              ug1y        Ladd (1980: 151)
```

　　注：母は、fat であることを認めている。

e. ［ある不慮の事故に対して自己を責めている相手に向かって］

```
        Nó                        ít's
    body's blaming   u,      not     your fault.
                   yó              your
```

f. ［John's mother complains to his father that he doesn't eat his spinach. She takes her husband to the dining room and points to John.］

　　Husband:
```
          He's                        why are you complain
              éating it!      So                        ing?
```
　　　　Bolinger (1986: 180 & 204)

(ii) その他、諸々の事例を紹介しよう。

a. A: I've never heard of it.

　　B: ↘ *Yes,* | *you* ↗ *have*.

b. A: She knows already.

　　B: ↘ *No,* | *she* ↗ *doesn't*.

c. ［A：母；B：幼児］

　　A: No more stories now. Get to bed. Come on.

　　B: ↘ *I* | *don't want to go to* ↗ *bed!*

56

d.　A: So what's John doing now?

　　B: Oh, I hear that he's teaching school in Boston.

　　C: ↘*John's* ｜ ˈ*not in* ↗*Boston*. He's in Denver now.

e.　[*Full House*]

　　Boy 1: Let's play superheroes.

　　Boy 2: OK. I'll be Batman.

　　Boy 1: I'll be Superman.

　　Girl:　 I'll be the Little Mermaid.

　　Boy 1: ↘*That's* ｜ ˈ*not a* ↗*superhero*. That's a fish.

f.　A: I'd like to meet your daughter some day.

　　B: ↘*No,* ｜ *you* ↗*wouldn't*. She's still in college. Besides she's not your type.

g.　A: I'd like to see where you live.

　　B: ↘*No,* ｜ *you* ↗*wouldn't*.

　　A: Oh, come on!

h.　A: I'll come with you.

　　B: ↘*No,* ｜ *you* ↗*won't!*

i.　[*Downton Abbey*. 貴族の跡取り息子が戦死した]

　　A: Mr. Patrick was his only son. Now he'd dead. What happens next?

　　B: I thought Lady Mary was the heir.

　　A: She's a girl, stupid. ↘*Girls* ｜ ˈ*can't in* ↗*herit*.

j.　[At a Chinese restaurant]

　　A: The food in this restaurant is great. I've eaten here so many times.
　　　　You're going to love this place.

　　B: Good. What did you eat before?

　　A: Well, my favorite is bird-tongue soup.

　　B: Bird-tongue soup? ↘*Birds* ｜ ˈ*don't have* ↗*tongues*.

　　A: I know. That's just the name of the dish.

k.　[*The Wizard of Oz*. Dorothy は道に迷っている]

　　Dorothy: Now which way do we go?

　　Voice: Pardon me. That way is a very nice way.

　　Dorothy: Who said that? [She looks around for the voice. Toto barks at the
　　　　　　　Scarecrow.] Don't be silly, Toto. ↘*Scarecrows* ｜ ˈ*don't* ↗*talk*.

ところで、I beg your pardon. には、相手の発言に対して反駁する意味もある。

l. [*Downton Abbey.* 使用人 O'Brien は自分が解雇される噂を耳にする]

    A: Miss O'Brien, we have the impression that you're planning a change of some sort.

    B: What do you mean?

    A: That you're leaving.

    B: ↘*I* | ˈ*beg your* ↗*pardon!*

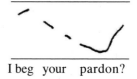

I beg your pardon?

    How dare you make such an assumption?

m. A: You're sitting in my seat.

    B: ↘*I* | ˈ*beg your* ↗*pardon.*

    Even when it is used with, say, an apology, the resultant meaning is still contradiction.　　Glenn (1977: 48)

参考：上記では、Girls can't inherit; Birds don't have tongues; Scarecrows don't talk. を反駁調で表記したが、それ以外のイントネーションも考えられる。例えば、Wells によれば、

    ˈBirds don't ↘have tongues!　（注：matter-of-fact 事務的な）

    Or, if you want to be very polite and deferential,

    ˈBirds ˈdon't have ∨tongues!

    The use of the exclamation mark suggests that this is not a polite response, but an exclamation. (2009.1.7)

    注：例文の末尾の下降上昇調に代わって上昇調（/）もあり得る。但し、前者のほうが more emphatic である。

　イントネーションは、話者の意思と談話の状況と密接に関連しているので、同じ文を言うのに、複数の「正しい」パタンがある。学習者には、反駁のイントネーションは極めて難関なので、その前段階として、上記の「参考」にある基本的なパタンを練習して、それに慣れた時点で、反駁に移るほうが得策である。

参考：今回は、反駁の音調曲線に見られる下降調＋上昇調を考察してきた。実は、この音調曲線が伝える意味は、話者の意思と談話の状況と密接に関係していて、反駁以外にも、いろいろな意味がある。それらは、伊達（2019）と本書の随所で論じている。

　　以下で述べる下降調＋上昇調のケースは、私が以前から関心があるものである。

I was walking along the street one day…and I saw a wallet on the pavement.
Well, I picked it up and I thought: I'll take it to the police… I had a look into
the wallet, and there was some money, and some cards and tickets and so on,
and a photo. I looked at the photo and suddenly I thought: I ↘ knew ｜ ↗ him.
It was an old friend from school.　　Marks (2007: 98)

　実は、私は、類似例 I ↘ know ｜ ↗ her. について課題 39 の中段で「話者が、*her* に
関心がある場合、そこに上昇調の文アクセントを置く。この場合、上昇調は minor
information——二次的重要度——であることを示している」と述べている。I ↘ knew ｜ ↗ him.
についても同じことが言える。しかし、ネーテイブスピーカー音声学者の意見を知り
たく思い、Mark Hancock——*English Pronunciation in Use* (*Intermediate*) の著者——
にメールを送り教示を求めた。以下は、返信（2010.9.21）の全文である。私は、関心
の観点から論じているが、彼は、対比の観点から解説をしている。

　注：ここでは音調単位の区切りは明示しない。

Hi, Tami

Thanks for drawing my attention to that example in Jonathan Marks' book.
Although Jonathan doesn't explicitly divide the discourse into tone units,
we can suppose that for each arrow, there is one tone unit. So the sentence *I
know him* has been divided into two units: //I know / him//

Why would the speaker want to place such emphasis here? Well, it's the
crucial moment in the whole story － a big surprising coincidence. Both
know and *him* could be seen as <u>contrasting</u> with alternatives:

　　-*Know*: not only do I have his wallet and photo in front of me, but on top
　　　of that, I actually *know* him.

　　-*Him*: I know many people, but who would have imagined that I would
　　　actually know the very person whose wallet I've found?

In order to make both of these contrasts, the speaker has to use two tone
units. As regards the tone, it may be analyzed as follows: *I know* is new
information, so gets a fall. *Him* is old information and so gets a rise.

　なお、話者が、特定の語を他の語と「対比」させるということは、その語に「関心」
がある証しなので、Hancock と私とは同じ観点を共有していると言える。

課題 14　I knew I would see you somewhere.

(i)　昔、会議で隣に同席したイギリス人と挨拶を交わしている時、私と同じマンションに引っ越してきたと聞き驚いたことがある。その後、暫らくお互いに顔を合わせることがなかった。ある日、マンションのエレベーターでばったり出会った。そのとき、彼は開口一番、次のように言った。

　① *I* ↘*knew* ｜ *I would* ↗*see you somewhere.*

後日、私はこの文のイントネーションを分析的に考え始めた。例えば、他にどのようなイントネーションが可能だろうか。

　② *I* ↘*knew I would see you somewhere.*

　これは、話者が、いずれ私と出くわすことを確信していたこと（certainty）を表す言い方である。では、①のイントネーションをどのように解釈すればいいのだろうか。これは、もう少し personal feeling が込められていて、自分の予想・期待が的中したことを伝えており、*see you somewhere* を 2 次的に重要であると見做している。そして、2 次的な内容（minor information）は、通例、上昇調で言われる。

　上記の ① と ② 以外に、3 つ目のイントネーションも考えられる。

　③ *I* ˈ*knew I would* ↘*see you somewhere.*

これは、客観的な発言（objective statement）である。

　以上のように、①に見られる下降調＋上昇調のパタンは、話者の prediction / expectation が的中したこと、換言すれば、真実性（factuality）があったことを示す。

　参考として、文献からの例を挙げておこう。各パタンは、それぞれ、上記の②、③、①に対応している。

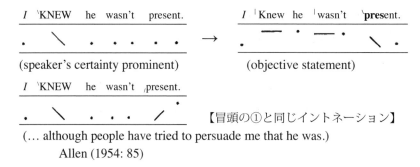

(... although people have tried to persuade me that he was.)
　　　Allen (1954: 85)

最後の下降調＋上昇調の例では、話者は、自分が正しかったことに――I told

you so.──ほくそ笑んでいるだろう。

(ii) 以下も、話者が言ったことの真実性に関わる例である。

A person coming upon a gravestone with the epitaph

I told the doctor

that I was sick.

is tempted to recite

I told the doc tor that I was si
ck.

（中略）which makes little sense. But if the epitaph is read as

told
I　　　the
doctor that I was sick!

the joke comes clear: I told him so and I was right and my being here
proves it.　　　　　　　　Bolinger (1989: 68-9)

墓標のメッセージは、故人が、生前に残したものである。日本語ならば、「私
は病気だと言ったのに」となるだろう。下降調の前者は、状況を反映しないの
でナンセンスである。なぜならば、それは、予想外れの意味を伝えるからであ
る。彼が医者に言ったとおりのことが起こった。自分の予想が当たるというこ
とは、予想した内容が場面に存在しており既知情報としての扱いになるので上
昇調で言われる。一方、自分の予想が外れるということは、言った情報内容が
場面に存在せず新しい情報として扱われるので下降調になる。
類例を示そう。
　サッカーの試合結果の予想が的中した場合、
・A: Manchester United 2, Arsenal 2.
　B: _I_ ↘ _thought_ ｜ _it would be a_ ↗ _draw_.
一方、予想外れの場合には、
・A: Manchester United 2, Leeds United 3.
　B: _You_ ｜ _said they'd_ ↘ _draw_.
注：上記で _tempted to recite_ とあるのは reading stereotype のことである。詳細は、課題
　　32 の「参考」欄を参照。

課題 15　How high are they?

(i) 以下は、旧版の中学検定教科書 *New Horizon 2* が出典である。

a.　Ken: What a great view!

　　Paula: You see, the Horseshoe Falls look like a big horseshoe.

　　Ken: Yes. *How high are they?*

　　Paula: 160 feet. The American Falls are higher, but the Horseshoe Falls are
　　　　　　wider.

斜体字の文について、ほとんどの人は、*high* が最も強調されて──核強勢を受けて──発音されると思うだろう。実際、How old are you? とか How tall are you? でも old と tall が最も目立って言われる。しかし、教員用指導書には、赤色の音調曲線で *are* に核強勢があると明示されている。なぜだろうか。それには、談話上の理由がある。換言すれば、それは、新情報 vs. 既知情報の概念と関係する。比較対照の例を紹介しよう。

① A: There's the famous Sky Tree.

　 B: Wow! ᐟ*How* ↘*high is it?*

② A: There's the Sky Tree. As you can see, it's very high.

　 B: ᐟ*How high* ↘*is it?* (or ↘*How high is it?*)

結論を先に言えば、a では、Ken と Paula は巨大な滝を目前にしており、それが高いことは、両者の間で shared information になっている。もし Paula が、The Horseshoe Falls are very high. と言っていたら、Ken は ↘How high are they? と言うかもしれない。富士山の高さを尋ねるときも、How ↘high is it? または How high ↘is it? となるだろう。どちらになるかは、会話中の context が決め手になる。Wells にコメントを求めた。

> I would explain by saying that both participants in the conversation already
> know that the falls are high, and treat this fact as being something that they
> both know (Gosh, they're high!) ─ so obvious we don't need to mention
> it. ─ And *how high ARE they, in fact?)
>
> 　　　注：*は強勢を示す。

b.　A: How old would you say I am?

　　B: I don't know. Maybe…51?

　　A: Oh.

B: ⌐*How old* ↘ *are you?*

c.　[Nursing home の入居者どうしの会話]

A: Would you like some grape juice?

B: I'd love it. Thank you. （薬の袋に気づき）Wow! So many pills!

　⌐*How sick* ↘ *are you?*

A: Well, sickness has become a relative term for me. I think of it now as more a general wearing-out process.

d.　[音楽学校での受付係（A）と受講生（B）とのやりとり]

A: Hi! Do you have guitar lessons today?

B: Yes, I do.

A: What time do they start?

B: At 3: 30.

A: Uh-oh! You're late!

B: Really? [In surprise] *What time* ↘ *is it?*

A: It's 3: 40.

(ii) 次は、How much is it? を含む対話である。

A: I need a couple of shirts. Grey Terylene, please.　注：Terylene は商標名

B: Certainly, sir. I'll just get some out. (After a while) Here's a nice shirt; we sell a lot of this one.

A: Yes. It's the sort of style I want. I'll take it. *How much is it?*

斜体字部では、どこに核強勢が来るだろうか。⌐How ↘ much is it? もあり得るが、通例は、⌐How much ↘ is it? である。なぜならば、much は、他の内容語（high, tall, old, etc.）よりも意味的に抽象的であるからである。Wells からコメントをもらった。

・This is the expected tonicity for *wh + be*. It is the same as in **What IS it?*, **Where WAS it?* (Though I agree that *How MUCH is it?* would be possible…The point is that *how much* counts as a kind of single interrogative wh-word.)　注：tonicity は核強勢配置と同義語である。

SUPRAS のメンバーからも返信があった。

・It is a little trickier with *much* and I can't explain it well… "How much IS it?" is the one that strikes me as <u>neutral</u> in this situation:

A: Here's a nice shirt.

B: How much *is* it? (2005. 3. 8)　　注：is に文アクセントがある。

しかし、以下のような短縮形では、

A: Was it expensive?

B: Quite expensive.

A: ˈHow ↘much?

B: A thousand pounds.

(iii) How young is he?

　愛らしい子どもを見かけて、How old is he? と言うのに、なぜ How young is he? とは言わないのかと、発音ワークショップで尋ねられたことがある。両者の違いは何だろうか。前者は、文脈なしで、唐突に発することもできるが、後者では、必ず何らかの前提が必要である。例えば、「彼は若い」という前提があり、「彼はどれほど若いのか」という質問に限って、How young is he? と言える。その場合、young は既知情報であるから、ˈHow young ↘is he? または↘How young is he? となる。

　以下の例では、*rich* と *smart* は、初出語であるが文脈上、既知語であると解釈できる。

a.　A: My! Is he rolling in money!　（金があり余っている）

　　B: Really? *How* ˈ*rich* ↘*is he?*

b.　A: When it comes to math, we have nothing on Tanaka.　（田中にはかなわない）

　　B: *How* ˈ*smart* ↘*is he?*

但し、他の核強勢配置も可能である。

参考：How much is it? では、通例、much には文アクセントが置かれないと述べたが、以下のように名詞主語を伴う文では、much には文アクセントが来る。リズムが影響する。How ˈmuch is the ↘doggie in the window?

課題 16　命令文（commands）

　My Fair Lady で、ロンドン下町の花売り娘 Eliza は、路上で Higgins から、自分の「汚い」発音を酷評される。彼女は、その場では憤慨したが、後に冷静になって、発音矯正レッスンを受けることを決断する。そして、将来は、高級住宅区域 Mayfair——下町訛りでは *Myfair*——の flower shop で働くことを夢見る。ある日、不躾に Higgins 宅を訪問する。彼の親友で同居人 Pickering と housekeeper の Mrs. Pearce は、丁寧に対応する。以下のやりとりでは、Sit down. が 4 回も発せられる。

　Pickering: [Gently] What do you want, my girl?

　Eliza: I want to be a lady in a flower shop 'stead of sellin' at the corner o' Tottenham Court Road.（中略）He said he could teach me. Well, here I am, ready to pay him

　Higgins: [Peremptorily] *Sit down*.

　Eliza: Oh, well, if you're going to make a compliment of it?

　Higgins: [Thundering at her] *Sit down!*

　Mrs. Pearce: [Severely] *Sit down*, girl. Do as you're told.

　Pickering: What's your name?

　Eliza: Eliza Doolittle.

　Pickering: [Very courteous] *Won't you sit down*, Miss Doolittle?

　Eliza: [Coyly] Oh, I don't mind if I do.

さて、状況から判断して、4 つの Sit down. のイントネーションは決して同じではないだろう。「高圧的に（peremptorily）」、「怒鳴りつけるように（thundering）」、「厳しく（severely）」、「丁重に（courteously）」はそれぞれ反映したイントネーションに分かれる。

これから命令文の様々なイントネーション型を紹介していく。
(i) 明白な命令の場合、下降調になる。

　ꞌPut it ↘down. (firm and authoritative)

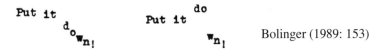

Bolinger (1989: 153)

65

しかし、例外もある。相手への配慮や利益（benefit）を表すときも下降調の command が使われることがある。以下の命令文は、command ではなく cordial invitation である。

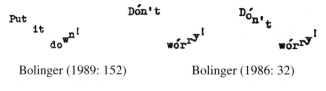

Bolinger (1989: 151)

(ii) なだめたり、助言したり、または励ましたりするときには非下降調－上昇調または下降上昇調－が使われる。

Bolinger (1989: 152)　　　　　Bolinger (1986: 32)

注：オンセットはしばしば高いピッチで言われる。

2 つの文献からの解説を紹介しよう。

・Leech & Svartvik (1994: 166):

[I]t is <not impolite> to use a command when you are telling someone to do something for his or her own good: *Have another chocolate; Make yourself at home; Just leave everything to me; Do come in*. These are in effect offers or invitations rather than commands. One way to tone down or weaken the imperative force of a command is to use a rising or fall-rise tone, instead of the usual falling tone:

Be ↘↗careful.

ˈDon't forget your ↗wallet.

・Demands take a falling tone, but 'coaxing/urging' which leaves the final decision to the addressee takes a rising tone; compare, e.g.

Come ↘on (= demand)

Come ↗on (= coaxing)　　　Tench (1990: 370)

参考：［挑発 / 疑念］ˈCome ↘on then, ∣ hit me! / Oh, ˈcome ↘on, ∣ don't lie!

　　　［激励 / 勧誘］ˈCome ↗on, ∣ you can do it. / ˈCome ↗on, ∣ cheer up!

(iii) 下降上昇は、警告を発するときに使われる。

Just ˈleave me a↘↗lone.

léave me alóne!

Just

Bolinger (1986: 233)

a. ˈWatch ↘↗out!

b. Well, ˈbe ↘↗careful. The roads are terribly icy.

c. There's a step. ˈMind you don't ↘↗fall. / ↘↗Mind.

(iv) 高上昇調で言うと威圧的（threatening とか imperious tone）になる。以下も Bolinger からである。

　ˈPut it ↗down.　　　　　　　　↗Hold it!（Stop it! は少し延ばし加減）

Put it down!

Hóld it!

(1989: 152)　　　　　　(1986: 257)

(v) 平板調で言うと、うんざりした口調になる。これは、〈高平坦＋中平坦調〉である。

If I wish to suggest that I am bored with the whole thing, I may say…

Put it

down!　(1989: 152-3)　　　　参考：

なお、平板調は短い型通りの command に用いられる。詳細は課題 33 参照。

では、冒頭で紹介した *My Fair Lady* での *Sit down.* は、上記のパタンのどちらになるのかと、読者の皆さんは知りたく思うだろう。そこで、実際の場面を観て調べたところ、「peremptorily」は (iv)、「thundering」は (i)、「severely」も (i)、「courteously」は (ii) に一致した。

　但し、「thundering」と「severely」には、それぞれ high fall and low fall という違いが聞かれる。前者はより高圧的である。

課題 17　Unity stress

(i) 初出の名詞主語と述語形容詞または述語動詞から成り立つ短い文において、両者間に意味的関連がある場合は、より重要な要素である主語に核強勢が来る。

A sentence consisting of a subject and a short predicate, both of which are new to the situation, often has the nuclear glide on the subject... Such a sentence forms a unity of communication with only one peak of prominence. The nuclear glide occurs on the most important word of this announcement, which is the grammatical subject.　注：nuclear glide 音調核

(At the window:)　↘*Father's coming*.　　概論の7と8を参照。

I've found out about that noise in the garage; the ↘*water was running*.

It's freezing cold in here; the ↘*windows must have been left open*.

Here are, for comparison, some sentences which have two peaks of prominence.

Mother (speaking of her children): |*Janet is in* ↘*Manchester*.

(Explaining why one has taken only an umbrella:) *My* |*raincoat's at the* ↘*cleaners'*.　　(adapted from Schubiger (1958: 84))　　下線は伊達が追加。

他の unity stress の例を挙げよう。主語と述語との間には、意味的な関連がある。

a.　A: Hurry up, Johnny.

　　B: Why? *Is* ↗*breakfast ready?*

　　A: Uh-huh, ↘*breakfast's ready*.

b.　A: Time to go to bed. *Are the* ↗*lights out?*

　　B: Yes, *the* ↘↗*lights are out, the* ↘↗*doors are locked*, and *the* ↘*windows are shut*.

上記の例では、主語名詞に prominence——文アクセント——がある。朝になって、母親が "Breakfast!" と言えば、Breakfast is ready. の意味である。家庭で照明と言えば on と off、玄関の扉と言えば locked と unlocked、窓と言えば open と shut は、predictable な語である。

一方、以下の文では、主語と述語両方に prominence がある。

c.　A: What's the news?

　　B: |*Mary is* ↘*pregnant again!*

d.　A: What's the matter?

　　B: *My* ⌐*ears are* ↘*ringing*.

e.　A: What's the matter?

　　B: *My* ⌐*nose is* ↘*clogged*. I can't breathe well.

　注意しなければならないのは、The door's open. である。この文でも主語と述語の間には意味的関連があり、*open* は、no real news、predictable な語である。しかし、この文を one peak of prominence のケースとして The ↘<u>door's</u> open と言うと、単に「ドアーが開いている」という意味にはならならない。言外の意味は、so you'd better shut it. という行動を示唆する。一方、two peaks of prominence として The ⌐<u>door's</u> ↘<u>open</u>. と言うと、単に *door* の状態の描写にすぎず、しばしば Come on in. とか So you can walk straight in. などの表現と連動する。

　ここで、one peak of prominence のケースに関する Knowles (1987: 151) の解説を紹介しよう。

[T]he DOOR's [open] may be interpreted not as a statement about the door, but as a command to shut it.

　参考：警告（warning）を表すイントネーションで言うならば、

　　The ↘↗<u>door's</u> open.

　また、reassurances の心的態度を伝えるならば、

　　The ⌐<u>door's</u> ↗<u>open</u>.

(ii) 他動詞と目的語の名詞との間にも unity stress が見られる。この場合、名詞目的語は predictable であり、no real news である。

a.　Somebody ↘<u>shot</u> *a gun*, but it missed me.

b.　The choir ↘<u>sang</u> *hymns* during the Easter service.

c.　The singer ↘<u>hummed</u> a tune for a while.

d.　He ↘<u>broke</u> *the seal* and opened the box.

e.　He ↘<u>opened the door</u> and left.

```
        broke the              broke      glas
He            se    (vs.  He        his      s
                al                            es
```

```
         opened the
He              do          (vs.  He   op      sto
                 or                  ened a      r
                                                  e)
```

[T]here is a degree of expectedness between one element and another, the typical case being the noun object which more or less suggests the action of the verb.　　　　　Ladd (1980: 60)　　[Bolinger (1965: 175-76)]

以下は、しばしば文献などで言及されるパタンである。

f.　Jenny ∣ gave ˈPeter inˎstructions to follow.

Ladefoged (2001: 16)

Instructions（使用書）と言えば、「従う」は予期される動詞であり、両者の間には unity がある。しかし、以下の例では、instructions の意味は「指示／命令」であり、*follow* は自動詞であり、「（後から）ついて行く」の意味である。この場合は、名詞よりも動詞の意味のほうが重要である。

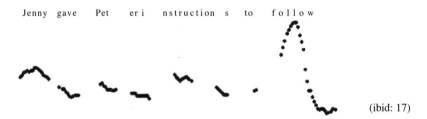

(ibid: 17)

g.　[John(B) goes to the reception desk. The receptionist(A) asks]

　　A: What have you got there?

　　B: I have some ˎ*orders to leave*.　（誰かに渡す注文品）

　　　(= John is carrying orders (to be turned over to somebody))

h.　A: Why aren't you staying?

　　B: I have ˈ*orders to* ˎ*leave*.　「退去せよという指示／命令」

参考：《遍在性（ubiquitous/ubiquity）》

　　　遍在性は、課題 12「時の副詞」で見たとおり私たちの脳裏に常に存在し、暗黙に了解されている概念である。そのような概念は、発話に際して、ことさら強

調する必要はない。例えば、life またはそれに類する語は、発話では初出であっても、焦点を受けない。

[E]xamples of ubiquity are the following responses to someone complaining about difficulties in getting along:]

a. *Times are TOUGH.* We'll have to wait things out.

b. *Life is HARD.* Don't expect a bed of roses!

c. *Your spirit is WEAK.* You must turn to God.

   Time, life, and *spirit* are always with us, and though each of these terms may be accented, none needs to be.　Bolinger (1987: 68)

気分が落ち込んでいる自分や他の人への激励の言葉がある。

d. My father passed away, and I miss him so. *But life goes ON.*　（頑張らなきゃ）

e. I'm so disappointed with the test results. *Oh, well, life goes ON.*

また、人生には、諸々の問題がつきものである。

f. A: How's old John doing these days?

   B: *He's got a MEDical problem.*

g. *John and his wife have a MARital problem*; they're separated now.

なお、遍在性は、不変の真理、生き物や物質の特性（permanent properties）や習性にも及ぶ。

　Penguins SWIM.　　Birds CHIRP.　　Milk is ANimal.（動物性）

課題 18　句動詞の強勢（1）

(i) 句動詞の強勢パタンは、英語のリズムとイントネーションを教えるときにつきまとう不可解な問題かもしれない。ネーテイブスピーカーは、幼い年齢の頃から物語の読み聞かせなどを通して句動詞を身に付けていく。しかし、外国人学習者の場合は、句動詞を習うのは学習が進んだ段階になることが多い。しかも、句動詞の強勢パタンの規則が分からないので、いろいろな動詞句に個別に対応せざるを得ない。それ故に、授業では強勢パタンを練習することはほとんどないだろう。

> Phrasal verbs are among the most perplexing pitfalls that dog the footsteps of teaching or learning English rhythm and intonation as in:
>
> > The mouse ran up the flagpole.　（旗竿を駆け上った）
> >
> > The government ran it up the flagpole.　（idiom：世間の反応を試した）
> >
> > The soldiers ran the flagpole up.　（旗竿を立てた）
>
> Used literally and figuratively, phrasal verbs are acquired early by native-speaking children, but late — if ever — by foreign learners. Such learners often regard them (or have been encouraged by their teachers to regard them) as irritating 'verb idioms' that have to be learned one at a time. What is still worse, so little attention is given to practicing the stress pattern of phrasal verbs in class.　McArthur (1989: 38)
>
> > 注：literally 文字通りの意味で；figuratively 比喩的な意味で

しかし、数多くある句動詞の強勢パタンは、個別に対応する必要はなく体系的に、かつ、比較的容易に対応できる。

① [The ˈmouse ˈran] ＋ [up the ˈflagpole]　（ran は自動詞；up は前置詞）

[The ˈgovernment ˈran it] ＋ [up the ˈflagpole]　（ran は他動詞；up は同上）

〜 The ˈsoldiers ˈran the ˈflagpole up.　（ran …up は分離型の句動詞）

② [He ˈlooked] ＋ [up the ˈflagpole]　（旗竿を見上げた）

[He ˌlooked ˈup] ＋ [the ˈanswer]　（正解を［辞書／参考書で］調べた）

〜 He ˌlooked the ˈanswer up.　（同上）

> 注：句動詞の第 1 強勢と第 2 強勢を、それぞれ [ˈ] と [ˌ] で示す。

但し、ˌlooked ˈup は、faster and natural tempo では、三連規則により副詞 *up* は強勢が弱まるので、前置詞 *up* と同じになる。

(ii) 以下は、Lewis の PhonetiBlog に掲載されている *People Speaking* シリーズからである。

A: Miss Jones is coming to lunch tomorrow. What am I to give her to eat?

B: What does she like?

A: That's not the question, really. She has all these dreadful allergies. So I'm terrified of giving her something that'll ˈ***bring her out in*** ˈ**spots**.

B: What can she eat?　　　　　　　　　　（湿疹を起こす）

A: Well, I imagine steak doesn't disagree with her. But I believe she ˈ***comes out in a*** ˈ**rash** if she touches onions.　（発疹する）

B: For goodness sake! ˈ***Ring up her*** ˈ**house** and ask them.

(2008.3.23)

音声を聴くと、斜体字部の句動詞 *bring out, come out, ring up* 中の副詞は、三連規則により強勢が抑制されている。以下でも、三連規則が働いている。

hi: ˈstɑːtid ˈʌp | ˈsnatʃt ʌ̣p (h)iz ˈkout | ənd ˈran aut əv ðə ˈhɑus
He started up　　snatched up his coat　　and ran out of the house　　Jones (1956: 287)

句動詞の発音に関わる少し amusing な逸話を紹介しよう。中年の女性 A（non-native speaker）が郵便局に行き封筒に貼るために切手を買った。以下は、彼女と応対した係員 B とのやりとりである。

A: Must I stick it on myself?

B: No, madam. It's much better to stick it on the envelope.

係員は女性を少しからかっている。この女性は、句動詞 *stick on* を発音する時に、*on* に強勢を置かなかったのだ。そのために、切手を「自分の体の部分に貼る」という意味に解釈された。

Must I ˈstick it on my ↗self?

しかし、彼女は次のように言うべきであった。

Must I ˈstick it ↗on ｜ my ↗self?　（自分自身で、封筒に切手を貼るべきか）

しかし、このようなイントネーションは、ネイティブスピーカーにも起こる可能性がある。Barbara Bradford（*Intonation in Context* の著者）によれば、

"Myself" has caused 'on' to be unstressed here — if this is natural, rapid speech. If the tempo were slower, 'on' could also be stressed. In rapid speech the stress is exactly the same — whether the stamp is destined for the envelope or the person. I think there are many, many more of these ambiguous utterances.　　(SUPRAS posting: 2003.8.24)

また、Rebecca Dauer（*Accurate English* の著者）の趣旨も同じである。

I also think that in fast speech there would be little difference between "*stick it / on myself*" and "*stick it on / myself*". Both 'stick and 'self' would have the strongest stresses; in my opinion, the main potential difference is in the length of 'on', which would disappear at faster speeds.

　　(SUPRAS posting: 2003.8.26)

(iii) 句動詞中の副詞が弱勢になるケースがもう 1 つある。それは、句動詞が反復されるときである。この場合は、動詞が強調されている。

[T]he particle is often non-prominent when we want to put special emphasis on the verb:

A: I can't remember Trudi's address.

B: Why didn't you WRITE it DOWN?

A: I WROTE it down. (or: I DID write it down.)

　　(adapted from Hewings (2007: 46))

a.　A: I wish they would ₗ*make* ˈ*up*.

　　B: They ˈ*made up*. *or* They ˈ*did* make up.

b.　A: I ain't telling you again. ₗ*Settle* ˈ*down*.

　　B: I am, I am. I'm ˈ*settled down*. *or* I ˈ*am* settled down.

c.　A: Did you ₗ*give* them ˈ*back*?

　　B: ↘Yeah, I ˈ*gave* them *back*.

課題 19　句動詞の強勢（2）

(i) 音声学の教本には、句動詞は二重強勢（double stress）で発音されると書いてある。そして、副詞のほうが動詞よりも強勢が強い。しかし、それは原則であって、実際の文脈上ではそのようにはならず、副詞の強勢が抑制されることが多々ある。

a.　I ˈ*got up* ˈlate in the afterˈnoon.

b.　Then she ˈ*sat down* and ˈlooked at the young ˈman again.

c.　"Now I must go," Teresa said. She ˈ*stood up* and ˈ*went out* of the ˈdoor.

d.　Hearing the sad news, she ˈ*broke down* in ˈtears.　（泣きくづれた）

e.　ˈSomeone *broke in* last ˈnight and stole my wife's jewels!

f.　I ˈ*broke out* in a ˌbig ˈsweat.　（大汗をかいた）

g.　I'll ˈ*pull in* at the ˈnext parking lot.　（停車する）

h.　ˈAll they ˈdo is to ˈ*sit back* and ˈlisten.

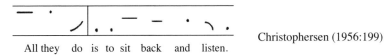

All they　do　is to　sit　back　and　listen.　Christophersen (1956:199)

これらの例でも、三連規則が適用されている。

(ii) 音調単位の区切りが、文の意味に微妙な影響を与える。

①　She ˈ*stood up* and ˈwent out of the ˈroom.

②　She ˌ*stood* ˈ*up*, | and ˈthen went ˈout of the ˈroom.

③　She ˌ*stood* ˈ*up*, | and ˈeverybody in the ˈroom | ˈturned in her ˈdirection.

①では、*stood up* と *went out of the room* は連続した動き（a continuous single action）である。一方、②では、*stood up* と *went out of the room* は、個別の行動（two separate actions）である。上記の f の場合、もし強勢配置を間違って I ˌbroke ˈout | in a ˌbig ˈsweat. と言えば、「大汗をかいて脱出した」という意味にとられるかもしれない。慣用表現に wake up and smell the coffee がある。その意味は、「なに寝言を言ってるんだ、いいかげんに目を覚ませ」（⇒現実を認識せよ）である。It's ˈtime to ˈwake up and ˈsmell the ˈcoffee. でも、continuous single action であるので、*up* の強勢が抑制される。

(iii) 以下は、高圧的な命令文である。句動詞中の副詞の強勢が抑制される。

a.　［麻薬取締官が 2 人の容疑者に］You chaps always say the same thing.
　　 |*Come on.* |*Hand it over.* Where is it?

b.　［母親が食事中に兄弟喧嘩をしている子供に］
　　 That's enough of that! |*Eat up!* It's getting cold.

c.　［店内で、買い物でぐずぐずしている友人に］
　　 |*Make up your mind.*

d.　［喧嘩中にパンチで倒した相手に］
　　 |*Come on.* |*Get up!*

e.　You aren't making sense. Listen, Larry, |*Wake up.* Face the facts.

f.　［警察官が現行犯に］
　　 Now |*get in there.* [He closes the door behind them, taking out his gun.]
　　 All right. |*Turn around. Now* |*sit down.*

g.　［強盗が］Freeze! |*Get 'em up!* （手を挙げろ）

h.　You there! |*Stand up!* Put your hands on your head!

i.　I'm sick of your crappy attitude. |*Get the hell out of here!* （出ていけ！）

Bolinger (1986: 317)

j.　A: Do you all know how many people they cremate out in California?
　　　　　　　　　　　　　　　　　　　　　　（火葬する）
　　 B: No. How many?
　　 A: 80 percent.
　　 B: |*Get out!* （嘘つけ！冗談言うな）
　　 A: I'm not kidding.

参考：高圧的な *Shut up!* の強勢を考えるとき、*shut* は下降調の高頭部（high falling head）であり、*up* は low fall（低下降調）の核を受けるという主張がある。しかし、本来、核は most prominent accent であるという大原則を考えると、*up* にはそのような卓立はない。むしろ、shut は最も目立って聞こえるので、ここに核が来ると考えるのが妥当である。上記の見解は、聴覚印象と全く合わない。伊達（2019）の課題 42 に関連内容がある。

課題 20　修辞疑問文など

(i) 修辞疑問文（rhetorical questions）の default pattern は、基本的には上昇調である。Is ⌐that a ⌐reason for de ↗spair? (No.)

しかし、以下のような諸ケースでは下降調になる。

① 発言に対して相手の同意を期待する（expecting agreement and not asking an opinion）。通例、下降調で言われる。

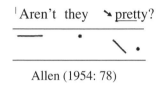

　　　Allen (1954: 78)

a.　⌐Isn't it ↘lovely today?

b.　⌐Don't they look ↘nice?

c.　⌐Isn't that ↘kind of her?

また、意味をさらに強調する場合、最初の語——be 動詞または助動詞——に核強勢が置かれる。

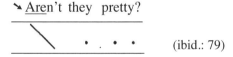

(ibid.: 79)

　　　注：核強勢のある語より後の部分は、尾部になり文アクセントを受けない。

d.　↘Isn't that kind of her?

e.　↘Don't they look nice?

② 時には、下降調は相手を問い詰める意味にもなる。

a.　A: Do you think this new guy will come to the party?

　　B: He's very charming; I'm sure you'll like him.

　　A: Yes, but ↘*will he come?*

b.　A: It is a very challenging assignment. I think I'll learn a lot from doing it.

　　B: Yes, but ↘*can you do it?*

c.　A: Oh, he'll come. Not to worry.

　　B: But ↘*are you sure?*

③ 軽い驚きを表す

　　(in question tags used as independent comments) mildly surprised

a. A: I like it here.

B: ↘*Do you?* I'm glad to hear that. I was afraid you might not.

b. A: Mr. Wilson is a robust man. I was wondering how old he is.

B: Oh, he's about 60, nearing the retirement age.

A: ↘*Is he?* I thought he was younger.

c. A: How did the exam go?

B: All of them passed it.

A: Oh, ↘*did they?* I'm glad for them.

d. A: He got a distinction.　（優の成績）

B: ↘*Did* he?

参考：↗↘*Did* he?　（上昇下降調；greatly surprised / impressed）

④ 強い賛同を表す（しばしば末尾に ever を伴う。一種の感嘆文）。

a. [子どもが昔懐かしい遊びをしているのを見かけ]

A: Hey, look, Jug! Remember?

B: Oh, boy! ↘*Do I ever!* Good old stickball!

b. A: Hawaii is a nice vacation destination. Would you care to go there?

B: ↘*Would I ever!*

c. [*How to Marry a Millionaire*]

A: Is she class? (elegant)

B: ↘*Is she!* Didn't I tell you she's been on the cover of a fashion magazine three times?

d. A: Darling, did you have a good time at Grandma's?

B: Oh, boy, ↘*did I!*

e. [セスナ機の前で]

A: Would you like to fly this plane?

B: ↘*Would I!*

f. A: Did you see how Bill came in to work this morning?

B: ↘*Did I ever!* Boy, *was* |*he* ↘*mad!*

g. The boss wants to see you right now. Boy, *is* |*he ever* ↘*mad!*

h. [久しぶりに再会して] Boy, *did* |*I ever miss* ↘*you!*

i. Hello, darling! Did you miss me? Oh, *am* |*I glad to see* ↘*you!*

⑤ 強い賛同を表す（though または just を伴う。一種の感嘆文）

a.　A: We did it at last! Now we can be really proud of ourselves.

　　B: Yes, ↘*can't we just!*

b.　［Sabrina (A) がパリから洗練されて帰国するとパーテイに招待される］

　　A: You didn't recognize me, did you? Have I changed?

　　B: You certainly have. You look lovely, Sabrina.

　　C: ↘*Doesn't she, though!*

c.　A: Appearances are deceiving.

　　B: ↘*Aren't they just!*

d.　A: What a lovely day?

　　B: ↘*Isn't it just!*

(ii) 修辞疑問文の慣用表現（idioms）

a.　And then he just walked out. |*Would you be* ↘*lieve it?*　（驚いたね）

b.　He refused to help me. |*Would you be* ↘*lieve it?*

c.　Well, |*what do you* ↘*know?*　（これはこれは）Look who's here!

d.　A: Who're you going out with recently?

　　B: |*What's it to* ↘*you?*　（余計なお世話よ）

e.　A: Did you hear the news? It was on TV. Carlos Ghosn was arrested. For phony business transactions.

　　B: Well, |*how do you like* ↘*that?*　（こりゃ驚きだ）

参考：To show interest and to encourage the speaker to continue, we can also use short questions such as *Did you? Were they? Haven' we?*, typically with a fall-rising tone:

　　A: Saw Helen in town today.

　　B: ↘↗*Did* you?

We can also use *Really?* with a fall-rising tone for a similar purpose:

　　A: Did you hear there's been another earthquake in Iran?

　　B: ↘↗*Really?*

　　A: Yeah, and another bad one, too.　　　Hewings (2007: 110)

但し、下降上昇調ではなく、上昇調もあり得る。Wells (2006: 52) を参照。

英語教師のための Intonation in Context 読本

課題 21　**Typical behavior を表す 'would'**

　助動詞 would の用法には habitual behavior を表すものがある。

・My grandfather *would* smoke three pipes before breakfast.

・He *would* just sit there and daydream for hours.

以下では、would は typical happening または behavior を表すが、上記とはニュアンスが違う。不満や批判の気持ちが込められている。

a.　The ⌐*bus* ⌐*would come* ↘↗*late*, │ just when I'm in a hurry.

　　（急いでいるときに、<u>決まって</u>バスが延着する）

b.　A: She says it was your fault.

　　B: *Well, she* ⌐*would* ↘↗*say that*, │ ↘*wouldn*'t she? She's never liked me.

この *would* の意味について、辞書での定義を見てみよう。

　　[spoken] to used to say that an action is typical or expected － usually used

　　to show <u>disapproval</u>:　　　　　　　　下線は伊達が追加

　　　・*You would go and spoil it, wouldn't you!*

　　　　（人の楽しみを台無しにするとは、お前らしいな！）

　　　・*She insists that she did nothing wrong, but then she would say that,*

　　　　wouldn't she?　　　　　*Longman Dictionary of Contemporary English*

　これらの例は、「～するなんて、君／彼女らしいよ」と非難している。

(Cynically) That's typical of you/her! である。注意しなければならないのは、

<u>*would*</u> には<u>文アクセント</u>が<u>置かれる</u>ことである。

SUPRAS 会員からの私信を紹介しよう。

　　We can use ***would*** like this when we are being critical of someone's past

　　actions or behavior. Note that <u>it has to carry strong word stress</u> when it is

　　used in this way.

他の例を見ていこう。

c.　A: Madeleine called to say she's too busy to come.

　　B: *She* ↘*would*. She always has an excuse.

d.　A: Betty forgot to type the reports up for her boss.

　　B: *She* ⌐*would for* ↘↗*get*, │ ↘*wouldn't she?*

e.　Oh, shoot! *It* ⌐*would* ↘↗*rain*, │ just when we want to play outdoors.

f.　*My son* ⌐*would run a* ↘↗*fever* │ just when we are about to go on a trip.

g. *You* 'would go and 'tell her about the ↘↗barbeque, | ↘wouldn't you?*
    I've never liked her. I didn't want to invite her.

h. [*Downton Abbey*, in the classroom]
    A: You see, boys. You must never think that education is only for special
       people, for clever people. Education is for everyone.
    B: *You* 'would ↘say that, sir*.
    A: Yes, but I'm not anyone special.
    B: You're a teacher.

Wells は blog の中で次のように述べている。

I have noticed one usage in which *would* seems to be obligatorily accented.
An example is in this complaint about a sudden change in the weather,
which I found myself saying the other day.

It ↘would start raining | 'just as we went out ᵛside.

The following examples don't sound right unless you accent *would*.

You 'would go and ᵧspoil it, | ↘wouldn't you?

She 'would say ᵧthat, | ↘wouldn't she?   (2008. 8.18)

蛇足ながら、have to にも、迷惑を伝える用法がある。

・Of course it *had to* start raining as soon as we got to the beach.

・Every time we go on a picnic, it *has to* start raining.

・Bad news, coach. Chester *had to* quit the team.

辞書の定義では

used when something annoying happens in a way that things always seem
to happen. --- *Longman Dictionary of Contemporary English*

課題 22　謝罪や遺憾の表現

(i) 英語音声学の教本には、真摯な謝罪は下降調で言われ、儀礼的な謝罪は上昇調で言われるとある。しかし、実際には真摯な謝罪でも下降上昇調または下降調＋上昇調になることもある。

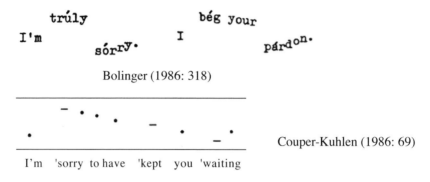

Bolinger (1986: 318)

Couper-Kuhlen (1986: 69)

a.　A: What a mess you've made of things!

　　B: *I* ｜*do a* ↘*pologize. I* ｜*won't let it* ｜*happen a* ↗*gain*.

b.　A: But why didn't you tell me?

　　B: *I'm* ｜*so* ↗*sorry*. I thought I had.

c.　A: How did this get broken?

　　B: *I'm* ｜*terribly* ↗*sorry about it*. I dropped it.

(ii) では、相手から長い時間待ちぼうけを食わされ謝られたとき、何と返答するか。"Never mind." と言って、その場を繕うのか、或いは、不満・怒りをあらわすのか。後者の場合、以下のようなやりとりが想像できる。

　　A: Oh, there you are, Tom. At last. You stood me up for an hour!

　　B: I'm terribly sorry I'm so late.　（待ちぼうけにした）

　　A: I'm ｜sorry, ↘too.

Aの2番目の発言は、「私こそ、すみません」ではなく、「それは当然だよ」／「そら、そうだろう」の意味である。怒りの気持ちは顔の表情にも出るだろう。校閲者 Rockenbach 教授に、I'm sorry, too. について敷衍してもらった。"I'm sorry about what happened, and I'm sorry to tell you this, but I don't forgive you for that." となる。類例を挙げよう。

a.　A: I'm sorry about the noise last night.

　　B: *I'm sorry, too.*

b.　A: I'm terribly sorry to have kept you waiting so long, sir.

　　B: Well, *I'm sorry, too.*

c.　[After a long, awkward silence]

　　A: Auggie, I'm sorry I've failed to make good use of your money.

　　B: [Scowling] Yeah? Well, *I'm sorry*, *too.* It took me three years to save up those 5,000 dollars, and now I'm broke.

インターネットでつぎのような書き込みを見かけた。

> One day I played a bit of a joke on a new friend of mine and he took it pretty seriously. He was really over-reacting, so I explained that it was a joke and said, "I'm sorry," to which he replied **"I'm sorry, too."** To me, it sounded a bit snobbish in the context.

ジョークをかけられた相手は、気分を害している。この書き込みについて、Rockenbach 教授にコメントを求めた。

> At first glance, I think that, although he said he was sorry and apologized for the joke, his new friend is probably NOT accepting the first person's apology. 'I'm sorry, too' probably means that the 2nd person is still disappointed and angry with the 1st person, and even though the 1st person wants to just 'forget about it' and let bygones be bygones with the poor joke, the 2nd person is still very much offended by the 1st person's behavior and is not in a forgiving mood.

とは言え、I'm に核強勢を置いて、↘I'm sorry, | ↘too. は、「私こそ、すみません」（It's ↘my fault, | ↘too.）と同義である。往年のコメディー *I Love Lucy* にぴったりの例があった。

　　Lucy: [At the door] I came over to apologize. Please don't be angry. It was an accident.

　　Tallula: Oh, all right. ↘I'm sorry, | ↘too. Come on in. I know it was an accident.

勿論、イントネーションだけでなく、声質（voice quality）、しぐさや表情（non-verbal behavior）なども、attitude や emotion の表明に関与する。

　蛇足になるが、イギリス英語では I should think so, too.（「それは当然ですね」「当たり前だよ」）が多いようだ。

David: Sorry to keep you waiting, Alan.

Alan: I ~~should~~ think so too.

　As you can hear, Alan's angry because David is late.

　　　　Thompson (1981: 10)

d.　A: My manager said you can get a refund on the item.

　　B: *I should* ⌐*think so,* ↘*too* — it arrived broken in two pieces!

e.　A: He finally apologized for what he said.

　　B: *I should* ⌐*think so,* ↘*too*.

f.　A: I owe you an apology.

　　B: *I should* ⌐*think so in* ↘*deed!*

　英語教育では、相手からの謝罪を赦す／受け容れる表現——That's all right. Never mind/Forget it.——しか学ばないが、いつかは、I'm sorry, too. や I should think so, too. と言ったり、言われたりする日が来るかもしれない。しかし、用心しなければならないのは、上記に挙げた言葉だけでなく、顔の表情やしぐさ（body language）、声の key も関与するので、相手の謝罪に対して I'm sorry, too. と答えること自体が、それを受け入れないというメッセージとは限らない。もし All right. I'm sorry, too. と言えば、「私こそすみません」の意味になる。

　ある会議で同席したアメリカ人男性とカナダ人女性に確認した。その方法は、まず私が、謝罪するべき状況を設定して、"I'm sorry." と言ったことに対して、2通りの方法で彼らに I'm sorry, too." を言ってもらった。基本的には、イントネーションは同じであった。

　言うまでもないが、相手に迷惑をかけてしまって謝罪する場合は、冒頭で述べた事実もあるが、I'm sorry. とか I'm terribly sorry. は下降調で言うほうが無難であろう。

課題 23　会話を誘導する（低）上昇調

低上昇調は、日本語には存在しない音調である。

Good morning.

This is a feature that is completely absent from Japanese.

(adapted from Ladd (2008: 28-29))

しかし、英語では、この音調は重要であり、幾つかの機能がある。その1つは、相手を安心させる（reassurances）機能である。

Dón't

wórry!

It's

éasy.

It's

ónly the wind.

Bolinger (1986: 32, 142 & 313)

　これらは、There's no reason to be concerned. というニュアンスを伝える。もう1つの機能として、会話を誘導する（低）上昇調がある。誰かが、あることを目撃して相手にコメントを呟くときにも、よく低上昇が使われる。その場合、目撃内容は、両者には一目瞭然のこととして共有されている。例えば、

[A] motorist passed two pedestrians on a rainy day and was careful to drive slowly through the puddles so as not to splash water. One pedestrian said to the other:

Thát's

consíderate.

The fact was obvious to both pedestrians.　(ibid.: 180)

話者は、相手に水を向けているのかもしれない。つまり、相手から何らかの反応を期待している。

[I]magine two friends visiting an art gallery. They pause before a canvas and one says to the other.

That's

an interesting picture.

[T]he terminal rise leaves the field open for the speaker to carry on with an explanation of his opinion, or for the hearer to respond with something like

Yes, I agree.

Bolinger (1989: 147)

　ここでも、発言者は、自分のコメントに対して相手から何らかの反応——同意——を期待している。次の地名についての発言も、話し手と聞き手との間に何らかの認識が共有されている場合に起こり、見知らぬ人に対して言われるものではない。その際、聞き手からのコメントが期待されている。

```
Den
    ver's a
         funny place.        (ibid.: 148)
```

これから、会話を誘導する低上昇調で発せられる他の例を見ていこう。

a.　A: What do you think of Jim?

　　B: He's a nice guy…

　　A: ↗*But*…?

　　B: Utterly boring.

b.　A: Can you believe what he did last night?

　　B: Tell me. *I'm* |*all* ↗*ears*.

c.　A: Hello, Sarah! *You* |*look* ↗*tired*.

　　B: Yeah, I'm afraid so. I've been very busy recently.

d.　A: Hi, Jane. *You're* |*dressed* ↗*up!*

　　B: Yeah, I'm on my way to a wedding.

e.　A: Good morning.

　　B: *You're* |*up* ↗*early*.

　　A: I couldn't sleep.

f.　A: So, are you going to enter a *karaoke* contest?

　　B: Do you think I should?

　　A: Well, why don't you? *You* |*have a* |*good* ↗*voice*.

g.　A: Hi, Jane. *You're* |*home* ↗*early today*.

　　B: Yes. The class got cancelled.

h.　A: What a glorious day!

　　B: *You* |*sound* ↗*cheerful*.

i.　A: You're kind of worried, aren't you?

　　B: *You're* |*very ob*↗*serving*.

以下の２つの解説を見てみよう。まず、O'Connor & Arnold (1973: 84) では、

> [W]e can say that the Low Rise constitutes <u>an appeal to the listener and invites him to say something more about the subject</u> of the previous conversation. So in the example:
>
> I'm going to Sheffield　　　　　ⵍReally? ‖ My ⵗmother came
> tomorrow.　　　　　　　　　from ⵍSheffield.
>
> *mother*, which is new, is clearly more important than *Sheffield*, which has already been mentioned, and <u>the way is open for the conversation to continue</u>.
>
> 下線は伊達が追加

次いで、Thompson (1981: 54) では、

> Harriet: I'd love to go to Australia, David.
>
> David: Oh, my ⵗsister | lives in Aus ⵍtralia.
>
> Notice that if David says *there* in place of *Australia*, the rising intonation at the end is not so common... But repeating the words *in Australia* at the end of the sentence means: 'Come on — let's talk about it'. This way <u>we can keep the subject open</u>.　　　　下線は伊達が追加
>
> 注：My ⵗsister | lives ⵍthere. というパタンも実際にはある。

但し、以下では下降調であった。

j.　A: Where did you go to school?

　　B: I went to Northwestern.

　　A: Hey, *my ⵗbrother went to Northwestern*.

実際、会話は、そこから発展せず、すぐ他の話題に移った。

課題 24　**Hopes and wishes**

　今回は、認識にかかわる動詞（epistemic verb）や心的状態（mental state）の形容詞（sorry, glad 等）が先導する文を採りあげる。そのような文は、複合イントネーション——下降調＋上昇調——で発せられる傾向がある。その際、hope, wish, glad, sorry など emotion を伝える語が主情報として下降調になり、後続する the topic of conversation は、何とか予測可能な副次情報として上昇調になる。以下は、Wells (2006: 81) からである。

> The fall-plus-rise pattern is particularly common where the first nucleus goes on a word referring to a mental state…:
>
> 　I'm ˯glad ｜ you found it /interesting.
>
> 　I ˯do wish ｜ you wouldn't com/plain so much…
>
> It is also found in cases where the second nucleus falls on information that is new though <u>fairly predictable</u>:　　　　　　　　下線は伊達が追加。
>
> 　ˈHow can we ˯get there?　　　・ ˯Maureen's ｜ got a /car.
>
> 　　　　　　　　　　　　　　　・ ˯Walking's ｜ the /easiest way.
>
> 　　　　　　　　　　　　　　　・ The ˯ tube ｜ would be /quickest.

次も、話し手と聞き手の間で共通認識されている状況を踏まえての文である。

Allen (1954: 94)

a.　A: We're off to France tomorrow.

　　B: Well, *I* ↘ *hope* ｜ *you get* ˈ*good* ↗ *weather*.

　　A: The problem is, my husband isn't feeling well at the moment.

　　B: Well, *I* ↘ *hope* ｜ *he* ˈ*feels* ↗ *better soon*.

ここでは、希望する topic は A と B に共有されているか、または、A がそのように捉えている。

b.　A: Oh, no! Look at this long line of people waiting to buy concert tickets!

　　B: How annoying! *I* ↘ *hope* ｜ *they* ˈ*won't be sold* ↗ *out*.

　　A: *I* ↘ *wish* ｜ *the* ˈ*girl selling* ˈ*tickets would* ˈ*hurry* ↗ *up*.

c.　A: What a lovely place this is!

88

B: Yes, indeed. *I ↘wish ｜ we could ꞌstay here for ↗ever*.

　実は、上昇調には、共有内容——既知内容——を伝える以外に、もう 1 つの働きがある。それは、相手に会話の続行を促す——相手の発言を引き出す——ことである。

A: Is something wrong, Alexandra?

B: No, nothing.

A: Yes, there is. I can tell. What's the matter? Come on. *You can ↗tell me*.

　　　注：詳細は、課題 23 を参照

I wish や I hope が先導する文においても、同じことが言える。下記の例文中の topic of conversation は、obvious to both the speaker and the hearer であるので、共通認識事項として minor information になる。

d.　A: It's a lovely present, Dick. Thank you very much.

　　B: *I'm ↘glad ｜ you ↗like it*.

e.　A: The pilot's turned on the "Fasten Seat Belt" sign. We may be having some turbulence.

　　B: Oh, *I ↘hope ｜ it doesn't get too ↗bumpy*.

f.　A: Yes, that was Ben Johnson all right.

　　B: *I ↘thought ｜ his ꞌface was fa↗miliar*.

g.　A: We must go now.

　　B: *I'm ↘sorry ｜ you can't stay ↗longer*.

h.　A: Oh, I like this. Who did it?

　　B: I did.

　　A: Really? *I didn't ↘know ｜ you ↗painted*.

i.　A: Hello, Jordan.

　　B: Nick! *I ↘hoped ｜ you'd be ↗here*. Great to see you!

　ただし、topic of conversation は、下降調になることもある。その場合、中立的（neutral）または淡々とした（matter-of-fact）ニュアンスがある。

　　・I ꞌhope you get ꞌgood ↘weather.

　　・I ꞌwish we could ꞌstay here for ↘ever.

課題 25　**Intonation of 'insists'**（1）

(i) 話し手は、時折、相手のことについて思い込みに基づいて質問することがある。以下では、A の思い込みに対して B がきっぱりと主張（insist）——実質上では否定——している。

a.　A: Why have you invited such a nasty man?

　　B: *But I ↘haven't invited him!*

b.　A: Why haven't you phoned me?

　　B: *But I ↘have phoned you.*

c.　A: Why don't you love me?

　　B: *But I ↘do love you.*

d.　A: The passbook should be updated.　（預金通帳）

　　B: *But it's ↘been updated already.*

e.　A: Which kind of beer do you like best?

　　B1: *I ǀdon't ↘like beer.*

　　B2: *I ǀdon't like ↘any kind of beer.*

f.　A: Why are you going to Ireland again?

　　B1: *I'm ǀnot ↘going to Ireland!*

　　B2: *I'm ↘not going to Ireland!*

これらの文における核強勢配置は論理的であるので分かり易い。

(ii) 以下でも、B は相手 A の早合点や思い込みを否定しているが、核強勢配置が論理的でない。

a.　A: I want you to apologize.

　　B: *But I've ǀnothing ↘to apologize for.*

　　A は、B が謝罪して当然であると考えている。B はそれに反駁している。

b.　A: What should we do now?

　　B: Do? *There's ǀnothing ↘to do.*

c.　A: Did you talk about it with Jane?

　　B: *No, there was ǀnothing ↘to talk about.*

d.　A: What did you say?

　　B: *There was ǀnothing ↘to say.*

e.　A: After you buy it, what will you do with it?

　　B: *I* ⌐*have no* ⌐*money* ↘ *to buy it.*

日本人学習者は勿論のこと教員も、きっと *nothing* や money に核強勢を置くだろうが、ネーテイブスピーカーは、通例、*to* に核強勢を置く。これらの例は、相手の思い込み（先入観）を否定する核強勢パタンであるが、概論で述べた核強勢配置の原則に反している。このような異例な強勢配置の現象を、Cruttenden (1997: 85) は ***insists*** と呼ぶ。次に、Wells (2014: 110-1) の解説を見てみよう。対話中の A は、B には何か食べるものがあったという前提（presupposition）で質問を発している。B は、それに対して反駁 / 拒絶している（counter/reject）。

　　One area of English intonation that is really difficult to explain is found in exchanges like this:

　　　　A:　⌐Have you /eaten?

　　　　B:　↘No, ⎮ there was ⌐nothing ↘to eat.

　　Why does B put the nuclear accent on ***to***, a function word that appears to have virtually no meaning of its own? …Here, A says something that *presupposes* that there was something available for B to eat…B's reply involves a rejection of this presupposition: it counters it… We know that in English it is usual to avoid putting the nucleus on a repeated item. So we don't expect a nucleus on ***eat***. Logically, we might expect a nucleus on ***nothing***. But that's not where native speakers put it. They usually put it on ***to*** (above), or sometimes, less commonly, on ***was***, or indeed on ***eat***:

　　　　B:　There ↘was nothing to eat.　　または

　　　　B:　There was nothing to ↘eat.

　このような強勢配置は論理的なものではない。Wells (2006: 184) は、それを謙虚に認めている。

　　It is appropriate to finish this chapter on a note of humility. Although we have made great strides in the study of focus, accenting and nucleus placement, we do not yet have all the answers. Examples like these exhibit patterns of <u>tonicity that still resist logical explanation</u>.

　　　　注：tonicity 核強勢配置　　　　　　　　　　　下線は伊達が追加

課題 26　**Intonation of 'insists'**（2）

(i) 相手の思い込みに対抗して主張することを *counterpresupposition* という。これは合成語であって、3 つの要素 counter+pre+supposition から成りたつ。まず、**counter** は、「カウンターパンチ」にもあるように「反撃、反駁」、**pre-** は接頭辞で「前もって」、**supposition** は、「想定、思い込み」（assumption）の意味である。従って、この合成語は、相手の思い込みや先入観に対して反駁する（拒絶する）ことである。そのような場合、旧情報の動詞に再び文アクセントを置くことがある。

a.　A: I found an article for you in a German journal.

　　B: *But I* |*don't* ↘ *read German.*

ここでは、A は、B がドイツ語雑誌を読むと思い込んでいる。B は、それを否定している。以下は、文献でしばしば引用される例である。

b.　A: Has John read *Slaughterhouse-Five*?

　　B: No, *he* |*doesn't* ↘ *read books.*　　　Ladd (1980: 52)

A の心理には John が読書する人間であるという想定（先入観）がある。B は、それを否定している。言い換えれば、B は、次のような暗黙のメッセージを A に暗に送っている。

　　What you're saying implies the possibility of John's reading books

　　－ well, he doesn't.　　　　　Fuchs (1984:146)

他の counterpresupposition の例を見てみよう。

c.　A: Do you want to do something tonight? Maybe go to the movies?

　　B: Hmm. I don't really like movies that much. *I* |*hardly ever* ↘ *go to the movies*.

d.　A: How about on Friday night? Do you like karaoke?

　　B: No, not really.

　　A: Hmm. OK. Let's watch TV at my place tonight.

　　B: But *I* |*don't* ↘ *watch TV*. I read books.

　　A: So… What do you want to do for fun?

e.　I brought her a bottle of whisky, but it turns out *she* |*doesn't* ↘ *like alcohol*.

f.　A: Have you seen *Brideshead Revisited*?　（イギリス映画）

　　B: *I* |*don't* ↘ *watch television*.

参考：［厳格な神父（father）が修行僧 monk を叱る］

　　　A: Monk Rufus, you watch television!

　　　B: No, ｜ *I* ⭦ *don't watch television*, *Father*.

(ii) 以下の「存在文」でも counterpresupposition の例が見られる。各文の second speaker が first speaker の presupposition（思い込み）を否定している。その場合、核強勢は、否定語ではなく be 動詞に置かれる。これも、Wells が後で言うように、不可解（weird）な現象である。

a.　A: What did you think of the garden? Were the flowers any good?

　　B: *There* ⭦ *were no flowers there*.

　　ここでは、A は「庭に花があった」という前提で質問している。

b.　A: Well, she'll do better next time.

　　B: *There* ｜*won't* ⭦ *be any next time*.

Wells は、blog の中で同じテーマについて論じている。

　Tamikazu Date sends some more examples of anomalous tonicity, similar to yesterday's:

(1) A: If something's right, how can it be a waste of time?

　　B: *There* ⭦ *is no right or wrong*. There's only opinion.

(2) A: I'm afraid your check to us this month will be rather large.

　　B: *There will* ⭦ *be no check*, Miss Minchin.

　　A: (In surprise) Excuse me?

(3) [*Music of the Heart*]

　　A: I'm putting your son on a two-day suspension. But next time he will be expelled.

　　B: *There will* ｜*not* ⭦ *be a next time*. I promise you that.

　　注：校則違反を繰り返す生徒の親（B）に、校長（A）が言い渡す。

(4) A: We'll transplant a new kidney.

　　B: In this hospital, *no organs will* ⭦ *be transplanted*.

Yep, in each case the second speaker rejects (counters) something implied by the first speaker. And in doing so the second speaker puts the nucleus on the verb **to be**. Weird, but that's how it is.　(adapted from the blog: 2007.2.22)

下線は、伊達が追加。

課題 27　前置詞への文アクセント配置

　英語では、一見して、より重要である語に文アクセントを置かずに、文脈上で重要でない前置詞に文アクセントを置くことがある。その intonational meaning の説明は難しいが、「surprise 効果」によって文全体の意味を強調していると考えられる。そこには、Bolinger（1986: 130）の言葉を借りると、'Note well this fact.' という意図がある。以下は、Wells の phonetic blog

Tami Date

に掲載された記事を本稿のために再構成したものである。
（2006.11.23）

Tami Date sends some more examples of prepositions bearing the intonation nucleus.

a.　She said it was in the fridge, but *there was* |*nothing* ↘ *in the fridge*.

b.　Why should we speak French? After all, *we're* |*not* ↘ *in France*.

c.　A: I've been by your house every Sunday for a month, but couldn't raise

　　　anyone. 　　　　　　　　　　　　　　　　　　　　　　　　　(wake)

　　B: *I'm* |*usually* ↘ *at home on Sunday*.

d.　A: Well, why don't you take some time off? I want you at your best.

　　B: *I'm* ↘ *at my best*.

e.　A: It's terrible! I don't know what to do.

　　B: Never mind. Worse things happen at sea.

　　A: *We're* |*not* ↘ *at sea*.

　　　注：Worse things happen at sea. は慣用表現で、Things are not as bad as they
　　　　　seem.（航海に出ると、もっと悪いことがある）という意味である。

f.　A: Did you get the toolbox from the car?

　　B: *It* |*wasn't* ↘ *in the car*.

g.　A: Why was Patty Grey in your car?

　　B: *Patty Grey was* |*never* ↘ *in my car*.

勿論、これらには強勢配置の定石ルールに基づいた言い方もある。

a'.　There was ↘ nothing in the fridge.

b'.　…we're |not in ↘ France.

c'.　I'm |usually at ↘ home on Sunday.

d'. I ➘ am at my best.

e'. We're ➘ not at sea.

f'. It ➘ wasn't in the car.

g'. Patty Grey was ➘ never in my car.

Wells の phonetic blog に関連記事がある。

The other day I overheard a snatch of conversation:

A father has just got onto a bus with his two children, a girl aged about five and a boy aged about seven. They sit right at the front of the upper deck of the bus, so they all have a good panoramic window view. The boy takes the seat next to the side window. The girl protests.

Girl: ∨Daddy, | I want to sit on the \window side.

Boy: But you're \on the window side!

If it were me, I think I would have said

But you \are on the window side!

General principles lead us to say that accenting ***on*** would be avoided, since it is a repeated item (it has just featured in the girl's utterance). Hence, I assume, my immediate reaction was that the boy's command of English intonation was not yet quite adult-like, and that the proper place for the nucleus is somewhere else, namely, on ***are***.

But on reflection I think this is not the whole story, and that adult native speakers probably **could** put the nucleus on ***on***, just as the boy did. (/Couldn't they?)　(2008.2.19)

実際、Lewis も同調している。

I don't find any problem with this accenting of ***on***. I could certainly do it myself and it doesn't sound at all juvenile to me.　(Blog 62: 2008.2.21)

一方、以下の文では *on* に文アクセント（核強勢）が置かれるのは理にかなっている。

A: Gosh! This is a steep mountain!

B: Yeah. And *we're ˈnot even* ➘ *on the mountain yet*.

既に紹介したように、例 a ～ g では、標準的な強勢配置が可能であるが、敢えて機能語に強勢を置くことによって、発言内容に注目させている。

"The accent on the preposition points up the fact more sharply."

　　Bolinger (1986: 130)

　類似例を挙げておこう。

h.　A: [In anger] Why can't you sell me fish and chips, dammit?

　　B: *Because we're* ˈ*out* ↘ *of them.* We're sold out.

i.　The bills were not large, *but there were a great* ˈ*many* ↘ *of them.*

j.　The mistakes you made were not big, *but there were a great* ˈ*many* ↘ *of them.*

k.　A: I love Osmond so. I want to marry him.

　　B: *But there is* ˈ*nothing* ↘ *of him*: no money, no name, no importance.

　　　Don't you care for these things?

l.　[Joke]

　　Officer (in the desert): Men, I've got some good news for you and some
　　　　　　　　　　　　　　bad news. Which one would you like first?

　　Men (having thought): The bad news, sir.

　　Officer: Very well. There's nothing to eat but camel shit.

　　Men: And the good news, sir?

　　Officer: *There's* ˈ*plenty* ↘ *of it.*

m.　A: I like Regency novels. I think I'll check out *Gone With the Wind*.

　　B: *But* ˈ*Gone with the Wind* ˈ*isn't* ↘ *of that period.*

　　　（adapted from Bolinger (1989: 376); Regency period は、George, Prince of
　　　Wales が摂政であった時代（1811 ～ 1820）

n.　A: Thank you for your help.

　　B: ˈ*Think nothing* ↘ *of it.*　　(idiom: You're welcome.)

o.　A: What should we do?

　　B: *Let us find a so*ˈ*lution* ↘ *to this problem.*

p.　A: John is a real go-getter in business. I admire him. Don't you, too?

　　B: Well, I don't know. *There is* ˈ*more* ↘ *to life than just making money.*

q.　It's nothing much, *but you're* ˈ*welcome* ↘ *to it.*

かつて、Lewis に、このような不可解な強勢について教示を求めた。その際、
以下の文章を紹介した。

　　There's a woman who sits opposite me at work ― she's really nice, but all
　　she ever talks about is food… She'll say "Do you know what I cooked for

Marianne and Marty last night? I got chicken, poured over a whole tin of mushroom soup. We had a bit of wine left － I put that in － it made this wonderful sauce," but the funny thing is, she's only about seven stones － *there's* ⌐*nothing* ＼*of her*, so thin.　注：seven stones は 98 pounds（約 44 キロ）以下は、Lewis からの返信内容である。

　　No easy explanation occurs to me immediately re:

　　　　There's nothing ＼of her.

　　Lots of prepositions behave this way, e.g.

　　　　There's nothing ＼to it.

　　　　There's nothing ＼in it.

　　　　There's nothing ＼for it.

　　　　I'm looking ＼at it.

　　　　I get nothing ＼from it.

　　　　Far ＼from it.

　　　　No doubt a ＼bout it.

　　　　Get ＼with it.

　　　　Think nothing ＼of it.　　(2006.9.21)

参考：前置詞の強勢について（追補）

　　　　He's déad and I'm glád of it.

　　　　He's déad and I'm glád because of it.

　　But if we want to point up 'cause' we may do so:

　　　　He's déad and I'm glád óf it.

　　[T]he extra accent so close to the end (especially in *glád óf*) is climactic.

　　One might think that, given the unimportance of *of*, emphasis is the only reason for putting the accent on that word.　Bolinger (1986: 107)

　　　　　　注：given = considering　　　　　　　　　　　　下線は伊達が追加

課題 28　文末の I think (suppose)

　主文（主節）の後に付け加えられる短いコメント（評言）として、I think, I suppose, I hope, I expect, you know などの表現がある。これらには3つのイントネーションの型がある。

a.　A: When will they get back?

　　B: To ↘morrow, *I think*.　（I think は尾部であり、実質的な意味はない）

この場合、「明日であること」に確信があるが、発言が独断的な（dogmatic）に思われないようにする言い方である。I think は尾部にすぎず、ピッチの変化を伴わない。

> [V]irtual certainty is indicated; so much so that *I think* could be omitted
> without substantially changing the meaning of the speaker's answer.
> 　　　　　　　O'Connor & Arnold (1973: 92)

b.　A: When's she coming?

　　B: To ↘morrow, | *I ↗think*.　(2 tone units)

「明日であること」に少し自信がない。

> [T]he speaker is fairly confident that his answer is the correct one,
> though there remains for him some slight element of doubt.　(ibid.: 92)

c.　A: When's she coming?

　　B: To ↘morrow, | *I ↘↗think*.　(2 tone units)

この場合、上記の2例よりも、話者の確信の度合いが低い。

> [T]he speaker is obviously much less sure of his ground than in [the
> other two]: it is as if he were saying that he is merely giving his opinion
> and that he could well be wrong.　　(ibid.: 94)

なお、I think に代わって、I should think も使われる。

I suppose, I hope などについても、3つの型がある。以下は、Bolinger (1989: 127-9) からである。

```
                com
      He's
           ing I suppose? (I hope, I gather)
```

ここでは、付加語は尾部であるので、大した意味はない。一方、上昇調になる

と、少々疑問の気持ちがある。

```
        com
  He's
          ing I suppose(?)
```

(a little higher on the scale of interrogativity (疑問))

下降上昇調では、確信がない。

```
        com                   po
  He's
          ing  I  sup
                        se.
```

("but I don't know for sure.")

　また、独立した文 I think so; I suppose so; I imagine so; I expect so; I hope so. も
ある。下降調の I ↘ think so. は自信ある言い方で、非下降調の I ↗ think so. と
I ↘↗ think so.（I ↘think ↗so）は自信の度合いが少し下がる言い方（but I'm
not quite sure.）である。また、I should think so. も用いられることがある。

参考：I hope not; I'm afraid not; I suppose not, I fear not. では、動詞 / 形容詞に核強
　　　勢が置かれる。

 a. A: Is there a charge for this?

   B: I ↘ hope not. *or* I ↘↗ hope not.（I ↘hope ↗not）

I hópe nōt.

 b. A: Do we get paid for our efforts?

   B: I'm af ↘ raid not. *or* I'm af ↘↗ raid not.（I'm af↘raid ↗not）

   I sup ↘ pose not. *or* I sup ↘↗ pose not.（I sup↘pose ↗not）

しかし、*not* に核強勢が来る場合、文全体を強調することになる。

 c. A: Were they satisfied with the explanation?

   B: I |fear ↘ not. / I'm af|raid ↘ not.

 d. A: Couldn't you make it some other day?

   B: No. I'm af|raid ↘ not.

The climax tone must come on the 'not' for both.

(personal mail from J. W. Lewis (2012. 9. 12))

課題 29　核強勢の異例な配置（1）

　序論でも述べたように、私は、イントネーション研究のために映画やテレビ・ドラマ中のセリフをコーパスとして利用している。時々、不可解に思えるイントネーションを聞く。これから文尾に位置する反復語を強調することによって、文全体の意味を強化する non-default form の例をいくつか見ていくことにする。核強勢を受ける語を大文字で示す。

a.　[*Lulu on the Bridge*；捕虜と捕獲者とのやりとり]

Captor: What's your favorite book?

Captive: *I don't have a favorite BOOK*.

Captor: What's your favorite movie?

Captive: *I don't like MOVIES*. I never go to them.

斜線部では、なぜ反復語 *book* と *movies* が強調されて――核強勢を受けて――いるのか。これは、話者のどのような心的態度（attitude）を表しているのか。私の打診に対して、いくつかのコメントが送信されてきた。たとえば

> My native speaker (US Midwest) intuition: The second speaker is a little put off by the whole idea of talking about books and movies, and thus stresses the words, as the kind of thing he doesn't bother with at all. He is maybe being a bit derisive of the whole idea, and implying that the first speaker has no business asking about such things at all; all this in addition to the assumed general resentment and anger he feels toward his captor.
>
> (2003.1.19)　　　注：be put off 不快になる；derisive 軽蔑的な

概して言えば、嫌悪感を表すのに反復語を強調するのは常套手段である。似た例が、Bolinger (1986: 90) にもある。

　① Raw fish is good for you, but after all, ˈ*who* ↘ *likes it?*

　② Raw fish is good for you, but after all, ˈ*who* ˈ*likes raw* ↘ *fish?*

　③ Raw fish is good for you, but after all, ˈ*who* ˈ*likes* ↘ *that?*

①は、特別な感情・態度を伴わない matter-of-fact の言い方である。それに対して②は、嫌悪感が込められている。*sushi* を食べる人が増えてきているとはいえ「生魚なんて」嫌だよ。③も、②と同じく emotionally colored であり、「そんなもの御免だよ」のニュアンスがある。

b.　[*Cape Fear*]

A: What did the doctor say?

B: That he was poisoned.

A: Poisoned? *What kind of POISON?*

以下は、SUPRAS のメンバーのコメントである。

To me, this communicates shock at the whole idea of 'poison' being involved. If just *kind* were stressed, as in the unmarked pattern, then speaker A would have sounded less shocked by the possibility of poison being the cause of death, implying that it was in the range of possibility he/she had already considered.　(2003.1.19)

この場合は、ショックを表すために反復語が強調して言われた。

c.　[*Full House*]

A: Let me quit the job.

B: I think maybe you're being a little hasty. Quitting isn't the right thing to do.

A: I've got to quit. We made a deal.

B: Look, the job is too important for you. *You're not quitting the JOB!*

（一種の命令文）

Lincoln 大統領の Gettysburg Address は、King 牧師の *I Have a Dream* と共に英語暗唱コンテストでは定番の題材である。Wells の my phonetic blog には、学童の頃の興味深い逸話が語られている。それは、"*that government of the people, by the people, for the people…*"の強勢配置について関するものである。

When I was a schoolboy my history teacher thought that there ought to be a repeated accenting of 'people': **that government of the ˈpeople, ǀ by the ˈpeople, ǀ for the ˈpeople, ǀ shall not ˈperish from the ˈearth**.

That is certainly an option the speaker would have had. We can repeat ourselves for emphasis, giving the same information more than once, and presenting it afresh each time, focusing on it anew. Arguably, Lincoln wanted to focus and refocus on the importance of democracy. Lincoln delivered his address before the days of sound recording. So we shall never know whether my history teacher was right or not.　(2007. 2.26)

但し、Lewis によれば、"My advice to the EFL advanced user is to go each time for stressing the preposition and not *people* to get the best shot at an idiomatic native-English-speaker-type effect."　(blog22: 2007.2.26)

課題 30　核強勢の異例な配置（2）

　英語では、反復語や代名詞は、対比用法以外では、文アクセントを受けないのが default pattern である。しかし、そこから逸脱するケースが多々ある。

(i) 反覆語

a.　A: What's the matter? What did he say?

　　B: It's |not what he ↘↗said, | but *the* |way he ↘*said it*.

b.　A: I like what you're wearing.

　　B: Thank you.

　　A: *And I* |love the |way you ↘*wear it*.

c.　A: Thanks for the advice.

　　B: What advice?

　　A: Well, it |wasn't so |much what you ↘↗said, | *it was the* |way you |didn't
　　　　↘ *say it*.

d.　A: I like city life.

　　B: *There are* |cities and ↘*cities*, you know.

e.　A: I want some money.

　　B: *You're asking* |me for ↘*money?* You must be mad! I'm a pauper.
　　　You're rich.

f.　|*Boys will be* ↘*boys* — they will wear the latest fashionable clothes, drive
　　the latest fashionable cars and acquire the latest fashionable goods.

g.　|*Tolerance is what* |makes |Britain ↘*Britain*. (i.e. makes the country the kind
　　of country it is) --- Tony Blair 元首相（人種差別事件を批判しての発言）

h.　A: John is often dressed rather sloppily.

　　B: Maybe so, but he's the kindest man I've ever met — |*Handsome is as*
　　　|*handsome* ↘*does*.　(i.e. How one acts is more important than how one looks.)

i.　A: Janice is pretty, isn't she? I envy her so.

　　B: She may have a pretty face, but |*pretty is as* |*pretty* ↘*does*; the way she
　　　behaves isn't pretty at all.

j.　A: It's very nice.

　　B: Yes. *As* |*nice as* |*nice can* ↘*be*.

k.　A: So how's he doing lately?

102

B: *He's as* ˈ*happy as* ˈ*happy can* ↘ *be*.

l.　The teacher invited Elsie into *the* ˈ*holy of* ↘ *holies* ― the staff room ― and offered her a cup of tea.

参考：以下のような慣用句においても、反復語に強勢が置かれる。

　　　ˈheart of ˈhearts（内心）; ˈKing of ˈKings (God); ˈon and ˈon; ˈday after ˈday; ˈmore and ˈmore; ˈinch by ˈinch; ˈarm in ˈarm; ˈback to ˈback（連続して）; an ˈeye for an ˈeye; ˈhome (away) from ˈhome; ˈhope against ˈhope（空頼み）;

(ii) 以下のケースでも、核強勢配置は非論理的である。

a.　A: I went home pronto.

　　B: ˈWhy did you go ↘ home?　(neutral reading)

　　　参考：↘Why did you go home? --- possible but marked　（有標の）

b.　A: We went into Manchester this morning.

　　B: ˈWhat did you ˈgo to ↘Manchester for?　(neutral reading)

　　　参考：↘What did you go there for? ---- possible but marked

　　　　　（a、b 共に adapted from Cruttenden (1997: 85)）

c.　If they can ˈsort it ˈout for them∨selves, | we'd ˈlike to ˈsee them ↘do so.
　　(neutral reading)

さて、c は Wells の blog からである。代動詞 ***do*** は、既知情報であるにもかかわらず、文アクセント（核強勢）を受けている。

　So why does ***do*** remain accented? In a neutral reading, it bears the nucleus.… But what I want to have is a set of rules…which will produce the correct intonation pattern. And the rules as I formulate them seem to lead to the pattern:

　　　If they can ˈsort it ˈout for them∨selves, | we'd ˈlike to ＼see them do so.

　― which is possible, but in fact marked…　Blog (2006. 8. 3)

Wells が学習者に提示するルールでは、核は see に来るはずだが、実際には、反復語 do に来る。ここに Wells の忸怩たる思いが読みとれる。

(iii) it を含む慣用表現

It is rarely prominent except at the end of a number of fixed phrases with *this* and *that*.

① ˈThis is ↘it. の通常の意味は「まさにこれだ／この時だ」（expected thing or moment）である。しかし、この idiom は、様々な意味合いで用いられる。

a. Here we are. *This is it.* This is my house.

b. *This is it* — the big sale!

c. ［結婚式を終え、娘が母に別れを告げる］

A: Well, *this is it.* You're finally rid of me.

B: No, I think you'll be back every now and then.

d. ［墜落していく爆撃機のパイロット］I thought, "*This is it!*"（万事休す）

All I could see was the ground flying up at me.

e. ［敵軍の総攻撃］It's an attack! *This is it!*（正念場、覚悟の時）

f. *This is it*, boys, the moment we've been expecting.（正念場）

最後の戦いや最後のチャレンジに立ち向かう時にも *This is it.* が使われる。

g. [Michael Jackson:] I just want to say that these will be my final show performances in London. *This will be it.* When I say *this is it*, it really means *this is it.*

② ˈThat's ↘it. という慣用表現がある。「その通り」、「それでおしまい」、「それが問題なんだ」という意味がある。低下降調で言われることもある。

a. A: It's the 14ᵗʰ today, isn't it?

B: *That's it.*

b. A: Do you need anything else?

B: *Oh, that's it.* Thanks.

c. *That's really it.* There's nothing more we can do.

d. *That's it then.* The situation can't be changed.

e. How could you do that to me? *That's it!* I'm leaving.

f. A: How can I get there? I don't see a bridge or a boat.

B: Just swim across.

A: *That's just it.* (That's the problem) I can't swim.

注：ただし、次のようなイントネーションもある。

・So ↘*that's it.* (adapted from Wells (2006: 26))

　　・A: So you fell off a horse. I suppose your pride hurt. Even more than your foot

　　　　and your shoulder. *Is ↗ that it?*　(*Is* |*that* ↗ *it?* も可)

　　　B: I suppose so.　(adapted from Arnold & Tooley (1971: 129))

(iv) 代名詞を伴う慣用表現

① 服飾に関する表現

　代名詞が核強勢を受ける短い慣用表現がある。例えば、It's so you! は、「とても君に似合っている」とか「とても君らしいね」という意味である。

a.　A: You must buy that jacket.

　　B: You really think so?

　　A: Yeah. *It's* |*so* ↘ *you*!

b.　A: Hi, Jane. Nice of you to come at such short notice.

　　B: No problem.

　　[A points to B's suspenders under his jacket.]

　　A: Wow, I like them.

　　B: |*Are they* ↗ *me*?

c.　[At a boutique]

　　A: Ah, you look fantastic! It's fabulous. Let's try some accessories.

　　B: Oh, I don't know.

　　A: Then, maybe a hat? Come on. Try this hat on.

　　B: Thanks, but *I* |*don't think it's* |*really* ↘ *me*.

② 乗り物に関する場面

a.　[The conductor announcing "Dobbs Ferry, next station. Dobbs Ferry."]

　　A: Well, |*this is* ↘ *you*.

　　B: Yeah. Thanks for seeing me off.

b.　[Seeing an approaching bus]

　　A: |*That's* ↗ *us*?

　　B: Yes.

c.　[In the hotel lobby, the concierge announces the arrival of a taxi.]

　　|*This is* ↘ *me*. Good bye. Take care.

課題 31　People have good clothes on.

(i)［エレベーターの中で］

　　You shouldn't be eating in here. *People have good clothes on.*

斜体字部は、どこに核強勢が置かれるだろうか。原則を言えば、核強勢は、文（厳密には音調単位）の最後の内容語に来る。これは、末尾焦点（end focus）と呼ばれる現象である。この原則に基づけば、副詞 *on* に核強勢が来るはずである。しかし、実際には *clothes* が核強勢を受ける。なぜならば、内容語の中でも、名詞は優先的に核強勢を受けるからである。そして、核強勢のある語（厳密には、音節）から以降は、尾部となる。

a.　ˈPeople have ˈgood ↘clothes *on*.

　　注：have は、三連規則により文アクセントを受けない。

この文は、ˈPeople ˈ*have on* good ↘clothes. と言い換えができる。

類例を挙げよう。

b.　I ˈ*look* the ↘answer *up*.　または

　　I ˈ*look up* the ↘answer.

c.　He ˈ*cleaned* his ↘desk *out*.　または

　　He ˈ*cleaned out* his ↘desk.

d.　They ˈ*put* the ↘meeting *off*.　または

　　They ˈ*put off* the ↘meeting.

しかし、slower, more deliberate speech では、それぞれ

a'.　People ˌ*have* ˈ*on* good ↘clothes.

b'.　I ˌ*look* ˈ*up* the ↘answer.

c'.　He ˌ*cleaned* ˈ*out* his ↘desk.

d'.　They ˌ*put* ˈ*off* the ↘meeting.

以下の 2 文では、faster tempo の場合、副詞 up と前置詞 on の強勢曲線は区別がつかない。つまり、共に弱強勢（reduced stress）である。

　　① I ˈlooked up the ↘answer.（参考書などで）正解を調べた

　　② I ˈworked on the ↘answer.（試験で）正解に取り組んだ

しかし、異なる構文では、slower または faster tempo 共に、up と on の強勢曲線に違いがある。つまり、up には強勢がある。

　　① ˈHere's the ˈanswer I ˈlooked ↘up.

② ˈHere's the ˈanswer I ↘worked on.

(ii) 慣用表現

以下のような成句では、副詞を移動させることはできない。

a.　*I* ˈ*walked my* ↘*legs off*, ˈlooking for a steady job.　（必死で歩いた）

b.　[Tom が久しぶりに Aunt Polly の家を訪れると]

　　Tom's Aunt Polly was right there. She jumped and *almost* ˈ*kissed his* ↘*head off*.　（猛烈にキスをした）

c.　Someone called out, "Who's there? Answer or I'll shoot!" But we didn't answer. *We just* ˈ*ran our* ↘*feet off*.

d.　When they heard his joke, *the audience* ˈ*laughed their* ↘*heads off*.

e.　You are leaving me? *I* ˈ*worked my* ↘*ass off* ˈ to provide you with a good life.　　　　　　　　　　　（必死で働いた）

f.　He was a working road manager. He took care of money, airplane reservations, getting the band to where they were supposed to go. *The cat worked his ass off*.　　　　注：the cat = the guy

```
            cat worked his  ass
     The
                       off      Ladd (1980: 65)
```

g.　There was a strange man on the bed, ˈ | *snoring his* ↘*head off*.

h.　*Our* ˈ*children* ˈ | *cried their* ↘*eyes out* ˈ | when our dog ran way.

i.　She waved goodbye to her parents, then went to the gate ˈ | and *sobbed her* ↘*heart out*.

j.　A: Good morning.

　　B: Afternoon is more like it. *You* ˈ*slept the* ↘*day away*.

しかし、以下の文では、off は句動詞の一部ではない。

・I'm going to ˈtake a ˈfew days ↘off.

・It's nice to ˈhave some ˈtime ↘off.

　これらの意味的区切りは、take/have + a few days off (= a few days' vacation)

　　Toˈday is my ˈday ↘off　(= holiday)

　　She ˈtook a seˈmester ↘off.　（one semester 休学した）

107

課題 32　**He left the door open.**

　標記の文では核強勢が *door* または *open* のどちらかに来る可能性がある。そのどちらかを決めるのは談話の状況である。一般に、第 5 文型 SVOC において O が新情報の場合にはそこに核強勢が置かれる。従って C は尾部となり文アクセントを受けない。ここにも名詞優先主義の原則が見られる。

a.　A: How's your new roommate Randy?

　　B: I can't trust him at all. *He* ⌐*always leaves the* ↘*door open* ⌐ and never pays his rent.

　　　　注：*leaves* は、三連規則により文アクセントを受けない。

b.　I think we could stand a little air in here. Tom, ⌐ ⌐*leave the* ↘*door open*. I felt a nice fresh breeze a moment ago.

一方、*open* に核強勢が来る場合、*door* の概念が文脈に暗示されている。または、話者がそのように推測している。

c.　A: [Slams the door.] Hi, Jane. I hope I'm not late.

　　B: Hello, Bill. I ↘wish ⌐ *you'd* ⌐*left the door* ↘*open*. It's stuffy in here.

次の 2 例は比較対照例である。

d.　[*The Secret of My Success*] I'm in trouble. I know girls like this. *They* ⌐*just can't* ⌐*keep their* ↘*mouth shut*. This news about me is gonna be all over New York.

e.　A: Is something wrong?

　　B: None of your business. *You* ⌐*keep your* ⌐*mouth* ↘*shut*.

Bolinger (1986: 256) には、以下のような模式図がある。

The first is more apt to be used when there has been no prior mention of 'window,' the second when 'window' is understood.

f.　Hey, *you* ⌐*left the* ↘*water running!* Come back.

g.　[From a distance, pointing to the car from which B has just emerged]

　　A: Hey! *You* ⌐*left the* ↘*lights on!*

　　B: What?

h.　A: The weather forecaster said we might have snow for Christmas.

　　B: That would be really romantic. I've never seen a white Christmas.

　　A: *Let's* ⌐*keep our* ↘*fingers crossed*. Maybe you'll get your first chance.

　次は、髪の毛が落ちたことを述べる言い方である。（189）では、自分の抜毛のなかに白髪があることに初めて気づき嘆いている時の言い方であり、白髪の存在は全くの新情報である。（190）では、以前から自分の頭髪に白髪が混じっており、そのうちの一本が抜け落ちたことを嘆いている。

i.　(189) I had a ⌐gray ↘hair fall out.

　　(190) I had a ⌐gray ⌐hair fall ↘out.

　　Sentence (190), but not (189), seems to presuppose that the speaker has numerous gray hairs. It sounds as if the speaker of this sentence is upset basically at the thought of one of these hairs falling out. Sentence (189), on the other hand, might be uttered by someone who was upset at discovering the presence of a gray hair…　　　　　Schmerling (1976: 92)

　しかし、注意しなければないことがある。目的語が生物や人間の意志ある言動の場合は、以下のようになる。　　詳細は、伊達（2019）の課題 45 を参照。

　　　・I ⌐heard a ⌐woman ↘scream.
　　　・We ⌐found a couple of ⌐men ↘arguing.
　　　・When I got home, I ⌐saw my ⌐mother ↘cooking.

参考：《reading stereotype》

　　　文のイントネーションを確かめるためにネーテイブスピーカーに発音してもらうときに留意するべきことがある。文脈を示さないと、reading stereotype の傾向が見られる。これは、「棒読み」のことで、citation reading とも呼ばれ、"a tendency for readers to apply, mechanically, the pattern that assigns a major *A profile* to the last content word" (Bolinger 1989: 68)。*A profile* とは下降調の核強勢のことである。例えば、event sentence では、＊There's a ⌐car ↘coming. とか＊My ⌐watch ↘stopped. となりがちである。また、Leave the door open. は、とっさの発話（out-of-the-blue utterance）の場合、door が核強勢を受けるが、文脈を説明しないで、彼らに読んでもらうと open に核強勢を置く。かつて、Cambridge University Press 出版の会話教材を聴いていたら、voice actor は door に核強勢を置いていたが、解説箇所 Grammar Focus では、解説者は、棒読みで open に核強勢を置いていた。関連内容が、課題 14 (ii) にある。

課題 33　**Calling intonation**

　短い発話に用いられる様式化（stylized）した特異なイントネーションがある。それは〈高平坦＋中平坦調〉である。2 つの平坦ピッチの最初のものが、核強勢を受け、2 番目の平坦ピッチへ step down する。模式図で示すと、以下のようになる。

[Calling a group of friends at a picnic]

```
Food's--                Come and get--
        ready--                       it--
```
                                      Ladd (1980: 173)

```
John-                ho-
    ny!                 ome!
                 Come
```
                                      Bolinger (1986: 8)

4 例のいずれも、末尾の pitch が下がり切らずに平坦調（level tone）になっている。このような音調は、伝統的に様々な名称で呼ばれてきた。例えば、stylized tone, level tone, calling intonation, calling contour など。本書では、以下のように表記することにする。

> ➔Food's ↳ready.　　ˈCome and ➔get ↳it.
> ➔John↳ny!　　　　ˈCome ➔ho↳ome.

注：強勢音節の後に尾部がない場合、それは 2 つに分割される。Jo-ohn!

　　a succession of two monotones (one syllable here is prolonged at each of two heights)　Bolinger (1986: 226)

しかし、この stylized tone は、call 以外でも使われることが多い。

(i) 常套表現や形式化した表現

a.　ˈGood ➔morn↳ing.

b.　A: See you soon.

　　B: ˈBye- ➔bye↳e.

c.　A: Thank you.

　　B: You're ➔wel↳come.

d.　A: Where are you, John?

110

　　B: |*Just* →*com*→*ing*.

e.　A: May I see your passport, please? OK. Enjoy your trip.

　　B: →*Thank*→*you*.

f.　[幼い子どもと父が「かくれんぼ」遊びをしている。父が鬼である]

　　A: Daddy, you be 'it' this time.

　　B: OK. One, two…nine, ten. Okay, ready or not, |*here I* →*co*→*ome!*

g.　[The phone rings.]

　　Good morning, |*Ace Travel* →*Agen*→*cy*. How can I help you?

h.　[In conversation with someone, the phone vibrates.]

　　→*Hang* →*on*. There's someone on the phone.

i.　[During a phone call] |*Hold the* →*li*→*ine*.

j.　[While playing tag]

　　Tag! →*You're* →*it!*

k.　[突然、背後から]

　　A: →*Peeka*→*boo!*

　　B: (Frightened) Oh, Mr. Baker, you scared me half to death!

　　A: Oh, I didn't mean to do that. I just thought you'd forgot about me.

l.　A: →*Ta*→*dah!* （ジャジャーン！）

　　B: What is that?

m.　[Comforting or reassuring someone, especially a child who is crying]

　　→*There*, →*there*, don't get so upset.

　　Thére,

　　　　　thére!　　　　Bolinger (1986: 260)

n.　A: Where's the phone book?

　　B: *On the* →*ta*→*ble*. (…right where it belongs [いつもの場所に])

o.　A: What did you have for dinner?

　　B: *Oh the* →*usual* →*thing*.

p.　A: There goes the money I won at the lottery!

　　B: |*Easy* →*co*→*ome*, | |*easy* →*go*→*o*.

(ii) 日常的な出来事について相手に注意喚起する (reminder)

　　[T]he stylized fall is appropriate for warnings that are essentially

111

reminders... It is used to inform the hearer of events considered commonplace or everyday... but not of surprises, emergencies, big news.

a. Jimmy, [|] *don't forget your* ➜ *lu* ➜ *unch!*

b. [|] *Look out for the* [|] *broken* ➜ *ste* ➜ *ep!* (reminder)

　(i.e., the step on the way down to the basement that's been broken for months)

```
Look out for the broken ste--
                              ep--        Ladd (1980: 174-5)
```

c. [From a distance, pointing to the car from which B has just emerged]

　A: *You* [|] *left the* ➜ *lights* ➜ *on!*

```
        left your lights--
    Y'                        on--        (ibid.: 177)
```

　B: What?

d. Oh, oh-h-h! [|] *Daddy for* [|] *got his* ➜ *brief* ➜ *case again!*

```
Oh            Daddy forgot his brief
    oh-h-h!                            case again!    Bolinger (1989: 285)
```

e. ［友人とジョッギングをしていて、お互い少々息が切れてくる］

　Just [|] *three* [|] *blocks to* ➜ *go* ➜ *o*.

　注：2人には馴染のジョッギングコース。もし友人には初めてのコースならば下降調になる。　（adapted from Bolinger (1986: 227)）

(iii) teasing （からかい）

a. Uh-oh! *Your* ➜ *fly's* ➜ *open!*

b. *You've* [|] *got a* [|] *hole in your* ➜ *pa* ➜ *ants*.

c. A: Hurry. Hurry. Comet's having puppies! （子犬を出産中）

　B: What?（犬のいるところまで走っていく）　Wait a second. Comet's a boy.

　A: Ha, ha. *I* ➜ *fooled* ➜ *you!* （上手く騙した）

d. [*Picnic*. 美貌ゆえに男性に人気のあるのが誇りの姉が、地味な妹から「男性なんて興味がないわ」ということばを聞いて]

　[|] *Beggars* can't be ➜ choosers.

e. [Bill はウエートレスの Katherine に気があり度々レストランにやって来る]

　Rosa: (to Katherine) *I* [|] *think you* [|] *have a* ➜ *custo* ➜ *mer!*

　Katherine: (to Bill) So what'll it be?

課題 33　Calling intonation

Bill: Would you have dinner with me tonight?

(iv) その他

a.　［駅員］*All a* →*bo*↴*ard*!　　注：上昇調もある

b.　［裁判所の廷吏］The court will be in session. *All a* →*ri*↴*ise*.　（全員起立！）

c.　［*High Noon*. 結婚の誓い］　　　　　　　　注：上昇調もある

　　Priest: Do you, Will Kane, take Amy to be your lawful wedded wife to
　　　　　　have and to hold from this day forward until death do you part?

　　Kane: *I* →*do*↴*o*.

　　Priest: Do you, Amy, take Will to be your lawful wedded husband to have
　　　　　　and to hold from this day forward until death do you part?

　　Amy: *I* ↘*do*.

　　Priest: The ring, please. Then, by the authority vested in me by the laws of
　　　　　　this Territory, I pronounce you man and wife.

d.　［教会での「主の祈り」斉唱（prayer in unison）］

　　　　ˈOur →fa↴ther
　　　　 Which ˈart in →heav↴en
　　　　ˈHallowed ˈbe thy →na↴ame
　　　　ˈThy ˈkingdom →co↴ome…
　　　　ˈThy ˈwill be →do↴one
　　　　 on ˈearth, ˈas it is in →heav↴en
　　　　…　　Tench (1990: 502)

　　注：上記は、イエスが弟子たちに教えた祈りで、祈りの模範とされ、キリスト教の
　　　　すべての教会において、家庭において、あらゆる時と所において唱えられる。
　　　　神の国の到来・糧食の恵与・赦罪・悪からの防護など 6 つの祈願を述べる。
　　　　「天にましますわたしたちの父よ、
　　　　み名が聖とされますように。
　　　　み国が来ますように。
　　　　みこころが天に行われるとおり
　　　　地にも行われますように …。」

参考：この stylized tone は (ii) a, b, c のように reminder のためによく用いられるが、

113

真の warning では用いられない。その場合は、下降調で言われる。

[One mountain climber to another]

$^|$ Look out for the cre ➘ vasse.

```
Look out for the creva
                     s
                      s
                       e          Ladd (1980: 174)
```

また、reminder を発しても相手に理解されず、再度、注意を促すときも下降調
で発せられる。

- A: [From a distance, pointing to the car] You $^|$ left the ➞ lights ⌐ on.

  B: What?

  A: (Louder) You $^|$ left the ➘ lights on.

```
            left your  lights
       Y'
                          on.        (ibid.: 177)
```

更に言えば、以下でも stylized tone から下降調に転じる。

- ➞ John ⌐ ny! [no response, louder] ➞ John ⌐ ny!

  [no response, still louder] ➘ Johnny!

  (adapted from Ladd (1980: 176))

課題 34　**Accent is predictable if you're a mind-reader.**

　標題の英語は、Bolinger の有名な論文（1972b: 633-44）のタイトルである。状況や文脈を正しく読めば、文アクセントを受ける語は容易に予測できるという主張である。

(i) 下位語と上位語との関係

a.　A: Do you like Picasso?

　　B: No, I ⌐don't ↘ <u>*care much for modern paintings*</u>.

　　ここでは、*Picasso* と *modern paintings* は同義語であるが、分類上では、それぞれ下位語と上位語との関係にある。

　　注：分類上、下位に区分される語句の後に、それより上位の語句が使われる場合、後者は旧／既知情報と見なされる。*Picasso* は下位にあり、modern paintings は上位にある。*Picasso* が言及されれば、***modern paintings*** という上位概念は、聞き手の頭にあるはずである。

b.　I wouldn't mind bacon, but *my* ↘↗<u>*wife*</u> │ ↘<u>*hates pork*</u>.

c.　A: Do you ever go running?

　　B: No, I ⌐can't ↘<u>*stand athletics*</u>.

d.　A: Have you seen *Oklahoma!*?

　　B: Sorry. I ⌐don't ↘<u>*like musicals*</u>.

e.　A: How do you like English phonetics?

　　B: I ⌐don't ↘<u>like *linguistics*</u>.

　　　参考：① X:　Do you like Italian food?　（上位語）

　　　　　　　　Y:　*I like spa*↘↗<u>*ghetti*</u>.　（下位語）

　　　　　② X:　Have you ever visited Scotland?　（上位語）

　　　　　　　　Y:　*I've been to* ↘↗<u>*Glasgow*</u>.　（下位語）

　　　　　③ X:　What's your family like? Do you come from a big family?

　　　　　　　　Y:　Not really. *But I* ⌐*have a* ⌐*twin* ↘↗<u>*brother*</u>.

　　　注：下位語が、上位語との関係において条件つき発言とか部分的発言の場合、下降上昇調になる。

(ii) 文脈上で明白な（contextually clear）語には文アクセントが置かれない。

a.　A: What do you do when you get home?

B: *I've │got to │take the ↘dog for a walk*.

  参考：I've │got to │take the dog to the ↘vet.

b. Harry wants a VW, but *his │wife would pre│fer an A↘merican car*.

c. A: Man, it's hot! Doesn't feel like it'll cool off till tomorrow at least.

  B: Yeah, *they ↘said it would be hot all day*.

d. *He's │taken his ↘son out to play*.

  参考：He's │taken his │son out ↘fishing.

e. I smiled at the supervisor and ↘↗*she │ greeted ↘me*.

> [G]*reeted* is merely a lexical variant of *smiled*: the smile was a greeting
> and there was some kind of greeting in response. This is prosodically
> indicated by *greeted* having no intonational prominence.
>
>   Greenbaum & Quirk (1990: 461)

f. It's not that Alan doesn't like Kate: ↘↗*she │ can't stand ↘him*.

> [W]e might say that the verb *doesn't like* means more or less the same
> as *can't stand*.   Knowles (1987: 154)

g. A: Marjorie's not very fond of books, is she?

  B: No, but Andrew's a great reader. *He's ↘always got his head in a book*.

最後に、mind reading できない男にまつわるエピソードを紹介しよう。

> An anguished young lady reported after a visit to a restaurant:
>
>   I asked the waiter where I could wash my hands and he showed me where
>   I could wásh my hánds!

Here *wash my hands* has two meanings, in contrast in the environment:
'toilet' and literally washing one's hands.

  (adapted from Bolinger (1986: 379))

課題 35　**Dogs must be carried.**

(i) イギリスは、動物愛護の国、愛犬国家とも呼ばれる。イギリス人の犬好きは世界的にも有名である。店内のみならず電車やバスでもよく見かける。エスカレーターに乗る場合は、抱きかかえなければならない規則がある。

　　　　Dogs must be carried on the escalator.

YouTube で Dogs must be carried を検索すると、ロンドンの地下鉄のエスカレーターの付近で係員が、犬連れの人たちに、この規則の順守を求めている、いろいろな場面が出てくる。写真のような滑稽な場面もある。エスカレーターの前には下図のような掲示をよく見かける。男性が、子犬を小脇に抱いている。

この掲示の英語は、発音の仕方によって 2 つの意味に解釈できる。

・You must have a dog and carry it.　(Absurd interpretation!)

　　（犬を連れていないとエスカレーターに乗れない）

・If you have a dog with you, you must carry it.

　　（犬を連れている場合、抱きかかえる必要がある）

これを発音する場合、それぞれ

①　↘Dogs must be carried.

②　↗Dogs ｜ must be ↘carried.

　　↘↗Dogs ｜ must be ↘carried.

勿論、掲示の意味は、②である。

Ladd (2008: 277) に詳細な解説がある。

> In the first case, where subject and predicate form a single intermediate phrase, there is a single primary accent; this accent is on *dogs*, in accordance with the principle of English that treats arguments as more accentable than predicates. In the second case, where subject and predicate each form a separate intermediate phrase, each has its own DTE and therefore its own accent (on *dogs* and *carried*, respectively). The accent on *carried* then becomes the main accent of the sentence.

117

注：arguments は、名詞の主語または目的語のこと；DTE (Designated Terminal Element) は、tone unit のこと。Wells (2006: 175) にも短い解説がある。

(ii) 商店や飲食店などの入り口には、マスクの着用を求める掲示を見かける。また、観光地のビーチにある店には、衣服着用とサンダル履きを求める掲示がある。

掲示の意味を表すイントネーションは、次のどちらであろうか。

① ↘Masks must be worn.

② ↘↗Masks ｜ must be ↘worn.

③ ˈShirts and ↘shoes must be worn on the premises.

④ ˈShirts and ↘↗shoes ｜ must be ↘worn on the premises.

両掲示の意味を表すのは、それぞれ①と③である。なお、②と④は、日常生活で言われる状況は考えにくい。

　さて、(i) ②では、看板は dog owners に向けられたものである。それを敷衍すれば、Dog owners, you must carry your dogs. であり、dogs は、表面上では初出の名詞のように思えるが、実際には dogs の概念は既に文脈にある。肝心なことは、carried である。一方、(ii) 中の掲示は、不特定多数の人に向けられており、mask/shirt/shoes. こそが肝心なことであり、wear は文脈からpredictable である。実際、ˈshoes to wear, shirts to wear などの強勢配置のパタンがあるように、この場合に限って言えば、wear は 'empty' verb である。

118

課題 36　**Unthinking intonation (1)**

　Wells は、公共の場所（電車や病院など）で流される recorded voice のイントネーションについて、しばしば批判的なコメントをしている。

(i) 以下は、Wells の phonetic blog からである。彼が車内で聞いたアナウンスのプロソディーを表記したものである（2008.10.9）。

　　　＼Passengers ｜ ˈmust be in pos/session ｜ of a ˈvalid /ticket ｜＼**or** ｜ /Oyster card for their journey ｜ be ∨ fore they board, ｜ or be ∨ liable ｜ for a ˈ**penalty** ＼**fare**.

Wells は、passengers に核強勢が置かれていることについて批判し、文脈を配慮していないと言う。既に文脈に存在している概念（passenger）に焦点を置く——下降調の核強勢を置く——のは不自然である。本来、文頭の名詞主語を独立した音調単位として下降調で言うのは、それが new and major information の場合である。車内の乗客のことは、既に文脈に存在するので、このような下降調のイントネーションは不適切である。従って、以下のように言うべきである。

　　ˈPassengers ⁽ˈ⁾must be in pos/session…

または ↘↗Passengers ｜ ⁽ˈ⁾must be in pos/session…　注：上昇調もあり得る。

　Wells によれば、このアナウンスには、もう 2 つ不自然な個所がある。まず、なぜ *or* に核強勢が置かれているのか。それは、and との対比でもないので、強調されていることに論理的根拠がない。機能語が不条理に強勢を受けるのは、従来から指摘されている珍現象である（課題 37 参照）。Wells は、次のように言う。

　　The accenting of function words is a habit about which people have been
　　complaining for decades.

次に、アナウンスでは複合語 *penalty fare* の強勢配置が間違っている。ˈ*penalty* ＼*fare* ではなく、ˈ*penalty fare* であるべきである。文脈上、fare は既知内容である。

(ii) Wells (2014: 117-8) は、自分が治療を受けている歯科クリニックがある建物のエレベーターで自動的に流れる recorded voice のイントネーションについて、以下のように述べている。

I was struck by the intonation patterns of the recorded voice as I went up to the top.

3 種類の音調（下降調、上昇調、下降上昇調）が見られる。

We have a fall on a declarative statement, followed by a non-final rise (because there is more to come), followed by another non-final tone, this time a fall-rise (bcause there's still another floor to go), then another fall-rise (a warning), a repeat of the second line, and finally a fall proclaiming that we've reached our desinaion.

Wells は、この recorded voice について「よくできました」と言っている。

以下は、核音調が伝えるメッセージである。

|Doors \closing. (*declarative statement*)

|Going /up… (*there is more to come.*)

|Floor ∨four. (*there is still another floor to go.*)

 Doors ∨opening… (*warning: Be careful.*)

|Going /up… (*there is more to come.*)

|Floor \five. (*we've reached our destination.*)

以下は、Wells の初期の phonetic blog からである。

Wednesday
19 July 2006

As I got off the tram on my way home yesterday, the recorded announcement went as follows.

∨This tram | is for 'Elmer's \End.

The ∨next stop | will be 'Morden \Road.

Deconstruction of the intonation patterns:

You know this is a tram, so the concept *tram* is 'given'. We focus instead on the contrast (therefore fall-rise tone) between this tram, whose destination we shall now tell you, and other trams that may be going to other places. We declare (therefore fall tone) its destination.

You know you're at a tram stop. So the concept *stop* is given. We focus instead on the contrast (fall-rise) between the next one and this one or other ones. We declare (fall) its identity.

注：deconstruction　分解・解体したもの

課題 37　Unthinking intonation (2)

(i)　Wells は、phonetic blog の中で、ロンドン地下鉄駅のアナウンスを批判している（2010.11.23）。

> Here is a recorded announcement I heard at a tube station recently.
>
> 　∨Customers are re∘quested ｜ to ˈtake their ˈlitter ＼home with them.
>
> 　　注：↘Customers are reques↗ted ｜ …

これは、*customers* が対比されている音調である。いったい誰と対比されているのか。Wells によれば

> [T]he lady making the recording spoke the right words but used the wrong intonation for them. The intonation pattern that she used bears an implication that the request is aimed at customers, but not at others. It implies a contrast between *customers* and some other possible subject. We might gloss this implied meaning as 'although those who are not customers can leave their litter behind'.

つまり、*customers* に対比強勢が置かれると、運賃を払っていない人——幼い子どもや年金受給者——は、ゴミを置き去りにしてもよいと解釈されかねない。

　また、*customers* は、既に文脈に存在しているので、そこに核強勢そのものを置くのは論理的でない。Wells によれば

> What she ought to have said was
>
> ˈCustomers are re ∨quested ｜ to ˈtake their ˈlitter ＼home with them.

次は、私が日頃利用する駅での英語アナウンスである。

> ˈPassengers going to ↘↗Namba ｜ should ˈchange trains
>
> at Amaga↘saki…

または、*customers* の直後に区切り（intonation break）を作って文を言う方法もある。これは、slow, more deliberate speech で起こる。

> ∨Customers ｜ are reˈquested to ˈtake their ˈlitter ＼home with them.

この場合の下降上昇調は、対比ではなく something more to follow の合図となる。

(ii) Wells の blog に対して多くのコメントが寄せられた。その中で、特に私が注目したものを紹介しよう。それは、不可解な強勢配置に関するものである。

① Actually this is a very mild example of inappropriate intonation used in public transport announcements. I've often noticed that announcers tend to emphasize prepositions, conjunctions and auxiliary verbs rather than nouns and main verbs.

Examples:
- ・"First Capital Connect WOULD like to apologize FOR this delay, and for ANY inconvenience it may cause…"
- ・"Please do not leave unattended luggage IN the train, or ON the station." (strangeness compounded by the fact we usually say ON the train and IN the station.)

また、飛行機内の safety announcements でも、不可解な強勢配置が聞かれる。Wells (2006: 183-4) は、次のように言っている。

② In-flight safety announcements are read aloud from a fixed script. But the flight attendant making them has discretion over the intonation used. One chose the following tonicity pattern:

∨<u>In</u> the event ｜∨<u>of</u> an emergency ｜ there∨<u>will</u> be emergency lighting ｜ ＼<u>in</u> the aisles ｜ …

Perhaps the attendant made these tonicity choices as a result of having to repeat the same formulaic words over and over again on successive occasions…

注：discretion over… に対して自由裁量；tonicity 核強勢配置；formulaic words 決まり文句

③ Another explanation might be sought in the speaker's wish to sound lively and avoid boringness, so that the listener is spurred into listening more closely.　注：spur 刺激する；closely 注意深く

④ I heard from a station announcer on the London underground this morning: "Customers are reminded that FULL service has now resumed ON the Waterloo and City Lines." Look at it from the announcer's point of view. He is bored with telling people over and over again that full service has now resumed after the suspension on the Waterloo and City Lines. He wants to take that as 'given'. So he finds somewhere else to place the tonics.

注：'given' 既知情報の　　tonics 核強勢と同義

課題 38　対比か反駁か

全米ライフル協会のロビイストは、以下のスローガンを掲げている。

　　↘↗<u>Guns</u> don't kill people.　|　↘<u>People</u> kill people.

この文では、guns と people との間に<u>対比</u>が見られる。まず、guns でピッチ
が高く始まり、それから下降に転じ低いピッチになり、最後に上昇する。これ
を模式図で示すと、

しかし、銃の所持規制派の発言「毎年、銃による死亡事件が多い」に対して

↘*Guns*　|　ᵎ*don't kill* ↗*people.* (↘*Guns don't kill peo*↗*ple*) と言って反駁するとき
の音調曲線（contradiction contour）も、上記の対比（下降上昇調）と同じで
ある。このように、対比と反駁のインネーションは、理論的には互いに異なる
が、音声的な差は曖昧である。

Ladd (1980: 152) の解説を見てみよう。

> [T]here are cases of actual ambiguity between the fall-rise and
> the contradiction contour, a sure clue that we are dealing with two
> linguistically separate categories....
>
> (15)　John's
> 　　　　not in Boston
>
> This can be interpreted either as the contradiction contour... or as the
> fall-rise with nucleus on *John*.

Ladd の説明によれば、以下のような明確な意味的相違（"sharp semantic
distinction"）がある。

　① 反駁の場合

　　↘<u>John's</u>　|　ᵎnot in ↗<u>Boston</u>. What're you talking about? He's right in the
　　next room, watching the tube.　(contradiction contour)

　② 対比の場合

　　↘↗<u>John's</u> not in Boston; it was Henry's turn to go this time.　(fall-rise tone)

　次の例でも、対比であるか反駁であるかの違いが曖昧である。

a.　A: This is urgent! Somebody must take care of it right away.

B: Don't look at me. *I can't do that*. I'm too busy.

$$^{I}\ _{can't}\ _{do\ that}$$

① 反駁の場合

    ↘I ¦ ꞌcan't do ↗that!　(contradiction contour)

② 対比の場合

    ↘↗I can't do that! Please ask someone else.　（対比：fall-rise tone）

以下の例は、課題 13 で反駁のイントネーションとして示したが、対比のイントネーションとも解釈できる。

b.　[*The Wizard of Oz*. Dorothy は道に迷っている]

    Dorothy: Now which way do we go?

    Voice: Pardon me. That way is a very nice way.

    Dorothy: Who said that? [She looks around for the voice. Toto barks at the
           Scarecrow.] Don't be silly, Toto. *Scarecrows don't talk*.

① 反駁の場合

    ↘*Scarecrows* ¦ ꞌ*don't* ↗*talk*.　(contradiction contour)

② 対比の場合

    I know animals can talk, but ↘↗*scarecrows don't talk*.　(fall-rise tone)

以下のストーリー中の *Turtles can't fly*. も、反駁なのか、または、対比なのか、区別がつかないだろう。

c.　Once upon a time, there was a young turtle named Harvey. Harvey told
    the other turtles, "I'm going to fly and go see the world," The other turtles
    laughed and said, "*Turtles can't fly*." Harvey didn't like the turtles laughing,
    so he told them, "I'll show you. I will fly higher than the birds."

課題 39　**Yes, I know her.**

(i) 1つの短い文が下降調と上昇調とに分かれて聞こえるときがよくある。

a.　A: Do you see that woman with short hair?

　　B: Yes, *I know her*. That's Meg.

斜体部を、動詞に核強勢を置いて *I ↘know her*. と言えば、default pattern になる。しかし、実際には、*I ↘know* | ↗*her*. または　↘*I know* | ↗*her*. もよくある。後者の場合、

↘I　　know ↗her.

> 注1：In this dialog, there is stress on **her**, but not strong, contrastive stress, just more than **know**. There is still stress on *I* also, but again not contrastive. So, the pitch starts out fairly high on *I*, then drops for the softly spoken **know**, then has a mild rise on **her**.　(SUPRAS posting)
>
> 注2：これは、突然、何かに気づいたときのパタンである。主語代名詞が高いピッチで始まる。詳細は、p. 127-8 を参照。

既知情報に文アクセントを置くケースは、珍しいことではない。話者が、*her* に関心がある場合、そこに上昇調の文アクセントを置く。この場合、上昇調は minor information——二次的重要度——であることを示している。

・I went to Kyoto the other day. I ↘loved it | ↗there.

・[Looking at an old photo album] Oh, I re↘member | ↗him! This is Joe Bessette. I once had a crush on him.

・A: I've got some chocolate here.

　B: Oh, good. I ↘like | ↗chocolate.　詳細は、伊達（2019）の課題 14 と 48 を参照。

　次に、a の斜体字部と同じパタンになる他の例を示そう。

b.　A: Are you going?

　　B: ↘Yeah, | ↘*I'm* | ↗*going*.

c.　Mother: Will you pick up your little brother? He's at Aunt Peg's house.

　　Daughter: ↘Sure, ↘*I'll* | *pick him* ↗*up*.

これら a, b, c 3つの対話を Wells に紹介し、イントネーションについてコメントを求めると、phonetic blog (2009.6.8) の中で以下の教示があった。

On balance, I think the most likely pattern for these utterances is **fall plus rise**…The problem is that the answers contain no new lexical or grammatical items. So there is no non-'given' item to place the nucleus on…. I have to say, though, that I don't feel very pleased with my explanation so far…. Or perhaps we just say they're yet more intonational idioms.

　　　注：non-'given' は、「既知内容ではない」つまり「新しい」の意味である。

　さて、これからが本論である。上記の対話中の例は、下降調＋上昇調のパターンであると述べてきたが、他の考え方——表記法——も考えられるのではないか。例えば、主語 I は、核強勢を受けるのではなく、むしろ high prehead とか high head であると考えるべきではないか。

　注：高前頭部に関しては、本課題の末尾の「参考」欄を参照、また、詳細は、伊達
　　　（2019）の課題 25 を参照。

　後日、私のコメントに応えて、Wells から次のような懇切丁寧な教示があった。

　Yes, there could be alternatively a high head or a high prehead followed by a rise.

　　　A: Do you know her?
　　　B: ＼Yes, ｜＼I ｜ know /her.　　[fall plus rise]
　　　B: ＼Yes, ｜ ˈI know /her.　　　[high head followed by rise]
　　　B: ＼Yes, ｜ ‾I know /her.　　　[high prehead followed by rise]

　　　A: Are you going?
　　　B: ＼Yeah, ｜＼I'm ｜ /going.　[fall plus rise]
　　　B: ＼Yeah, ｜ ˈI'm /going.　　[high head followed by rise]
　　　B: ＼Yeah, ｜ ‾I'm /going.　　[high prehead followed by rise]

　　　A: Will you pick up your little brother?
　　　B: ＼Sure, ｜＼I'll ｜ pick him /up.　　[fall plus rise]
　　　B: ＼Sure, ｜ ˈI'll pick him /up.　　　[high head followed by rise]
　　　B: ＼Sure, ｜ ‾I'll pick him /up.　　　[high prehead followed by rise]
　ところで、私は伊達（2019）の課題 58 で、

課題 39　Yes, I know her.

↘<u>Here you</u> ↗<u>are</u>.

↘<u>There you</u> ↗<u>are</u>.

↘<u>There you</u> ↗<u>go</u>.（音調の区切りの棒線は付けていない）

と表記している。Wells (2006: 146-7) での表記は、

[|]Here you /<u>are</u>.

[|]Here it /<u>is</u>.

となっている。しかし、Wells (2014: 112) では以下のような異なる表記法が見られる。2つの音調単位に分けている。

\<u>That's</u> ｜ /<u>funny</u>.

\<u>That's</u> ｜ a re/<u>lief</u>.

\<u>That's</u> ｜ a /<u>pity</u>.

It is sometimes difficult to decide whether a falling pitch movement represents an accent in the head (high falling head) or a separate nucleus (fall tone)　Wells (2006: 249)

　これらの例文のイントネーションの表記法について Tench に意見を求めた。彼は、That's funny は fall+rise ではなく、むしろ high onset+rise であると言う。このように、Wells と Tench は表記法について意見を異にする。

John suggests fall+rise for these comments in a given situation; I think it is a high onset+rise within a single intonation unit.　(2007.6.18)

注：onset は音調単位中の最初の文アクセント（head）のこと。

このように音調表記法が異なる理由は、音調分析ソフトで計測して得られた physical evidence（物理的根拠）からは、決定的な結論を引き出せないからであろう。録音された、または、実際に耳にした話しことばの一節のイントネーションの型を分析するのは容易でないことも多い。なぜならば、聴覚印象に基づくイントネーション表記と音声分析ソフトによるピッチの結果がしばしば不一致になるからである。この場合には、有能な人間の耳による分析のほうが信頼できると言われている。音声分析ソフトによる physical evidence がどうであれ、実際の音声を聞くのは、生身の人間の耳である。それが音調分析に重要な役割を果たす。そうであっても分析者の解釈に微妙な誤差が見られるのは避けられない。

　参考までに、冒頭の a と同じ音調曲線をとる他の例を幾つか挙げておこう。日本人学習者には全く馴染がないだろうが、比較的頻度の高い型である。<u>突然、何かに気づいたときに使われる</u>。これらも、3 種類の音調表記が考えられる。

まず、解説を紹介しよう。

① If the person answering the question has difficulty remembering his new address, and it <u>suddenly</u> comes back to him, he may say, brightly,

Bolinger (1989: 88)

② This intonation is used if, after thinking about the matter for some time, we <u>suddenly</u> have an idea, or remember a fact.

I know. 　　　　　＼ ／ 　　　　Schubiger (1935: 71)

③ This is an intonation idiom. When "I know" is used to say that you have <u>suddenly</u> had an idea or <u>suddenly</u> thought of a solution to a problem, it has two nuclear accents, fall plus rise. ＼I ⏐ know. 　　(Personal mail from Wells)

下線は、伊達が追加。

a. 　A: And who do you work for?

　　B: I work for AJ dot com.

　　A: Ah, *I know*. Do you sell computers?

b. 　A: Who was it?

　　B: Kinkaid.

　　A: *I knew him*.

c. 　A: Hi, I'm Sonny Webster. You used to come in my Mom's bakery.

　　B: Sonny Webster?

　　A: Yeah.

　　B: Sonny Webster! *I remember you!*

(ii) また、このような下降調＋上昇調のパタンは、状況から見て明らかなこと、または、とりとめないことに関して質問をされたときにもよく用いられる。

a. 　A: John, are you free on Sunday night?

　　B: Sunday night? ↘<u>Yeah</u>, ⏐ ↘<u>I'm</u> ⏐ ↗<u>free</u>.

　　A: Listen. I've got some tickets for a great concert on Sunday night.
　　　 Do you wanna come with me?

b. 　A: Are you getting off at the next stop?

　　B: ↘<u>Yes</u>, ⏐ ↘<u>I'm</u> ⏐ getting off ↗<u>there</u>.

c.　A: There's a big sale on at the mall now. I'm going to check it out.
　　　Are you coming?

　　B: ↘Yeah, | ↘I'm | ↗coming.

文献からの説明を見てみよう。

> Often answers with this intonation are given to questions that may seem
> pointless or silly. The <u>rising intonation</u> indicates that the answerer has
> decided to treat the question with courtesy and patience and to assume
> that the questioner had a legitimate reason for the asking of it.

English Language Services (1967: 48)　　　下線は伊達が追加

もし下降調で↘Yes, | I'm ↘coming. と言えば、単なる確認の返答である。

d.　Mike: Look at this Christmas card!

　　Shin: What's Santa doing? Is he swimming?

　　Mike: ↘Yes, | *he's ↘swimming.*

　　Shin: In winter?

　　Mike: In Australia, Christmas is in summer.

　　Shin: Oh!

以下は、SUPRAS のメンバーのコメントである。

> The (low) fall on SWIMming is not in the least surprising, especially in this
> context. Mike knows that Christmas is warm down under, so he simply confirms
> the fact, as anyone else could do, knowing what he knows, so, yes, "Of course
> he is." If the fall seems abrupt, perhaps it is (or is at least just matter-of-fact),
> compared to the rise.　　　(SUPRAS posting: 2009.5.30)

e.　A: I got an invitation to your wedding, Mary.

　　B: Are you coming?

　　A: Of course.

　　B: Good.

　　A: Mary, are you happy?

　　B: ↘*Yes,* | *I'm ↘happy.*

しかし、下降調は、<u>時には</u>「当たり前だよ（*Yes, but why ever are you asking
me that?*)」という impatience を伝える。

f.　A: Are you coming?

　　B: *Of ↘course I'm coming.*

129

Listen to these examples, with the same kind of questions and answers, but with falling intonation in the answer. This indicates displeasure and impatience, and under the wrong circumstances would be quite discourteous.　　　　English Language Services, INC. (1967: 48)

参考：今回は、high prehead（高前頭部）という言葉がよく出てきた。高前頭部は談話においてどのような働きをしているのか。この疑問に答えるには、友人から私への質問に対する回答を紹介するのが得策であろう。以下が質問の趣旨である。

　　「小学校外国語活動教材『Let's Try! 1』Unit 1 にあいさつの Hello. が出てきます。デジタル教材には第一音節が高ピッチで第二音節が上昇調も何回か出てきます。Hello を高ピッチ＋低上昇調で発音した場合の意味合いをお教えいただけましたら幸いです。」

　　私からの回答：問題の Hello! の intonation には、2 つの要素が関与している。

　　① 発話に liveliness、animation を加味する働きをする高前頭部（prehead）

　　② reassurances, friendliness を加味する low rise

　　①＋②＝ ‾Hel ↗lo!　（注：横棒 ‾ は、高いピッチを示す。）

　　また、prehead に限らず、頭部（head）を高く言うときも同じ効果がある。

　　　　‾Good ↗morning.　‾Good ↗bye

追加説明：挨拶ことばに限らず、発話の冒頭の prehead を高く言うと、発話全体が強調され "gives a liveliness to the whole word group" となる。

　　　　O'Connor & Arnold (1973: 36)

a.　‾I |get up |early every ↘morning.

b.　Hey, ‾I re|member ↗you. We went to the same high school.

c.　[Do you like rice wine?] ‾I ↘love it.

　　なお、‾Hel ↗lo! における末尾の（低）上昇調は、friendliness、または reassurances を表す。

d.　Hi, Jane. ‾You |look ↗lovely.

e.　There's |no ↗hurry. |Take your ↗time.

Hello. の 3 通りの言い方：

　・Hel ↘lo!　(fall; matter-of-fact, businesslike)

　・Hel ↗lo!　(low rise; friendly, lively)

　・‾Hel ↗lo!　(high prehead + low rise; still more friendly /lively)

課題 40　下降上昇調と「下降調＋上昇調」との聴覚的区別

　イントネーションが果たす様々な機能の1つとして、意味を区別するものがある。音声学の教本には、しばしば以下のような例が挙げられている。

a.　① A: This is John' wife.

　　　B: I ↘*thought* ｜ *he was* ↗*married*.

　② A: This is John's fiancée.

　　　B: *I* ˈ*thought he was* ↘*married*.

　　　　　Oakeshott-Taylor (1984: 1)

Bolinger (1989: 381) は、それぞれについて以下の音調曲線を示している。

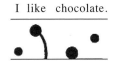

しかし、時には、イントネーションが意味の区別に役立たないこともある。

b.　① A: Here's some chocolate, Susan.

　　　B: Oh, dear. *I* ↘↗*like chocolate*, but I'm on a diet.

　　　　　（実際には I ↘like choco ↗late となる）

　② A: Here's some chocolate, Jane.

　　　B: Oh, good. *I* ↘ *like* ｜ ↗*chocolate*. Thank you.

まず、各 B は、理論的には音調が違う。違いを意識して発音しても、聞き手には同じように聞こえる。その理由は、どちらも最後の音節 -late が上昇するので、聴覚的には両者の区別ができないからである。O'Connor & Arnold (1973: 28-9) の解説を見てみよう。

> This compound Fall-plus-Rise tune may be very similar to some forms of the simple tune containing the Fall-Rise, but… the two tunes are very different in their meanings. So it is necessary to keep them separate. The first example above *I* ˋ*like* ˌ*chocolate* represents a pattern like this:
>
> I like   chocolate.
>
> But so too does the notation *I* ˅*like chocolate*. So there may be no difference of pattern between the two tunes.

このような場合、イントネーションではなく、文脈が意味の区別をする。

c. ① A: I found out that John was married. You said earlier that he was a
         bachelor.

     B: Sorry. *I* ↘↗*thought so*. (I↘thought↗so)

   ② A: I found out that John was a bachelor.

     B: I ↘*thought* | ↗*so*. [And I was right.]

理論的——音韻的——には、I ↘↗thought so. と I ↘thought | ↗ so.は違うが、どちらも、音声的には *I*↘*thought*↗*so* となるので両者の意味の区別ができない。しかし、thought を高上昇、so を低上昇で *I*↗*thought*↗*so*. と言えば、but I was wrong. の意味が明確になる。

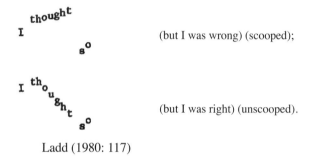

(but I was wrong) (scooped);

(but I was right) (unscooped).

        Ladd (1980: 117)

Rockenbach 教授からコメントをもらった。

> For "but I was wrong" it would be a bit more complex, with a bit of rise during each of ***thought*** and ***so***, segueing into the 'but I guess I was [seem to have been] wrong,' which is almost certainly sure to follow it. I think that the multiple 'rises' on ***thought*** and ***so*** would convey the kind of *tentativeness* which might accompany a kind of *apology*, which would carry the message that 'I'm sorry that the mistaken advice/suggestion/action inconvenienced you, and I hope you'll understand and forgive me'.

他の例を見てみよう。

d. ① A: Why did you keep insisting that John had a wife?

     B: I ↘↗*thought he was married*. (I↘thought he was mar↗ried)

   ② A: This is John's wife.

     B: Yes, *I* ↘*thought* | *he was* ↗*married*.

ここでも、両者の音調曲線は以下のようになり、音声的には、どちらかの区別ができない。

```
I
  thought
          he was married.
```

しかし、thought を高上昇、married を低上昇で、以下のように *I ↗thought he was ↗married* と言えば、But I was wrong. の意味が明確になる。

```
      thought
I           he was married.
```

Bolinger (1989: 382)

しかし、以下の① B と② B では、区別が難しい。

e.　① A: You come from Sheffield, don't you?

B: ˅No, ｜ *my* ˅*mother came from Sheffield*, (but not me.)　（対比）

② A: I'm going to Sheffield tomorrow.

B: Really? ｜ *My* `*mother came from* ˌ*Sheffield*.

①と②に近い発話文をそれぞれ模式図で示すと、

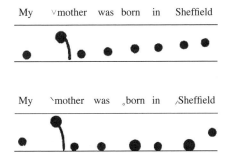

O'Connor & Arnold (1973: 84 & 30)

参考：Wells は、下降上昇調と下降調＋上昇調との区別の難しさについて次のように言う。

It is notoriously difficult to decide between a single fall-rise spread over nucleus plus tail, on the one hand, and a fall followed by a rise on the other (which... necessarily involves an IP boundary between them).

I ˅wish I was rich. (...but I'm not.)

I ＼wish ｜ I was /rich. (That's what I wish.)

注：IP = intonation phrase (i.e. tone unit)

(adapted from Wells (2006: 249))

133

課題 41　She might have told me.

(i) この文は、2 通りの意味が考えられる。それは、① possibility「〜したかもしれない」と② impatience や reproachfulness「〜してもよかったのに」「〜してくれてもよかったのに」の意味である。模式図を紹介しよう。

— ＼ — ＼ ＼　　　　Hirst (1977: 48)

She might have told Mary. (She should have told Mary.)

上図は、② の意味を示している。同様にして、

a.　You ˈmight have kept some for ➘➚me.

　　You ˈcould have asked me ➘➚first.

　　　　Kingdon (1958: 194)

b.　(1) She might have ˇtold me.　('indignation')

　　(2) She ˋmight have ˊtold me.　('doubt')　　Bolinger (1989: 15)

② の意味をもつ《might/could have+ 過去分詞》の構文は「〜しようと思えばできただろうに、（実際は）しなかった」という批判的な含意がある。

下降上昇調は、時には disapproval, displeasure の含意を伝えることがある。

・A: Oh, what a beautiful morning!

　B: *It's* ˈ*bitterly* ➘➚*cold, though*.

・A: How did you enjoy the boat race?

　B: *There were* ˈ*awful* ➘➚*crowds*.

・A: Did you have a nice time with Betty?

　B: *She* ˈ*didn't turn* ➘➚*up*.

・A: I'm going home by train.

　B: ˈ*Not in this* ➘➚*rain*.

本論に戻って、標題の構文をもつ例を挙げよう。

c.　A: Did you mind him coming to tea?

　　B: *You* ˈ*might have* ➘➚*warned me*. The room was untidy.

d.　A: How could he let you know? You were absent from the meeting.

　　B: *He* ˈ*could have* ➘➚*texted me*.　（メールを送れたのに）

e.　A: Did you mind my inviting Eve?

　　B: *You* ˈ*might have asked me* ➘➚*first*. I don't like her.

課題 41　She might have told me.

また、at least を伴うと、「せめて〜できたはずなのに」という意味がより明確になる。

f.　[*Wuthering Heights*]

　　A: Edgar, I think you behaved abominably.

　　B: What do you mean?

　　A: *You ⌐could have at ⌐least been* ↘↗*civil*. You dismissed him as if he had
　　　been a servant.

g.　A: Hey, Cathy! Where were you all weekend?

　　B: *You ⌐could have at ⌐least begun with 'Good* ↘↗*morning'*.

h.　A: But I haven't had time to write to them.

　　B: *You ⌐might at ⌐least have* ↘↗*phoned them*.

なお、課題 11(ii) の対話の最後近くにある文 "Driver, I think you could have
spoken to her in a little more friendly manner."（p.51）の場合も、上記と同
じイントネーションで言われる。

(ii) 次は、《might/could + root verb》の構文の例である。この場合は、非難・
抗議・遺憾の意味がある。（〜してくれてもよさそうなのに）

a.　*You ⌐might ⌐give me a* ↘↗*chance*.
　　You ⌐might ⌐tell me a ↘↗*bout it*.
　　(adapted from Kingdon (1958: 194))

b.　Why are you holding out on us?　（隠し事をする）　Tell us the truth. *You
　　⌐might at ⌐least* ↘↗*trust us*.

c.　A: I'm getting married.

　　B: Are you?

　　A: I'm 24. It's time I settled down. *You ⌐might con* ↘↗*gratulate me*.

　　B: Congratulations! Well, who are you to marry?

d.　[*The Great Gatsby*]

　　Tom's got a woman in New York. *She ⌐might have the ⌐decency not to
　　⌐phone him at* ↘↗*dinner time*.

(iii) 下降調が用いられることもある。ある日、知人のカナダ人牧師に下記の例
文のいくつかを朗読してもらった。

a.　A: I'm sorry, honey. I couldn't get away for three hours.

B: Four hours. *But you could have phoned me.*

A: Yeah, I know, I know. *I could have phoned.*

b. ［デートに出かける時に、相手の男性の身なりがカジュアルすぎる］

A: Hello, Rosemary! You sure look pretty.

B: Seems to me *you might at least have your coat on.*

c. A: Where's Cousin Edgar now?

B: I think he's gone.

A: Oh, yeah? *He at least could have said good bye.*

当初は下降調であった。そこで、私が下降上昇調で発音すると、彼は、それも妥当であると言い、自らそれを確認するかのように、下降上昇調で繰り返した。

　以上が、暗に非難や不満を表す際に用いられる標準的なイントネーションであると思われるが、他の言い方もある。例えば、*Intonative Features* の著者 Hirst は、私の質問に応えて、SUPRAS にコメントを発信した。

　　She might have bought some chocolate.

With a down-stepping head and a **fall・rise** on *chocolate*, this is likely to be interpreted as a possibility (*but then she might not…*). With a sequence of **falls** on *might* and *bought*, the interpretation is more likely to be one of reproach (*she might at least…*) Of course there might be many intonation patterns possible with this sequence with either interpretation.　(2003.6.30)

　念のために、**a down-stepping head and a fall・rise** と同じパタンをもつ他の文を紹介しよう。

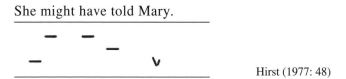

She might have told Mary.

Hirst (1977: 48)

この場合は、possibility「言ったかもしれない」という意味である。頭部（head）中の *might, have, told* は徐々に down-stepping し、Mary で fall・rise という音調になっている。しかし、Hirst も言うように、possibility にしろ、reproach の意味にしろ、他の言い方もあるということである。それは、上記の牧師と私とのやりとりからも明らかである。また、Hirst は reproach には下降調が使われると言っているが、本課の冒頭の図を見ると、reproach の意味では、下降上昇調になっている。

課題 42　**It's not what he said.**

　英語のネーテイブスピーカーは、外国人が犯す単語発音の間違いには寛容で あるが、そのような寛容さはイントネーションの間違いにまで及ばないと言 われる。彼らは、外国人が単語レベルの発音にかける努力と苦労をよく認識 している。しかし、彼らは、イントネーションにも間違いがあることに気づ かない。イントネーションは、話し手の気持ちと深く結びついているだけに、 感情の行き違いや誤解を招くことがある。困ったことに、外国人が間違った イントネーションで何かを言ったとき、ネーテイブスピーカーは、それが言 い間違いであることに気づかず、本人の意図とは全く違った意味に受け取り、 It's not what he said, but the way he said it (that bothered me). と不満を漏ら す。しかし、話し手は、「そんなつもりで言ったのではない」（I don't/didn't mean the way I might have sounded.）。

> What is very noticeable is the tolerance that native speakers show when a learner fumbles over consonants, vowels and word stress. This tolerance derives from the native speaker's awareness of word phonology and possibly from their familiarity with other learners' efforts (or indeed their own) of the problems of pronouncing the words of another language.
>
> 　But such tolerance does not always extend to intonation, for two reasons. Firstly, native speakers are not usually so aware of intonation…secondly, and possibly more alarmingly, a mistaken intonation still **means** something; it might well be that you intended to convey one particular meaning but they interpreted it quite differently.　Tench (1996: 11)

・あるイギリス人のグループが、カフェテリアで、アジアからの移民のウエイ ターの話し方に気を悪くした。

> John Gumperz, while consulting, met a group of English native speakers who felt mistreated because the cafeteria servers were always rude to them. Among various cross-cultural issues, Gumperz found a solid specific complaint: the servers, all immigrants from South Asia, tended to offer side dishes using a falling pitch, perhaps ↘*gravy*　rather than the more typical rising pitch for offers: ↗*gravy*.
>
> For the native English speakers, the falling pitch was clearly rude,

137

conveying a cold "take it or leave it" attitude, but the servers, of course, had no such intention. This trivial difference in behavior caused bad feelings.

注：John Gumperz はアメリカの言語学者　　　　　　　　Ward (2019: 196)

確かに、"but the servers, of course, had no such intention." とあるように、ウエイターは、全く誤解されている。

・インド人が銀行の窓口で "Excuse me. I want to deposit some money." を下降調で言ったことが teller に押しつけがましい（pushy）印象を与えた。

```
        cuse                                    mon e
Ex    m    e.    I want to deposit s  o  m  e
                                              y.
```

イギリス人なら、以下のように言っただろう。

```
I  want to deposit some
                      m  o  n
                            e  y. p  l  e  a  s  e.
```

Bolinger (1989: 62-3)

　下降調は、文末で最も頻繁に使われ、完結、断定が基調である。下降調を使うとき、話し手の伝えたい情報が完結しており、そこには確信があるという趣旨のことが、音声学の教本に書かれているが、これを短絡的に捉えると、とんでもない社交的ミスをおかしかねない。

　Wells は、ジョッギングを日課としていた。以下のようなエピソードを紹介している。以下は、彼の phonetic blog (2006.7.17) からである。

As I was jogging in a local park, a man coming from the other way asked me,

　　You ⎮*haven't got the* ↗ *time on you, have you, mate?*

Since I was indeed wearing a watch, I duly answered him,

　　E⎮*leven fifty-* ↘ *seven.*

The wording and intonation of his question was appropriate for the situation of an English person addressing a stranger. But an EFL student would probably have cast the question differently:

　　⎮*What's the* ↘ *time?*

— which in this context would have sounded rude.

Why is this? We use the simple wording and the fall when we wish to be

課題 42　It's not what he said.

businesslike with someone we are already talking to…But when starting
a conversation, particularly with a stranger, we prefer to be indirect.

これは極めて重要な指摘である。日本の英語教育では、疑問詞疑問文と命令
文が下降調で発音されると、短絡的に教えられていることが多いからである。
見知らぬ人に向かって、What time is it? や What time do you have? を下降調
で言うと、rude であると誤解されるかもしれない。

```
How
   do I
       get
          to the Em
                    pire
                        State Build
                                   ing        (polite)
```

```
How do I get to the Empire State
                                 Build
                                      in
                                        g    (abrupt)
```

　　　　Ladd (1980: 123-4)

参考：イントネーションの怖いところは、話者が意識しようと否かにかかわらず、聞
　　　き手に特定の心的態度を伝えてしまうことである。英語がたどたどしい場合、
　　　wrong intonation であっても相手は大目に見てくれるけれども、流暢になって
　　　くると、事情は違ってくる。自分では気づかずに wrong intonation で何かを言っ
　　　た場合、相手はその intonational meaning に反応し、心証を悪くすることもある。
　　　告白すると、昔、ある学会の懇親会の宴席で、イギリス人女性が、私をジョー
　　　クで少しからかった。一同大笑いした。私は、ジョークに機嫌よく対応した。
　　　いや、そう思っていた。ところが、驚いたことに、翌朝、プログラムが始まる
　　　前に、彼女は緊張した表情で私のところへ来て昨晩のことを謝った。私は当惑
　　　した。どうやら、ジョークに対する私の言いかたがまずかったので、気分を害
　　　したという印象を与えたようだった。私はそれを否定し、真意を伝え謝罪した。
　　　思わぬところで彼女に辛い思いをさせてしまった。もう 20 年も昔の逸話であ
　　　る。勿論、こんな出来事は些細な social faux pas（社交上のミス）であったの
　　　で、それで友情が破綻したのではない。しかし、イントネーションを研究して
　　　いる者としては、誠に忸怩たる思いだった。

課題 43　Exclamations / interjections

(i) 話し言葉は、必ずピッチの高低変化を伴う。それは、個人によって異なる相対的な高低である。一般に、強勢がある音節は、それがない音節よりも高いピッチで言われ、卓立している。アメリカ英語では、通例、4 段階のピッチを認めている。話し始める時の高さは /2/ であり、それより低い /1/ は、下降調で話し終える際のピッチである。/3/ は、発話中の情報の中心点－情報の焦点－に、また、上昇調の末尾に現れる高さである。

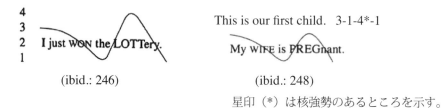

Celce-Murcia, Brinton & Goodwin (2010: 233)

(ii) 更に、/4/ のピッチレベルもあり、これは驚きや感動を伝える exclamation に現れる。例えば、以下は、宝くじが当たった時の興奮状態を伝えるイントネーションである。

I just WON the LOTTery.　　(ibid.: 246)

This is our first child.　3-1-4*-1
My WIFE is PREGnant.　　(ibid.: 248)

星印（*）は核強勢のあるところを示す。

Exclamation は、日本語では感嘆文とか感嘆詞と訳されているが、exclaim されるものをすべて含み、特定の文法形式に限られているのではない。その意味では、interjection も exclamation に含まれる。

a.　[At the breakfast table]

　　A: Oh, Tony, *2look at the 4*1*time*!

　　　You said you had a first-period class.

　　B: So I do. I've got to go.

b.　A: Marcus has left his job.

　　B: *4*1*Really?*　(surprise)

参考：$_{2}$-^{3}<u>Really?</u>　(doubt: I'm not sure I believe you.)

c.　A: I'm actually a black belt.

　　B: *Is ^{4}$_{-1}$<u>that</u> so!*　How amazing!

d.　A: The boss wants the report by tomorrow.

　　B: *You're ^{4}$_{-1}$<u>joking!</u>*

e.　A: Jack's just bought a new car. It's pink.

　　B: *^{4}$_{-1}$<u>Pink!</u>*

f.　A: Welcome back, Joe. How did you find the heat in Malaysia?

　　B: *$^{|}$Utterly ex ^{4}$_{-1}$<u>hausting!</u>*

g.　A: What a beautiful day!

　　B: *^{4}$_{-1}$<u>Isn't it!</u>* Just like May!

また、/4-1/ は、時には、皮肉や非難を表すこともある。

h.　［だらしない夫に、いちいち注意しなければならないことについて妻が］

　　A: It makes me feel like an old hag or something.　（意地悪な老婆）

　　B:　Sometimes you are an old hag or something.

　　A: Oh, *^{4}$_{-1}$<u>great!</u>*

i.　［夫が帰宅すると、家じゅうが散らかっている］

　　Oh, my God, Betty! What the hell's going on here?　Todd, Doug!

　　I don't believe this! What's going on here? Oh, *^{4}$_{-1}$<u>great!</u>*

j.　A: You left your little child all alone at home, didn't you?

　　B: Yes, but…

　　A: *$^{|}$Some parent ^{4}$_{-1}$<u>you</u> are!*

k.　A: Roses! Are you planting roses?

　　B: Yeah.

　　A: *$^{|}$Fine farmer ^{4}$_{-1}$<u>you</u> are!* Not a turnip or a cabbage or a potato.

l.　A:　The trouble with you is you're lazy.

　　B: *^{4}$_{-1}$<u>You're</u> a fine one to talk.*

　　　　参考：^{4}You're a $_{2}$fine one to ^{3}talk. もあり得る。この場合、末尾が上昇するので
　　　　　　　　softening effect がある。一方、^{4}$_{-1}$ 下降調は more cutting（辛辣）に聞
　　　　　　　　こえる。

m.　A: I think you should quit smoking.

　　B: *^{4}$_{-1}$<u>You</u> can talk.* You used to be a heavy smoker when you were young

141

yourself.

参考：[4]You [2]can [3]talk. もあり得る。こちらのほうが less cutting である。

n.　A: Oh, there he is. At last.

　　B: *About [4]-[1]time!*　(sarcasm or irritation)

(iii) 一方、ピッチ /2-1/ も、皮肉や失望、無関心などを伝える。

a.　A: The flight's been cancelled.

　　B: [2]-[1]*Great*.

b.　A: The car broke down again.

　　B: [2]-[1]*Super*.

c.　A: What do you think of our new boss?

　　B: [2]-[1]*Charming*.　課題 11 の「参考」を参照。

参考：oaths and epithets

　　本来、oath は、誓い、誓約、（法廷における）宣誓の意味であるが、時には、の
　　のしり、悪口、人を非難する意味もある。また、epithet は、あだ名、通り名、
　　軽蔑の言葉、悪口の意味である。相手を非難する表現は、低上昇調が多い。

　　a.　[無謀な運転するドライバー腹を立て] |*Those drunken ↗drivers !*

　　b.　[市役所に行って、申請を断られ] |*Those stupid ↗people at City Hall !*

　　c.　He |wouldn't |lend me his ↘car. |*Stupid ↗bastard!*

　　しかし、下降調の言い方も存在する。

　　d.　[ドライブ中に、猫が突然飛び出してきた] |*Stupid ↘cat!*

　　e.　[女性が男性の愚行に愛想尽かして] |*Oh, ↘men!*

　　なお、冒とく的または卑猥な語や表現は、expletives とか swearing と呼ばれる。
　　驚き、怒り、苛立ちなどの強い感情を表すときに用いられ、exclamation が変化
　　したものである。

```
God                  God                 You                   You
    damn  it     or      damn it--            bastard    or        bastard--
```

　　Ladd (1980: 181)

課題 44　イントネーションの談話的意味

　今日、イントネーションの話題になると、必ず Brazil の理論（1994）が紹介される。彼は、イントネーションを proclaiming tone（宣言音調）、referring tone（言及音調）、neutral tone（中立音調）という 3 種類に分類している。宣言音調は、新情報を伝えるときに使われ、下降調とその強調形である上昇下降調で発せられ、一方、言及音調は、既知情報・旧情報に言及するときに使われ、下降上昇調とその強調形である上昇調で発せられる。中立音調は、宣言と言及の区別をしないときの音調で、平坦調または低上昇調で言われる。

　Brazil 論に基づいた例を挙げよう。

a.　A: When are you going to New York?

　　B: *I'm* ↘↗*flying* ｜ *at* ˈ*ten o'* ↘*clock.*

　　注：*flying* は既知（旧）情報であるので referring tone（下降上昇調）、一方、*at ten o'clock* は新情報であるので proclaiming tone（下降調）で言われる。

b.　A: What do you think of Picasso?

　　B: *I don't* ↘*care* ｜ *for* ˈ*modern* ↘↗*paintings.*

　　注：I ˈdon't care は新情報であるから proclaiming tone（下降調）、一方、modern painting は既知（旧）情報であるから referring tone で言われる。

また、yes-no question の場合、

c.　If you say:

　　// ↘ are YOU the new SECretary//

　　You are saying something like 'I don't know you. Please tell me who you are'; but

　　// ↘↗ are YOU the new SECretary//

　　means something like 'Am I right in thinking you are the new secretary (the person I've heard so much about)?'

　　　　　　Brazil (1994: 44)

読者には見慣れない表記であるので、本書の表記法に倣って書き換えると、

　　　　・*Are* ˈ*you the new* ↘*secretary?*

　　　　・*Are* ˈ*you the new* ↘↗*secretary?*

d.　① DOCTOR: // ↗ now we've HAD you on the TABlets// ↘ for a WEEK now// ↘ ARE you feeling BEtter at all//

② AN OLD FRIEND: // ↘LOVEly to SEE you// ↘↗ are you feeling BEtter now//

　　　・ ˈAre you ˈfeeling ↘better at all?

　　　・ Are you feeling ↘↗better now?

e. 　// ↘IS there a BUffet on the train//

　　// ↘↗IS there a BUffet on the train//

　　　・ ˈIs there a ↘buffet on the train?

　　　・ ˈIs there a ↘↗buffet on the train?

　　　注：アメリカ英語では、buffet の強勢は第 2 音節に置かれる。

Brazil (p.43) は、yes-no questions を 2 種類のイントネーションに分け、下降調は、全く予備知識のない純然たる質問であり、下降上昇調は、あらかじめ予備知識があり確認のための質問であると言う。

しかし、Wells (2006: 45-6) によれば、

　　・ The default tone for a yes-no question is a **rise**.

　　・ It is also possible for a yes-no question to be said with a **fall**. This makes the question more insistent. It is more businesslike, more serious, perhaps more threatening… The insistent yes-no fall is also regularly used when a speaker repeats a question because the other person didn't hear it properly.

既知情報が非下降調で言われるというならば、新情報は非下降調で言うことができないということになる。これは、上記の Wells の解説と齟齬をきたす。宣言音調は新情報を伝え、言及音調は既知情報を伝えるという論は、いちおう納得できるが、それを yes-no question にまで適用するのは無理がある。少なくとも英語教育においては、下降調の Is there a ↘buffet on the train? は、上昇調と共に、yes-no question の一般的な音調であり、また、相手がこの質問を十分に理解しなかった場合の repeat question である。課題 9 を参照。

　そもそも音調と特定の文構造との間には密接な関係はないということは常識になっている。特定の構文は特定の音調をとる傾向があることは認められているが、Brazil 論で説明できない事例も多くある。

課題 45　You'll see. と You'll be sorry.

(i) You'll see.

この表現の意味は、「今に分かるよ」であるが、そのイントネーションは、以下のようになる。

Yóu'll

　　　ßée!　　　　　Bolinger (1986: 185)

a.　A: Do you think he will change his mind?

　　B: I don't know. ↘ *You'll* ｜ ↗ *see*.

b.　A: Monica, why have you brought me here of all places?!

　　B: ↘ *You'll* ｜ ↗ *see*.

c.　Kindness begets kindness, Cinderella. ↘ *You'll* ｜ ↗ *see*.

d.　A: He's running rather slowly. I think he's tired.

　　B: Oh, no. He's in great shape. He'll do well. ↘ *You'll* ｜ ↗ *see*.

　　参考： ˈYou'll ↗ *see*. (high head followed by a rise) という表記も可能である。

　　　　　課題 39 を参照。

時には、捨て台詞「見ていろよ！」の意味で用いられることがある。映画 *The Phantom of the Opera* では、バイオリン演奏技術が落ちたためにオペラ楽団から解雇された Eric が、起死回生を図るために書き上げた協奏曲がある。それを出版社に売って資金を得ることを考えている。それに懐疑的な劇団関係者に向かって捨て台詞を吐きながら退出する。

e.　I have written a concerto. I have faith in it. They are certain to publish it and they will give me a substantial advance. [On leaving]

　　↘ *You'll* ｜ ↗ *see*!

(ii) You'll be sorry.

　この表現は、相手が間違ったことを言ったり、していると思ったとき、忠告する意味を込めて使うが、時には「後悔しても知らないぞ」「覚えていろよ」となり、言い方によってはかなり喧嘩ごしに聞こえることもある。

Yóu'll

　　　　sór

　　be

　　　　　rʸ•　　　(ibid.: 325)

a. A: I'm gonna make his life miserable!

   B: Don't do that. ↘*You'll* | *be* ↘↗*sorry*.

   A: I don't care.

b. Let me go, or ↘*you'll* | *be* ↘↗*sorry*.

(iii) I see ［下降調＋上昇調］

　I understand, I follow. の意味である。但し、ピッチは下降する直前に上昇するので、実際には、rise+fall+rise となる。

　　　　Ｉ

　　　　　se^e•　　　　　Bolinger (1989: 27)

a. A: He lives here but works in London during the week.

   B: Oh, ↘*I* | ↗*see*.

b. A: Excuse me, but how can I get to the downtown New York?

   B: You can take either a bus or a taxi.

   A: ↘*I* | ↗*see*.

c. A: It's you, isn't it?

   B: What is?

   A: In the novel. Isn't it meant to be you?

   B: Oh, ↘*I* | ↗*see*. Yeah, it's me all right.

   参考：|I ↗*see*.（high head followed by a rise）という表記も可能である。

   　　　課題 39: p. 126 と Wells (2006: 254) を参照。

(iv) I see.［下降調］

通常は matter-of-fact, businesslike の心的態度を表す。

a. A: I'd like to meet Mr. Brown, if I may.

   B: I'm sorry. He is in conference now.

   A: *Oh, I* ↘ *see*.

   しかし、see が少し延ばし加減になると、disappointment, acquiescence（しぶしぶの了承）を表す。

　　　　　　se

　　　I

　　　　　　e•　　　　（ibid.: 27）

b. A: May I pay by credit card?

146

B: Sorry, we don't accept credit cards.

A: *Oh, I ↘ see*.

I see. の様々な音調曲線と意味について、Schubiger (1935: 71) は、以下のような音調曲線を示している。

・I understand, I follow.

　　　注：図は 3 つのパタンを示している。

・I understand. This intonation is used if we understand only after a certain time, if it suddenly dawns upon us.

・I understand, with an added note of reassurance.

・Disappointment or incredulity. This intonation is often combined with lengthening of the "s" and of the "ee."
Note: "Oh" and "I see" are often combined.

　以上のように、イントネーションは、話者の意思と談話の状況と密接に関連しているので、同じ文を言うのに、複数の「正しい」パタンがある。

課題 46　話題を変えるときの **by the way** など

日本人は、by the way を上昇調で言うことが多いようだが、ネーテイブスピーカーは、下降調を用いる。

> …[T]he phrase *by the way*, used in spoken English to introduce a side issue not connected with the main subject you were talking about before, seems (at least for me) always to have some kind of fall (high fall, low fall, rise-fall), never a rise or fall-rise.　　Wells (2014: 105)

a.　A: Some more coffee, dear?

　　B: Yes, please. Are you planning a busy day?

　　A: Yes, I have to do some shopping today. Is there anything you want?

　　B: I don't think so. Oh, ⌐*by the* ↘*way*, I'll be a little late for dinner.

同様にして、新しい話題に入ったり、話題を変える場合は、incidentally, anyway, right, besides なども下降調で言われる。

b.　*Inci* ↘*dentally*, have you seen Cathy recently?

c.　A: I haven't seen Joe for a while. Is anything the matter?

　　B: I don't know, but he seems to be down in the spirits lately.

　　　↘*Anyway*, that's what they told me.

d.　A: ↘*Anyway*, how're things with you?

　　B: I couldn't complain. So far so good.

e.　A: I really like this town square.

　　B: Lovely, isn't it? ↘*Right*, so what would you like to see next?

　　A: Maybe we could go into the safari park?

　　B: It's really expensive to get in. *Be* ↘*sides*, it's only open on weekends.

一方、既に述べられた内容と繋がりのあることを加える場合には、上昇調または下降上昇調が用いられる。下降上昇調のほうが more emphatic である。

f.　A: Mr. Jenkins should be back in a few minutes.

　　B: *In* ↗*that case*, I'll wait for him.

g.　A: Perhaps we could meet and have lunch?

　　B: ↗*Otherwise*, we could just have a coffee.

h.　A: We could go to Paris by train rather than taking the car.

　　B: ↗*Better still*, we could travel first class.

i.　A: Did your Dad see you drinking in the room?

　　B: ↗*Worse still*, he caught me smoking.

蛇足になるが、新しい話題を言い出すとき、listen とか look が用いられることがある。相手の注意を引くための間投詞のようなものである。

j.　↘Listen, I want you to come with me.

k.　↘Listen, there's something I want to tell you.

l.　↘*Look*, why don't you come over to my house?

m. A: There's a meeting this afternoon.

　　B: ↘*Look*, I won't be able to get there, so can you tell me what happens?

(ii) また、now も話題を変えるときに用いられることがある。その際、会話の流れを主導したり、問い詰めたり、苛立ちの気持ちを伝える。この場合の now は下降調で言われる。

　　Now is a discourse marker basically for change of topic…The effect of *now* [is] in opening up a new topic... Its effect [is] in "taking command," even hectoring the hearer.

　　　Now what do you mean by that!

　　　Now I'm not going to take that any more.　（もう我慢ならないぞ）

　　(adapted from Bolinger (1989: 291-2))

a.　A: Johnnie's pulling my hair!

　　B: ↘*Now stop it*, you two!

b.　A: I've got another question.

　　B: ↘*Now what?*

c.　A: I'm sorry to trouble you.

　　B: ↘*Now what's the matter?*

d.　［不注意でヘマをした人に向かって］↘*Now you've done it!*

e.　A: Watch me juggle with these plates.

　　B: Careful!［A が皿を落とす］↘*Now look what you've done!*

以下は、Wells (2006: 115) の解説である。

　　If someone has been doing a number of foolish things, you might greet the latest foolishness with:

　　　＼Now what's she done?

149

課題 47　疑問詞疑問文（1）

　初対面の挨拶のことば How do you do? は、末尾の動詞 *do* に核強勢が置かれるのが定石である。しかし、それ以外のパタンもある。

a.　A: Endora, I'd like you to meet Mr. Gregson.

　　B: How do you DO?

　　C: *How do YOU do?*

b.　A: Sara, this is Mr. Geoffrey Hamilton. This is Miss Crewe, our new pupil.

　　B: How do you DO?

　　C: *How do YOU do?* I believe I am to teach you to ride.

c.　"Good day," said the Scarecrow in a rather husky voice. "Did you speak?" asked the girl in wonder. "Certainly," answered the Scarecrow. "How do you DO? "I'm pretty well, thank you," replied Dorothy politely. "*How do YOU do?*"

これらの例において you に核強勢が置かれているのは対比のためである。では、以下ではなぜ助動詞 do が核強勢を受けているのだろうか。

d.　A: Benjamin, this is Mr. Weatherby-Price. Mr. Weatherby-Price, this is Lord Gostwycke Cunningham.

　　B: *How DO you do?*

e.　A: George, dear.

　　B: Yes?

　　A: Let me introduce you to our new neighbor.

　　B: (To the neighbor) *How DO you do?*

f.　Mrs. Higgins: Eliza, this is Lord and Lady Boxington.

　　Eliza: How do you DO?

　　Mrs. Higgins: And this is Freddy Eynford-Hill.

　　Eliza: How do you DO?

　　Freddy: [Instantly infatuated] *How DO you do?*

　実は、疑問詞疑問文で対比の意図もなく助動詞や be 動詞が核強勢を受ける場合、文全体が強調されている。*How DO you do?* は、emphasis の 1 例である。

　　In question-word questions, extra emphasis (showing interest or urgency) is often produced by putting the nucleus on the verb *be* or an auxiliary verb, e.g.

(We can't let that happen.) What SHOULD be done?

(That's a very expensive ring.) How much IS it?

(I expect the family to come tonight.) How IS your wife?

[Thinking you recognize someone] Who IS that man over there?

(adapted from Cruttenden (2014: 288))

他の例を挙げよう。

g. *What DID you say to Miss Gage?* She's furious.

h. Oh, *what HAVE you done?* I'm spoilt! I can't go! My hair! Oh, my hair!

i. A: Hello.

B: Philip! *Where HAVE you been?* I've been worried.

j. ［*Gone with the Wind*. 2 人の決別の場面］

Rhett: I'm going, my dear, to join the army.

Scarlett: Rhett! *How COULD you do this to me?* Why should you go now?

k. ［夫（B）の横で妻（A）が友人の女性と Yak, yak, yak（ぺちゃくちゃ）話している］

A: Bye now, Jane. Been lovely seeing you.

B: [A little later] *Why DO you both talk at the same time?*

A: How else can we get in everything we have to say?

l. [In a bar]

A: Say, *what IS that girl's name?*

B: Joan. What is it to you?

A: I'd like to know her.

m. ［身持ちの悪い男が帰宅すると、愛犬以外は、家族の誰も迎えに出てこない］

Hello. I'm home! *Where IS everybody? Where IS anybody?* Hi, ya, Bennie. Come here, sweetheart. *Where IS everybody, huh?* I guess you're the only one who cares about me in this family.

n. ［*The Glass Menagerie*. 娘が social life もなく、家で一人ガラス細工などをいじっている。それを見て母が嘆いている］

All she does is fool with those pieces of glass and play those worn-out records. *What kind of life IS that for a girl to lead?* (personal concern)

o. ［*Rebel Without a Cause*. 父親は、なぜ息子が反抗するのか理解できない］

I try to get to him. What happens? I buy everything he wants. A bicycle? He gets it. We give him love and affection, don't we? *Then what IS it?*

(reproach, petulance)　　　　　注：父親は、憤慨して is を目立って高く言っている。

p. ［女子高生 Elizabeth は、人が羨むような生活環境にありながら、ふさぎ込んでいる。母親 (A) が夫 (B) に向かって］

A: Don't talk to Elizabeth for a while, John… She's a little depressed.

B: Again? She has a good home, a nice room, good family, nice friends. She goes to a good school, she sings in the choir, she swims at the YMCA. *What IS it with this kid?!!* (reproach, petulance)

> There are some formal connecting words, such as **be**, which have little or no meaning in themselves, and are therefore incapable of independent emphasis. Hence a strong－ that is, in this case, an extra － strong－ stress on such words is felt to be equivalent to <u>emphasizing the whole sentence</u>:　　　　　下線は伊達が追加
>
>   What áre you doing?
>
>   What dóes he know about it?
>
>   You are late. － I ám rather late.
>
>   He will be angry. － Lét him be angry.
>
> 　　　　Bolinger (1986: 128-9, quoting a passage from Sweet, H. *A New English Grammar, Logical and Historical, Part II － Syntax*)

152

課題 48　疑問詞疑問文（2）

(i) 文頭の疑問詞は、文アクセントを受けることがあっても核強勢を受けないという特徴がある。例えば、

a. A: I went shopping.

B: ˈ*Where did you* ↘ *go*?

(↘ Where did you go? は possible, but rare)

b. A: I hate him.

B: ˈ*Why do you* ↘ *hate him*?

(↘ Why do you hate him? は possible, but rare)

これら 2 例は、default pattern であり、話者の心的態度は matter-of-fact である。しかし、文頭ではなく文中の位置（sentence-medial position）では、

c. A: I don't see John around anywhere — Where did he go?

B1: *I don't* ↘ *know where he went*. (logical and calm response)

B2: *I don't* ˈ*know* ↘ *where he went*! ('where' is the point of interest)

(adapted from Bolinger (1989: 236-7))

(ii) さて、ここでは non-default pattern を考察することにする。Why doesn't somebody do something? という idiomatic phrase がある。この疑問文には 2 つの意味がある。

① used to make a suggestion:

例えば、*Why don't you sit down and relax for a while?*

② used to say that someone should do something. (literal question)

例えば、*Why don't you mind your own business?*

では、このような用法の違う文は、同じイントネーションで言われるのか、または、違ったイントネーションで言われるのかという疑問が思い浮かぶ。それを検証してみよう。

a. You know, Henry, the climate here is really bad for you. I've got a suggestion. ˈWhy don't you ˈmove to Cali↘fornia?

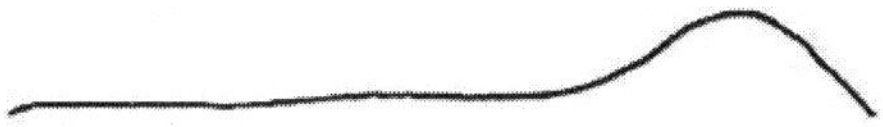

Why don't you move to California?

Henry, I'm curious. ↘Why don't you move to Cali ↗fornia?

Why don't you move to California?

Is it because you don't want to leave all your friends in Boston?

Couper-Kuhlen (1986: 166)

前者は、上記の①──提案（suggestion）──である。一方、後者は、② ──文字通りの疑問文（literal question）──である。

では、次のペアーでも同じことが言えるだろうか。

b. ・A: I certainly hate making all this racket.

　　B: ˈWhy don't you be ↘quiet?

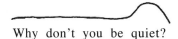

Why don't you be quiet?

　・[To a child who has been talking too much]

　　↘Why don't you be quiet?

Why don't you be quiet?　(ibid.: 165)

　前者はむしろ literal question であり、後者は suggestion──ただし angry suggestion──である。もう 1 例を示そう。

c. ↘Why don't you butt ↗out?

Why don't you butt out?　(ibid.: 166)

これも、b の 2 つめの文と同様に、literal question ではなく、angry suggestion である。換言すれば、command を表す修辞疑問文である。その意味は、冒頭で紹介した Why don't you mind your own business? と同じである。

　結論として、fronted WH-word に核強勢が来る疑問文は、文字通りの疑問文になることもあり、また、修辞疑問文になることもある。どちらであるかは文脈による。以下は、後者のケースである。

d. ↘Why don't you keep your ↗mouth shut?

e. Oh, ↘why don't you come on time for ↗once?

f. 　↘ Whydon't you watch where you're ↗ going?

　　（どこ見て歩いているんだよ！）

g. 　↘ Why don't you keep your nose out of ↗ my business?

h. 　Oh, ↘ why don't you ↗ listen, Charles?

(iii) 他の疑問文でも、fronted WH-word に核強勢が置かれることがある。それは、emotional emphasis を表す文である。

a. 　A: Hullo, dear! I have done all your shopping for you.

　　B: Done my shopping? But ↘ *how did you know what I* ↗ *wanted?*

b. 　［占い師 (B) と客 (A) とのやりとり］

　　A: What kind of man do you think my husband will be? Can you really tell me?

　　B: Of course, I can. I always tell the truth.

　　A: Wonderful! ↘ *What* will he be ↗ *like?*

　　B: Well, probably he'll be a middle-aged man about…

以下は、下降調なので、more demanding である。

c. 　［妻が家出しようとしていると、夫が］

　　Hey, hey, hey! Enough, enough, all right? What are you doing?

　　↘ *Where are you going?* Come on, just tell me what I did that's so terrible.

d. 　［迷い子の息子が見つかって］

　　Well, ↘ *where have you been?* I've been worried to death.

e. 　［*Lucy Show* で、事務員の Lucy が机上のラジオを音量を大きくして執務していると、上司の Mr. Mooney が猛然とやってきて、叱る］

　　Mrs. Carmichael, turn off the radio! ↘ *What's that thing doing here?*

SUPRAS とのメール交換から得たコメントの一部を紹介しよう。

・↘ *How did you know what I* ↗ *wanted?* について

　The stress on **'how'** shows how <u>really surprised/impressed</u> she is about his doing such a difficult thing as going and buying the right things, something only she should know how to do well, and/or be willing to do.

・↘ *What will he be* ↗ *like?* について

　The stress on **'what'** expresses her <u>great curiosity</u> about the matter — one can imagine her cocking her head, looking up with a wistful smile and stars in her eyes.

・ ↘ *Where are you going?* について

This is said to someone who appears to be going somewhere he shouldn't.

　伊達（2019）には、「疑問詞は、内容語の範疇にあり文強勢を受ける資格があるが、通例、文（音調単位）の<u>冒頭</u>では核強勢を受けないという特異な特徴がある」とある（課題 1）。ところが、本課題では、全く逆のことを提示している。この矛盾の説明が必要である。実は、対比以外の目的で、疑問詞に核強勢が来るのは、異例なことである。実際、O'Connor & Arnold（1973: 87）は、"This tune is perhaps better avoided by the foreign learner." と警告している。とは言え、私は、このような異例なケースを映画や sit-com で何度も聞いてきた。

The use of the High Dive with questions of any kind is unusual. When it occurs, the High Fall is normally placed on the *wh*-word… and the effect is of considerable emotion. This emotion may take the form of *plaintiveness*, *despair* or the like.

　　Example: Oh, no! ↘ <u>What</u> have you done ↗ <u>now</u>?

Or it may be a matter of gushing warmth.

　　Example: ↘ <u>What's</u> the ↗ <u>matter</u>, darling?

　(adapted from O'Connor & Arnold (1973: 87))

注：High Dive とは High Fall + Low Rise のことである。

課題 49 **Reassurances** と **appeals**

(i) まず、標題の最初の語の定義を示そう。Reassurances are all those words and expressions that make the other person more comfortable, less worried.

Someone is worried about how long a job will take, and the speaker says,

Don't   It won't take a

     wor^{ry}·   minute·   Bolinger (1989: 76)

a. A: Hey, look at the time! We must hurry, or we'll miss the train.

   B: *I* ⎡*won't be* ↗ *long*.

   これは、reassuring な応え方であり、"Don't worry. We'll catch the train." という心的態度が込められている。イントネーションは、通例、低上昇調である。一方、default pattern の下降調は、matter-of-fact（事務的な、淡々とした）響きがあり、場合によっては abrupt（ぶっきら棒）の印象を与えるだろう。

b. A: Well, it's been nice meeting you.

   B: ⎡*Good* ↗ *bye!*

      参考：⎡Good ↘ bye! （注：dismisses someone）

c. A: I couldn't get any real orange juice — only canned stuff.

   B: Well, ⎡*that's* ⎡*better than* ↗ *nothing*.

      参考：Well, ⎡that's ⎡better than ↘↗ nothing. (more emphatic)

d. A: Tell me what's on your mind. *I'm* ⎡*all* ↗ *ears*.

   B: I'm afraid somebody's listening.

   A: ⎡*No one's* ↗ *listening*.

      参考：⎡No one's ↘↗ listening. (more emphatic)

e. A: Do hurry up, or we'll miss the flight.

   B: Well, *it's* ⎡*only six o'* ↗ *clock*.

f. A: I feel very bad about it.

   B: *But it* ⎡*wasn't* ↗ *your fault*.

g. A: Will he be all right?

   B: *There's* ⎡*nothing to* ↗ *worry about*.

h. A: I'm so sorry.

　　B: *It ˈdoesn't ↗matter*.

i. ［歯医者が子どもに向かって］

　　It ˈwon't ↗hurt.

j. A: Sorry to keep you waiting, Sarah.

　　B: *ˈThat's all ↗right*.

(ii) 嘆願したり（appeal）、または、反対するのに最もよく用いられる音調は、softening effect のある上昇調である。但し、下降上昇調もありうる。

　　An appeal is an attempt by a speaker to get the hearer to consider further the information provided and/or the reality or belief expressed.

　　　　　Tench (1990: 354)

a. A: He's late again. I shall have to sack him.

　　B: *You ˈcan't do ↗that!* He is too useful to our project.

b. A: Don't bother me any longer.

　　B: *I ˈonly ˈwanted to ↗help you*.

c. A: You disturbed me a lot the other day.

　　B: *I ˈcouldn't ↗help it. I ˈdidn't ˈdo it on ↗purpose*.

d. A: I've had enough of him! I'm gonna give him a piece of my mind.

　　B: *ˈDon't do ↗that*.

e. A: He's an idiot!

　　B: *You ˈshouldn't talk like ↗that*.

f. A: He's all talk and no action!

　　B: *I ˈwouldn't say ↗that*.

```
                                  thát|
          thá t|
Don't do              I wouldn't say        Bolinger (1986: 219)
```

Even quite fierce contradictions are normally expressed by native English-speakers with final rises, as in ↘*Oh, I'm* ↗*not*. Final fully-falling tones in such situations would tend to sound altogether too crushing. They might possibly even sound so angry as to provoke the complete termination to a friendship!　　　(Lewis' blog 365: 2011.10.26)

158

課題 50　**Emotional emphasis**

(i) 英語音声学の教本には、機能語が対比の文アクセントを受けるケースの解説がある。対比には明示的な（explicit）なものと暗示的な（implicit）のものがある。対比は、大抵、前者のケースであるが、後者の場合、文アクセントが置かれている機能語が、何と対比されているかが不明なことがよくある。このような場合には、対比という名称ではなく情緒的強調（emotional stress/ emphasis）と呼ぶほうが妥当であると思われる。文アクセントを受けている機能語そのものに重要な意義があるのではなく、むしろ、文全体が強調されていると考えるとよい。伊達（2019）でも多くの用例を示してきたが、これから述べる様々な構文でも、代名詞が文アクセント（しばしば核強勢）を受ける。

　一般に、文アクセントの配置がイントネーションの default pattern から逸脱すればするほど、それだけ感情移入が高まり、不満、苛立ち、驚き、喜びなどの感情を表す。

> There seems to be in highly emotional language very little limit to the shifting of stress. Also, in gushing speech the intonation turn can fall on almost any word of the sentence. The more unusual an intonation, the greater its emotional value, e.g.: "You ˈare a devil" is more emphatic --- and in this particular instance, more usual --- than "You are a ˈdevil" (with unemphatic intonation). "ˈYou are a devil," which is intoned

> is more unusual and therefore most expressive.　　Schubiger (1935: 44)

注 1：gushing は、「感情吐露を伴った（emotional）」の意味で、intonation turn 核
　　　音調のことである。
注 2：模式図は、本書の表記法では ↘↗You are a devil!　（↘You are a ↗devil）。
　　　参考として、*My Fair Lady* で、Eliza は Higgins の非情さに対して抗議する。
　　　"Ooh, you are a devil. You can twist the heart in a girl the same way some
　　　fellows twist her arms to hurt her!"

(ii) 叙述文（statements）の場合

a. A: ↘↗ *You're looking tired.*　注：personal concern

   B: Well, it's been a busy day.　　Wells (2006: 182)

b. A: Hullo, everyone.

   B: ↘↗ *You're late.* [Where have you been?]　O'Connor & Arnold （1973: 171）

皮肉を表す幾つかの例を挙げよう。

c. ［妻 Jane が娘の結婚式の準備でおおわらわの最中、夫が帰宅する］

   A: Hi, Jane. I'm home!

   B: Well, ↘↗ *you're a big help.* Where have you been?

d. A: Those kids are no good.

   B: ↘↗ *You're a fine one to talk*, considering all the trouble you caused when you were young.

e. A: You left your little child all alone at home, didn't you?

   B: Yes, but…

   A: |*Some parent* ↘ *you are!*

f. A: Roses! Are you planting roses?

   B: Yeah.

   A: |*Fine farmer* ↘ *you are!* Not a turnip or a cabbage or a potato.

以下は、一種の感嘆文である。

g. A: Jack!

   B: Katherine! Oh!

   A: Boy! *Did* |*I ever* |*miss* ↘ *you!*

h. A: Welcome home, Sabrina!

   B: You didn't recognize me at first, did you?

   A: Boy, *have* |*you* ↘ *changed!* You look lovely!

i. A: I really hate flying in these jumbo jets. They cruise so high you can't see any scenery.

   B: Boy, *are* |*you* ↘ *wrong!* You can see fantastic scenery aboard these jumbo jets.

(iii) 疑問詞疑問文の場合

　日頃の様子とは違った相手に対して、What's the matter with you?；What's

160

up with you?；What's with you? と尋ねる疑問文がある。この場合、you を強調すると、emotionally involved の心的態度の表明になる。例えば、surprise, personal concern など。なお、What's with you? の辞書定義は、[AmE] used to ask why a person or a group of people is behaving strangely である。

SUPRAS のメンバーが、次の posting を発信した。

> [A very alert ESL teacher in Los Angeles related the following exchange, which she overheard while riding an elevator in the giant LA Unified School District administrative building. Person A entered the elevator and looked at person B.]
>
> A: *What are YOU doing here?*
>
> B: I'm cleaning out my desk.
>
> A: Oh, ummm, uhh, when are you leaving?
>
> B: Now.

A は、B の行動に何か異常を感じて、あのような質問した。それもそのはず、B は仕事を辞め、机の中身を整理している。このように、you を強調することによって、<u>文全体の意味を強調している</u>。

　以下の漫画では、母親は息子の早い帰宅に驚き、*What are YOU doing home?* と言っている。

注：I have to go は、「トイレに行きたい」の意。他に、Can I go on this train?

a.　A: |*What are ↘ you doing up*? It's the first day of vacation. I thought you'd be sleeping in.　（朝寝坊する）

　　B: I tried. But my body clock is still on school time. I woke up at 6:45.

b.　[日頃、飲酒には無縁の友人が、突如パブに姿を現すと]

　　Mr. Roberts! What a surprise! |*What brings ↘ you here?*　(idiom)

c.　[*Downton Abbey*]

A: ᵢWhere have ↘ *you* been?

B: I'm not late, am I?

A: You're late when I say you're late.

d. ［B は、サッカーチームの補欠選手に降格されて意気消沈している］

A: ᵢWhat's the ᵢmatter with ↘ *you*?

B: What do you think? I'm playing in the reserves. I don't like playing with children.　　　　注：reserves　補欠組

e. ［決勝戦が迫っている］

A: ᵢWhat's ᵢwrong with ↘ *you*? You look really down.

B: I'm feeling nervous.

f. ［A（若者）は、B（女性）に好意を寄せていて、彼女の交友関係に干渉してくる］

A: So where does he give you a ride from?

B: ᵢWhat's it to ↘ *you*?   (= Mind your own business.)

A: Just curious.

しかし、注意しなければならないのは、*What is it to you?* は、下降調の場合に限って hostility の態度が表出されるということである。もし末尾を上昇調で言えば、単に好奇心の含意が込められている。渋谷の忠犬ハチ公がモデルになったアメリカ映画 *HACHI*（Richard Gere 主演）の中で、街での評判を聞き、新聞記者（A）がやってきて、street vendor（B）に話しかける。

A: Excuse me, sir. The dog up there. Is that the dog we hear so much about?

B: Uh-huh. ᵢWhat is it to ↗ *you*?

A: Oh, I'm sorry. I'm a reporter from a newspaper.

蛇足になるが、下降調の ᵢWho are ↘ *you*? は、suspicion または challenge の態度が表出されるが、ᵢWho are ↗ *you*? は、好奇心を伝えている。

参考 1：be 動詞の強意用法

　　　本課題では、代名詞の強意用法における emotional emphasis を扱ってきたが、be 動詞も話者の心的態度の表明に寄与する。冒頭付近で "You ᵢare a devil" is more emphatic…" という文を紹介したが、話者は be 動詞を強調することによって文全体を強調し、話者の心的態度を表すことがよくある。

　a.　［音信不通となっていた Brian が突如姿を見せる］

Roberta: *It ↘ is you!* Oh, my Gosh.

b.　I'm sorry to be late. I couldn't catch a bus. *It ↘ is Easter Sunday*, you know.
　　I walked.

c.　[Laura suddenly stumbles. She catches at a chair with a faint moan.]
　　Laura! Why, Laura! *You ↘ are sick!*

d.　A: Goodbye, Mr. Jones.
　　B: Well, *it ↘ was nice to meet you*. Goodbye.

参考 2：心的態度を反映する代名詞の強意用法

　　一般に、話し手の心的態度や感情を伝えるのに、日本語は表意文字で表す範囲が広く、それ以外の表情をつけても、つけなくとも用が足せる。他方、英語では、単語や、句、文の特定の場所にイントネーションを自由にかぶせることによって、話者の態度を伝えることが多い。日本語では、「が、ね、でしょう、だろう、のに」などの助詞（particles）を使えば、普通の文字で心的態度を表せる。例えば、I thought it would snow. では、自分の予想が当たったときと外れたときは、英語ではイントネーションによって、それを区別するが、日本語では、「やっぱり」と「〜のに」をつけ足しさえすれば区別ができ、所期の目的は果たせる。これを、安倍 勇（1962: 120）は、いみじくも「可視イントネーション」と呼んだ。また、日本語では、場面や敬語に頼って、できるだけ主語を省略した話し方をする。これは、クドクドと主語を明示する英語とは全く対照的である。例えば、英語の歌を聞いているとき感じるのは、何と主語——特に代名詞主語——が多いかということである。一方、日本語では、主語が明示されるのは、拒否、不満、焦燥、怒りといった心的態度を表す場合が多い気がする。その際も、自分や相手のことを言うのに、「私なんかには関係ない」とか「あなたなんかには分からない」、「人の気持ちを知らないで」とか「人の顔をじろじろ見るな」といった言い方をする。代名詞にアクセントを置いても、置かなくても話者の気持ちが伝わる。鈴木孝夫（1996: 132-148）は、話者が相手に対して自分のことを「ひと」と呼ぶ現象について、文学作品を通して考察を行っている。英語では、代名詞にいろいろな音調をかぶせて、話者の心的態度を表すことが極めて多い。日本人学習者は、代名詞への関心が薄く実際に使うことが稀なので、英語での代名詞の強意用法は大きな弱点である。

課題 51　**Climactic accent**

　　Bolinger (1987: 96) が **climactic accent** と呼ぶ現象がある。それは、文全体の強意（climactic purpose）のために核強勢を文末に移動させることである。

- ・The high pitch means that the speaker is "keyed up," but its position ― shifted to the right ― suggests a buildup or climax. From the hearer's standpoint there is impact by virtue of final position, on the psychological principle of last-heard-best-noted.　　　注：keyed up (= excited)

  　　　　　　　Bolinger (1986: 48-49)

- ・An accent at or near the end has a greater impact than one toward the beginning, which is useful for arousal in any of its interpretations – anger, involvement, surprise, enthusiasm.　　　注：arousal (= excitement)

  　　　　　　　Bolinger (1987: 96)

(i) 以下の各ペアーの B1 は default pattern、B2 は climactic pattern である。

a.　A: Can I bring my girlfriend?

　　B1: *By* ˈ*all means*.

　　B2: *By all* ˈ*means*.

b.　A: Uh-oh! Look what happened.

　　B1: *It's* ˈ*my fault*. I'm sorry.

　　B2: *It's my* ˈ*fault*.

c.　A: What's the fuss all about?

　　B1: Cockroaches are *all* ˈ*over the place*!

　　B2: Cockroaches are *all over the* ˈ*place*!

d.　A: Whew! It's finished at last.

　　B1: All your hard work will be worth it *in the* ˈ*long run*.

　　B2: All your hard work will be worth it *in the long* ˈ*run*.

e.　A: How do you know there was a fire at the barn?

　　B1: *I've just* ˈ*been there*. That's how.

　　B2: *I've just been* ˈ*there*.

f.　A: Hi, Jane!

　　B1: Good morning. *How* ˈ*are you?*

　　B2: *How are* |*you?*

g.　A: You're not old, Lydia.

　　B1: Well, I'm almost 60. It's no fun to grow old, *be*|*lieve me.*

　　B2: It's no fun to grow old, *believe* |*me.*

h.　A: Are you ready?

　　B1: |*Almost.*

　　B2: *Al*|*most.*

i.　A: What do think of Russia's Putin?

　　B1: His rule is |*absolute.*

　　B2: His rule is *abso*|*lute.*

j.　A: How big is the portrait?

　　B1: It's |*life-size.*

　　B2: It's *life-*|*size!*

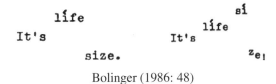

Bolinger (1986: 48)

　　参考：　A: How was he?

　　　　　B1: He lay *sick and broken* in his bed.

　　　　　B2: He lay in his bed, *sick and broken*.

(ii) 離れたところにいる人に声をかけたが返答がないので少しじれったくなると 2 回目は語末の無強勢音節が強調される。

a.　[『アラバマ物語』*To Kill a Mocking Bird*、少女が父を呼んでいる]

　　　→Atti↴cus! ↴Atti→cus!　　　注：彼女は、父を呼ぶのに first name を使う。

b.　→Ba↴sil! ↴Ba→sil!

　　→Ro↴ger! ↴Ro→ger!

　　→Hen↴ry! ↴Hen→ry!

```
        ger!           ry!
   Ro            Hen
```

(adapted from Bolinger (1986: 75))

[A]n impatient caller is apt to vary it (= the calling tune) in the expected

165

direction up, if it is necessary to repeat:

li / **Fe cia !**   **cia !** / **Feli**

Bolinger (1998: 46)

(iii) 課題 25 の例文でも、以下のように文尾の反復語を強調して、文全体の意味を強化する。各 B2 は、climactic accent を表す。

a. A: I ˈwant you to apologize.

B1: But *I've ˈnothing ↘to apologize for*.

B2: But *I've ˈnothing to a↘pologize for*.

b. A: What should we do now?

B1: *There's ˈnothing ↘to do*.

B2: *There's ˈnothing to ↘do*.

c. A: What did you say?

B1: *There was ˈnothing ↘to say*.

B2: *There was ˈnothing to ↘say*.

次の例では、話者 A の苛立ちが感じとれるだろう。

［映画 *Exodus*］

d. A: Karen, would you like to go to America?

B: Of course. Everybody likes to go to America.

A: Then you will go. I'll take you with me.

B: You mean right away?

A: Perhaps in the next week or so. What's the matter?

B: Nothing.

A: You do want to go, don't you?

B: Yes, but I must think a little about it.

A: *ˈWhat is there to ↘think about?*

参考：Logically, we might expect a nucleus on ***nothing***. But that's not where native speakers put it. They usually put it on ***to*** (above), or sometimes, less commonly, on ***was***, or indeed on ***eat***:

B: There ＼was nothing to eat.　または

B: There was nothing to ＼eat.（課題 25 を参照）

課題 52　Come with ME.

　私が知る限りでは、下記のような短い表現では、通例、核強勢の配置は以下のようになる。核強勢を受ける語を大文字体で示す。

Come WITH me.

I'll go WITH you.

Please bring it WITH you.

You can take it WITH you.

実際、Wells（2006）でも、with に核強勢が置かれている。但し、動詞の目的語が名詞のときは、with には強勢はない。

Take your umBRELla with you.

Bring your FRIEND along with you.

参考までに言うと、Stay WITH me. または STAY with me. である。

　しかし、映画や sit-coms を観ていると、Come with ME. をよく聞く。特に、人をどこかに案内する場面でよく聞く。このような言い方は、前課で述べた climactic accent であると思う。昔、ロンドンの金融街を歩いていて、セント・ポール大聖堂に行く道順を通行人に尋ねたら、You're almost THERE. OK. Come with ME と言って案内してくれた。当時、高校英語教師であったので、このような言い回しが印象に残り、今でも覚えている。それが契機になって、Come with ME. をいろんな機会に聞くたびに、頻度の高さを確認している。

a.　[At the motel]

A: Do you want a room?

B: Yes, please.

A: *Then come with ME.*

更に言えば、同じ意味で、Follow ME. があり、これもよく使われている。

b.　［路上での道案内］

A: How can I get there?

B: *Just follow ME.*

しかし、高圧的な場面でも Come with ME が聞かれる。

c.　Suddenly I felt a hand on my shoulder. It was Colonel Emsworth.

"*Come with ME, sir.*" he said in a low, angry voice.

d.　［路上で、警察官が挙動不審な男に職務質問をする］

Mister, you're not making any sense. *You'd better come with ME.*

話題が変わるが、人に何か親切な行為をする場合、Allow ME. という言い回しも定着している。

e. ［パーテイで着席しようとしている女性に向かって］

　　・ *Allow ME, miss.*

　　・［自分の肩マウントを脱ぎ、寒さに震える女性の肩にかけながら］*Allow ME.*

f. *Excuse YOU.*

　　相手に抗議する言い方である。「失礼な！」

注：burp (belch)　げっぷの音
詳細は、伊達（2019）の課題 12 を参照。

Two other stereotypes involving pronouns that are often accented <u>climactically</u> are *Excuse mé!* and *Believe mé*!　　　下線は伊達が追加。

　　　Bolinger (1986: 80)

g. ［くしゃみやげっぷのときの謝罪］

　　・ *Excuse ME*!

　　・ *Pardon ME*!

h. Believe ME. など

　　・It's no fun to grow very old and become frail, *believe ME.*

　　・Oh, boy, we're pretty upset, *let me tell YOU.* Who wants another four years with that Trump guy?

i. *Excuse ME?*

　　相手の無礼な発言に反駁する言い方

　　Excuse ME? WHAT did you just say?　（共に上昇調）

課題 53　**Adverbials**（副詞相当語／句）

　節または文全体を修飾する副詞および副詞句は、通例、個別の音調単位を構成する。

(i) 文頭では下降上昇調または上昇調をとり、文末では上昇調をとる。この位置の adverbials の大部分は、主文の意味を制限する（limit）働きをする。

文頭では

a.　*Un↘↗fortunately* ｜ he couldn't ace the test.

b.　*On ↘↗Fridays* ｜ I go to Jennifer's place.

c.　*In ↘↗Manchester* ｜ we do it this way.

d.　*In the ↘↗kitchen* ｜ the staff were busy.

e.　｜Strangely e↘↗nough ｜ it doesn't work like that.

文末では

a.　He couldn't ace the test, ｜ *un↗fortunately*.

b.　He drives to work, ｜ *↗usually*.

c.　He met her then, ｜ *↗probably*.

d.　I like ice-cold drinks, ｜ *↗actually*.

e.　She came home while I was sleeping, ｜ *per↗haps*.

f.　Babies often cry during the night, ｜ *from ↗my experience*.

g.　I'm satisfied with the results, ｜ *on the ↗whole*.

h.　We have very little snow here, ｜ *as a ↗rule*.

i.　He's late, ｜ *as ↗usual*.

(ii) 特定の adverbials は、文頭または文末に来て主文の意味を強化する（enforce）――断定する――場合は下降調になり、聞き手の同意を期待している場合は上昇調または下降上昇調になる。

文頭では

a.　A: Are you coming with us?

　　B: *Of↘course I am*.

b.　A: Does she know?

　　B: *↘Surely* ｜ she must.

c.　A: How much do you think it's going to cost?

169

B: ↘*Obviously* ǀ quite a lot.

d. A: So you didn't like the beef.

B: *On the* ↘*contrary*, ǀ I enjoyed it.

e. A: Katie was angry with him.

B: ↘*Naturally* ǀ she would be.

比較対照例：下降上昇調のほうが、より強調的である。

f. ① ↘↗*Obviously* ǀ we can't tell you what to do.

② ↘*Obviously* ǀ we can't tell you what to do.

g. ① ↘↗*Clearly* ǀ he'll be disappointed at the news.

② ↘*Clearly* ǀ he'll be disappointed at the news.

h. ① *In* ↘↗*my opinion*, ǀ he is something of a genius.

② *In* ↘*my opinion*, ǀ he is something of a genius.

<u>文末では</u>

a. A: There's a rip in the new pants I bought at the shop.

B: You can ask for a refund, ǀ ↘*obviously*.

b. A: Do you think he knows about the problem?

B: He must know about it, ǀ ↘*surely*.

c. When I'm in London, I visit my mother ǀ ↘*regularly*.

d. When he heard it, he turned red ǀ ↘*literally*.

(iii) 時には、adverbials が個別の音調単位を形成しないで、尾部として、先行する主文のイントネーションの中に組み込まれることがある。これは、話者が文脈上の理由で adverbials を重要視しないときの optional なケースである。

a. I ˈlike the ˈdress you're ↘wearing, *by the way*.

b. I ˈlike your ˈhouse so ↘much, *by the way*.

c. He ˈdoesn't drive to ↘work, *normally*.

解説を紹介しよう。

・It should not be imagined that clause-modifying adverbials must have a separate intonation-group; merely that they very commonly do. In very general terms, <u>it depends on how prominent the speaker wishes the modification to be.</u>　　　　　　　　　　　　下線は伊達が追加

注：modification は adverbials のこと

Cruttenden (1997: 69)

・Very commonly, a linking adjunct in clause-final position does not have its own separate intonation unit but is integrated intonationally into the preceding clause, for example:

86　He can read <u>French</u> *however*

87　You can <u>go</u> *then*

88　They <u>smell</u> *perhaps*　　　斜体字は伊達が追加

Tench (1990: 83)

(iv) adverbials ではないが、主文の内容を制限する表現がある。それは、いわば afterthought として主文の後に来る。特に、認識にかかわる動詞（epistemic verb）や心的状態（mental state）の形容詞（afraid, sorry 等）を伴う表現が多い。

a.　A: How much holiday will you get?

　　B: Three weeks, ｜ *I ↗<u>hope</u>*.

b.　A: What're you guys doing this evening?

　　B: We're not doing anything, ｜ *as ˈfar as I ↗<u>know</u>*.

c.　A: Instant coffee today, ｜ *I'm af↗<u>raid</u>*.

　　B: OK. It's better than nothing.

d.　A: What happened to Muriel?

　　B: She's resigned, ｜ *so it ↗<u>seems</u>*.

しかし、afterthought が尾部になることもある。これも、上記の Cruttenden の解説 "it depends on how prominent the speaker wishes the modification to be." が関わっている。

e.　A ↘<u>storm</u> is coming, *I'm afraid*.

f.　A: Hello, Sarah! You look tired.

　　B: Do I?

　　A: You've been over ↘<u>working</u>, *you know*.

g.　She ˈlives in ↘<u>Kennington</u>, *as far as I know*.

171

課題 54 虚辞（**empty words**）

(i) ある種の名詞や動詞などは、文脈中で取るに足らない意味であったり、特定の意味がないことがある。それらは、empty words（虚辞）と呼ばれ、通例、文アクセントを受けない。しかし、紛らわしいケースもある。

  Gasoline is expensive. ˈDon't waste a ˈ*drop*.

ここでは *waste* のほうが *drop* よりも重要であるので、ˈDon't ˈ*waste* a drop. となるかと思えば、実際には上記のように言う。重要な意味をもたない虚辞であるはずの *drop* に核強勢が置かれる現象をどのように説明すればいいのか。この場合、not... a drop は nothing を言い換えたものであると考えるのが妥当である。*Don't waste a drop.* は、ˈWaste <u>noth</u>ing. と同義である。多くの類例がある。

a. Time is money. ˈDon't waste a ˈ<u>*minute*</u>.

b. I ˈcan't see a ˈ<u>*thing*</u>.

c. I ˈdidn't hear a ˈ<u>*word*</u> about it.

d. ˈDon't tell a ˈ<u>*soul*</u> about it.　（誰にも言うな）

e. I'm broke. I ˈhaven't got a ˈ<u>*dime*</u>.　（一銭もない）

f. It ˈdidn't cost us a ˈ<u>*penny*</u>.

g. So you ˈhaven't touched a ˈ<u>*drop*</u> for years, have you?
  （アルコールを一滴も飲んでいない）

(ii) things, people, place(s) などの empty words には、しばしば文アクセントが置かれない。

a. Wasn't that a knock at the door? Or am I iˈ<u>magin</u>ing *things*?

b. I'm worried. Iˈkeep ˈ<u>see</u>ing *things* these days.　（幻覚）

c. You didn't hear that? Am I ˈ<u>hear</u>ing *things*?　（幻聴）

d. I like you. You're sensitive. You ˈ<u>feel</u> *things*.

e. Washing dishes and ˈkeeping *things* ˈ<u>ti</u>dy ǀ is the worst work in the world.

f. We've got a ˈlot of *things* ˈ<u>go</u>ing for us.　（事態は順調に進んでいる）

g. Well, I'm sure ǀ the ˈboss will ˈmake *things* ˈ<u>fine</u> for you.　（事態を改善する）

h. A: What should I do about it?

  B: ˈTry to ˈlook on the ˈbright ˈ<u>side</u> of *things*.

i.　A: What's it like being a nurse?

　　B: Nursing is a good job for me. I ˈlike ˈhelping *people*.

j.　A: How's he doing at the new job?

　　B: He'll ˈgo *places*. （出世する）

k.　A: What's new?

　　B: We're ˈhaving a ˈbarbecue at ˈour *place*. （自宅）

l.　He's comfortable now │ because he ˈbought a *place*.

　　　　Cf … because he ˈbought a ˈhouse.

m.　A: [On the phone] Hi, Bill. Sorry to disturb you at this hour.

　　B: For God's sake, ˈthis is ˈsome time to ˌwake ˈup a *guy*! It's 4 o'clock in the morning!

n.　I must go now. I've ˈgot to ˈsee a *guy*.

o.　ˈTime and ˈtide wait for ˈno *man*. （歳月人を待たず）

p.　He was arˈrested because he ˈkilled a *man*.

　　　　Cf. He was arˈrested because he ˈkilled a ˈdoctor.

q.　We ˈbought ˈcheese and *stuff*.

(iii) しかし、thing と things が文アクセントを受けることもある。

a.　I'm proud of him. He ˈdid *the* ˈright ˈthing.

b.　ˈWhat's the ˈpoint of *the* ˈwhole ˈthing?

c.　ˈChange is *a* ˈgood ˈthing. It shows that you are not bound to your former self.

d.　ˈWhy did you ˈdo such *a* ˈsilly ˈthing?

e.　I just want to live my own life │ and ˈdo *my own* ˈthing. （すきなようにやる）

f.　Audrey Bartlett was *the* ˈnearest ˈthing │ Vera had to a friend.

g.　[Trump 大統領の熱烈な支持者の弁]

　　ˈTrump is *the* ˈbest ˈthing │ that ever happened to America since Lincoln.

　　参考：f と g のように、人のことを thing と言うには、学習者には違和感があるが、Wells にコメントを求めた。その際、私は、Queen Elizabeth II is the best thing that ever happened to Britain since Victoria. という文を作って送信した。以下は、Wells からのコメントである。"It's OK and idiomatic in Britain just as in the States. The 'thing' is not the person but the fact of their being there."

h. Shakespeare is *a* ⌐*thing of the* ⌐*past* ⌐ to many English literature majors.

i. ⌐*You poor* ⌐*thing*, you've had a hard time of it, haven't you?

j. It wasn't really the driver's fault; it was just ⌐*one of those* ⌐*things*.

k. Hi, James! ⌐*How're* ⌐*things*?　　　　　　（idiom：よくあるやむを得ないこと）

(iv) 虚辞としての動詞

　文脈から判断して予測可能な動詞には文アクセントを置く必要がない。

　　⌐books to *write*; ⌐work to *do*; ⌐clothes to *wear*; ⌐food to *eat*; ⌐lessons to *learn*; ⌐groceries to *get*; A dis⌐covery was *made*; A ⌐question was *asked*; An ⌐accident *happened*. 等。

次に、Bolinger (1986: 124) の解説を見てみよう。

　　A routine verb such as *get* is often deaccented:

　　　　Téll 'im to get lóst.

　　　　I've gótta get on the tráin.

　　　　Trý to get a pícture of him.

　　How regular deaccentuation is with *get* can be seen in the folk spelling *giddap* for *get up* (to a horse)…　　　　注：*giddap*　進め！

　　The verb *go* also has a folk spelling, *gwan*, for its deaccentuation in the phrase *go on* and a similar deformation occurs in

　　　　[gə] 'wáy! (*go away*)

　　　　[gə] hóme! (to a dog)

他に、文脈上で predictable または small and common と見なされる動詞は、しばしば文アクセントを受けない。

　a. ⌐Try to **get** ⌐*hold* of him.

　b. Is ⌐that the ⌐opening you **got** ⌐*through*?

　c. What's the matter with you? ⌐What **got** ⌐*in*to you?

　d. What's the matter? ⌐What **came** ⌐*o*ver you?

　e. Move away from the door. We're **coming** ⌐*through* it.

　f. I ⌐told you not to **go** ⌐*through* there.

(v) Miscellaneous

　a. There was a ⌐*wo*rried *look* on his face.

174

b. I noticed a ˈweary *look* about her.

c. I'm afraid old Fred has a ˈmedical *problem*.

d. Jack and Jane have a ˈmarital *problem*; they're separated now.

e. This is a ˈlegal *matter*. It does not concern you.

f. They did it on ˈJohn's *behalf*.

g. In ˈmy *opinion*, he should be fired!

h. In ˈhis *eyes*, the manager should be fired.

i. We're lost. It's ˈyour *fault*.

j. In ˈsome *cases* the answer is obvious.

k. They did it for ˈJohn's *sake*.

(vi) 不定代名詞は、具体的な意味がないので虚辞と言えるが、以下のような構文では、核強勢を受ける。

a.　A: Here you are at last.

　　B: Hullo, Susan. Sorry to be late. But we had a bit of trouble with the car.

　　A: A bit of trouble?

　　B: ↘*Everything went wrong*. The car wouldn't start,…

　ここでは、'had trouble' は 'went wrong' と同義語である。

b.　A: What's the next move?

　　B: ↘*Anything can happen*.

c.　A: Now we're in trouble.

　　B: ↘*Anything can happen*.

　ここでは、happen は文脈から予測可能と見なされている。伊達（2019）のp.121 を参照。

課題 55 I've never been there.

ある中学校の教科書には以下の一節があった。

The place I want to visit is Korea. My email friend, Mina, lives in Seoul. She writes to me about schools, movies, and music in Korea. I write to her about life in Japan. Korea is close to Japan, but I have never been there.

さて、*I have never been there.* では、どの語が最も強調されて——核強勢を受けて——発音されるか。強勢の原則は、それが新情報の内容語に来るというものである。大まかには次のような考え方になるだろうか。

「副詞 there は既知情報であり、強勢を受ける資格なし。be 動詞は機能語である。否定詞 never だけが強勢を受ける資格がある。結論として、

I have ↘never been there. となる。」

実際、教科書でも、そのように示されていた。しかし、これは大間違いである。タイミングよく、共同研究仲間がこれを問題視し Wells にメールした。早速、彼の phonetic blog (2010.9.24) で取り上げられた。

The first thing to say is that the textbook is clearly wrong. It seems to me that native speakers would virtually always choose to place a nuclear accent on *been*.   aɪv nevə ↘biːn ðeə

この文脈での *been* は visited という意味であり、full verb である。

[In response to *John sees lots of bullfights*]

No, John's ˈnever ↘been to Spain. Or Mexico.

(adapted from Bolinger (1989:374))

なお、伊達（2019: 39）でも述べたように、日本人は、文中では否定語が最も重要であると思い込み、文脈も考えずに機械的に、そこを強調する悪癖がある。ただし、

I've ↘never been (= visited) there.

という場合、必ず前提がある。

A: Have you been to China?

B: No, I've ↘never been there. （対比）

以下の斜体字の文でも、日本人は否定語を強調するであろうが、実際には、表記のようになる。

a.　A: Why didn't you invite John to the party the other day?

　　B: *Be ǀ cause I ǀ don't ↘ like him.*

b.　A: I don't like him.

　　B: *You've ǀ never even ↘ spoken to him.*

c.　A: Have you talked to John recently?

　　B: No, *I can't ↘ stand the man.*

以下は、存在文である。

d.　I wanted some cheese. *But there ↘ was no cheese.*

e.　A: You should try to look on the bright side.

　　B: *There ↘ is no bright side.*

f.　A: She's lost the game, but she'll do better next time.

　　B: *There won't ↘ be any next time.*

g.　[In class]

　　A: Jim, you haven't handed in your report yet. For your assignment, you were supposed to do a report on the Lincoln-Douglas debates.

　　B: But I couldn't!

　　A: Why?

　　B: *Because there ↘ is nobody ǀ named " ǀ Lincoln ↘ Douglas"!*

h.　[On the phone]

　　Hi, Teddy? What's the math homework for tomorrow? Oh, wait a minute! *There ↘ isn't any homework!* It's summer vacation.

　　詳細な説明については課題 26 (ii) を参照。伊達（2019）の p.66 にも関連内容がある。

参考：地域によっては、I've ǀ never ↘ gone there. という言い方もある。以下は、上記の Wells の phonetic blog に対して読者が寄せたメールである。

Apparently I speak a different dialect then. **I'd say 'gone' more often than 'been' in this context.** In fact, I don't consider the two sentences completely equal per se (but almost). For me, "I've never been there" states that one has never *existed in*, and thus never experienced the marvels of, that location before regardless of how one got there. It places emphasis on the novel experience of a location rather than the journey.

課題 56　選択疑問文

授業で教えられる選択疑問文は、通例、2つのタイプがある。

　　Will you have ↗tea ｜ or ↘coffee?　（Which drink?）

　　Will you have ｜tea or ↗coffee?　（Any drink?）

前者は、二者択一の疑問文であり、聞き手は、どちらかを選ぶことを求められ
ている。一方、後者では、聞き手は、他の飲み物を頼んでもよい。

　実は、2つの上昇調単位で言われることもある。

　　Will you have ↗tea ｜ or ↗coffee?

　これは、特にサービス関係の仕事に就いている人に見られる言い方である。
気遣いが込められている。

　　↗Chicken ｜ or ↘beef?

　　↗Chicken ｜ or ↗beef?

Wells（2006: 75）は、前者の上昇調＋下降調について次のように説明する。

　　[T]he addressee (the passenger on an airline, perhaps) is being invited to
　　choose between the two possibilities, chicken and beef.

次に、後者の上昇調＋上昇調の場合、

　　[S]he is being invited to choose one of those two, or　− if she prefers −
　　some other option.

後者の言い方は、yes/no 疑問文（yes なのか no なのか）と、選択疑問文（yes
ならば、どれを）との混合の意図が含まれている。それは、下記の Bolinger
(1989: 114) の解説中にも表れている。

　　Someone asking *Would you like coffee or tea?* with B + B is most likely
　　seeking a yes or no answer, not a choice, though this shape is sometimes
　　met with in blends: a stewardess on an airplane might use it to elicit a
　　reply like *Yes, thank you, I would − coffee, please.*

　　　注：B+B は、上昇調＋上昇調のこと；下線は伊達が追加。

上記と似た事例が病室でも見られる。

　　A nurse in a hospital brings two urns, one with coffee and one with tea, to
　　the door of a patient's room. She wants to ask, "Will you have coffee or
　　tea?" As an alternative question, this is normally spoken:

　　Will you have ↗COFfee or ↘TEA?

しかし、このようなイントネーションは不躾に聞こえるだろう。なぜならば、どちらも欲しくなかったり、ほかに何か欲しいこともあるからである。

> But saying it that way would be rude, for it would close the door to a third alternative, which is to have neither. So she says
>
> > Will you have ↗COFfee or ↗TEA?
>
> a normal yes-no question, leaving it up to the hearer to supply, after "yes", the additional information of which one, or perhaps both.
>
> > Bolinger (1968: 328)

以下は、international students を対象にした英語教材からの対話である。この場合、明らかに二者択一の疑問文であるのに、上昇調＋上昇調になっていた。

a.　A: Majestic Theater. How could I help you?

　　B: I'd like to book two seats for tonight, please.

　　A: ↗ORchestra or ↗BALcony?

　　B: Balcony, please.

　　A: Can I have your name?

　　B: William Porter.

b.　A: May I take your order?

　　B: Could I have a chicken sandwich, salad and a medium ginger ale, please?

　　A: Okay. One chicken sandwich, salad and a medium ginger ale.

　　　Thousand ↗ISland, ↗FRENCH, or i↗TALian dressing?

上昇調は、相手に押しつけがましい印象を与えない配慮だろう。

　教本の記述では、最後の選択肢は下降調、それ以外は上昇調になるとあるが、時には平坦調のこともある。例えば、Will you have coffee or tea? では、最初の選択肢 coffee が平坦調になることもある。Wells (2006: 225) には、

> Would you prefer ↗coffee | or ↘tea?
>
> 　→ Would you prefer →coffee | or ↘tea?

　また、速いテンポでは、最初の選択肢 *coffee* は、独自の音調単位を形成せずに、文全体が1つの音調単位になる。それ故に、以下のようなトラブルが起こる。

[The customer (A) can't hear very well, which makes the waiter (B) impatient.]

    A: Let's see now. What can I have to start with?

    B: Soup or salad?

    A: What's *super salad*?

    B: What do you mean, *super salad*?

    A: Didn't you say you have *super salad*?

    B: No, we don't have anything like that. Just plain green salad. Or you can start with tomato soup.

B（ウェイター）は、*Soup or salad?* を一気に上昇調で言ったのだろう。だから、*soup or* は、super と同音（homophone）になる。

Rebecca Dauer から教示を得た。

Dear Tami, I think in fast speech in normal circumstances, i.e. with background noise, these sound almost the same to most people and to virtually all non-native speakers. So as a teaching material, it's fine. However, in a careful style there is a difference.　(2004.8.16)

参考：Rebecca Dauer のこと

　　　　海外で出版される英語音声学の教本は、圧倒的にイギリス英語に関するものが多いが、Dauer の *Accurate English: A Complete Course in Pronunciation* は、アメリカ英語を扱っている。B5 版よりも少し大きな本で、難解な専門語の使用をできるだけ控えていて、とても読みやすい。また、演習のページが多い。

　　　　彼女は、20 数年前、British Council Tokyo の招きで講演来日した。私は、著書にサインをしてもらった。それと、2 人とも創立して間もない SUPRAS の会員であることが縁となり、以後、連絡を取り合ってきた。私が SUPRAS に発信すると、たびたび懇切丁寧なコメントを返信してくださった。私の著書でもよく引用している、彼女は、アメリカ英語について貴重な情報源であった。

　　　4, 5 年たった後、彼女は音信不通になった。2007 年 3 月に、御主人 Mr. Dauer からメールがあった。Becky は天に召された。まだ 60 歳だった。メールには、日本が大好きだった彼女の思い出になるものがあれば送って欲しいという要請があった。私は、彼女が制作した音声キットを贈ってもらっていたので、思い出の品と写真と共に送った。

課題 57 慣用的イントネーション

(i) Bolinger (1986: 4) は、あるグループを対象に行った音声認識実験の結果（一部）を紹介している（課題 6 を参照）。その中で、参加者の多くが、ピッチの上昇と下降との区別ができなかったと言っている。そして、聞き分ける耳をトレーニングするには、まず、定型化したイントネーション（set intonation）を聞くことから始めることを勧めている。

> To train one's ear, the best place to start is with expressions that carry with them a set intonation. There is only one "way" to say them － or maybe two, or a very few － if they are to have the meaning we intend.

そして多くの慣用的表現の例を挙げている。それらを私のコメントを加えながら紹介していく。

a. Take the expression *all right* tagged at the end of a sentence to signify 'It's true, there's no doubt of it.'

```
          he's smart
   Oh,
                     all right.
```

この文は、「確かに彼は賢い」という意味である。この idiom は文末に来て、通例、低上昇調で言われる。

・A: Are you sure it was Bill?

B: Oh, yes, it was him all right.

但し、時には尾部になることもあり、独自のピッチ変化を伴わない。

b. The exclamation *A fine thing!* when used ironically generally has the same tune as *Hell's bells!*:　　　　注：Hell's bells!　畜生／いまいましい！

```
      fine
   A
         thi
            ng!
```

これは、皮肉的に言う「ご立派なこと」である。

・That's a fine excuse!

・A fine teacher you are!

この場合の *fine* は原義とは正反対の bad という意味である。

c. The phrase *for a change* is generally tagged at the end of a sentence, as

181

all right is, but instead of having a rise on the last word the whole phrase remains at a low pitch:

```
        this
  Try
            tie, for a change.
```

　この idiom は「たまには」とか「珍しく」の意味である。

・How about going walking for a change?

・Look! He's come on time for a change.

但し、この idiom は、alternatively can be accented, taking the nucleus in its own IP (usually a rise) となる。

　　(adapted from Wells (2006: 159))

d.　We often use the expression *in no time* to mean 'very quickly.' We then say it with *no* at the highest pitch.

```
      no
  in
        time
```

名詞句の強勢規則では、*time* が最も高いピッチになるはずだが、この idiom はそれに反している。

・We'll be there in no time.

　ついでながら、これは in time「まもなく」と対比される。

e.　When the word *rather* is used to signify strong agreement, it carries the same intonation as *Yes, sir!, You bet!, Right on!*, and other expressions of agreement. The second syllable, which is normally weak (as in *It's rather good*), thus becomes as prominent as the first.

```
  Ra the
     a   r!
```

これは、Yes, indeed!, You bet!, Right on! などと同じく、強い同意を表す。

・A: Wasn't it lovely weather?

　B: Rather!　(=Yes, indeed!)

　　但し、今では old-fashioned である。*Rather!* は、上記の模式図では下降調になっているが、（低）上昇調になることもある。

Rather.

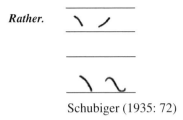

Schubiger (1935: 72)

f.　To convey the idea of ignorance, someone who is asked for information may reply *Search me*!, with a glide up on *search* and a slight drop from the highest pitch on *me:*

Search me
　　　　e}

これは、I don't know. の意味である。少し上昇気味で *search* を言い、ピッチが最も高い時点の *me* で下降する。

・A:　Where is she?

　B:　Search me!

同じイントネーションが、Search me! と同じ意味をもつ idioms Don't look at me! や Don't ask me! にも用いられる。

Don't look at me!

Bolinger & Sears (1981: 28)

g.　When someone pushes ahead too fast or take too much for granted, the expression *(Now) wait a minute!* makes an effective protest when said like this:

Wa-a-a-it　min
　　　　　a　　ute!

Here timing is a factor: *wait* is drawled, and *min-* is uttered forcefully following a slight pause after *a*.

これは、抗議を表す idiom である。

・Wait a minute! That's not what we agreed on!

以上のほかに、Wells（2006）には多くの set intonation で発せられる成句が挙げられている。

(ii) Wells (2014: 105-6) には、以下のような慣用的イントネーションの例が示

183

されている。

English has various tone idioms — words or phrases for which the choice of tone (rise, fall or fall-rise) is fixed rather than free. For example, the interjection **oops** or **whoops**, used when you've fallen, dropped something or made a mistake, can only have a rise. You can't say it with a fall…

/Oops!
× \Oops!

On the other hand the phrase **by the way**, used in spoken English to introduce a side issue not connected with the main subject you were talking about before, seems (at least for me) always to have some kind of fall (high fall, low fall, rise-fall), never a rise or fall-rise.

You can say **hello!** With any tone. But its newer equivalent **hi!** seems to demand a fall.

Hel\lo!
Hel/lo!
Hel\/lo!
\Hi!
× /Hi!

You can use any tone for **goodbye**, though probably the most usual one is a rise. But its informal equivalent **see you** sounds odd with a simple rise: it seems to need a fall-rise… A rise seems OK if we add an adverbial. So is a fall.

\/See you!   'See you to/morrow!
?? /See you!   'See you to\morrow!

(iii) 他の慣用的イントネーション（tone idioms）を紹介しよう。

a. 失敗したり、困ったときに発する間投詞

　　Uh-oh　（第 1 音節は声門閉鎖音を伴う）

　　[ʔoʔou]　　　Cruttenden (1997: 175)

　　参考：*Wells* の表記では、第 2 音節が低上昇調になる。

　　　　　　Longman Pronunciation Dictionary 3ʳᵈ Edition

b. 相手の話への同意や相づちを表す間投詞

　　Uh-huh　（低上昇調で言われる）

c. 質問に対する否定を表す間投詞

Uh-uh　（両音節とも声門閉鎖音を伴って下降調で言われる）

d.　Nurse: How was your night?

　　Patient: ꞌ*Not* ↘ *bad*.　(ꞌ*All* ↘ right.)

　　Nurse: That's good.

以下で、*all right* と *not bad* に関する解説を紹介しよう。

> On their own these phrases are non-committal, and fairly neutral on the scale from good to bad. With a raised voice and a falling nucleus, they mean 'very good', e.g.
>
> 　　A: How did you like the film?
>
> 　　B: It wasn't ↘ BAD　(it was all ↘ RIGHT).
>
> On the other hand, with a lowered voice and rising nucleus to suggest 'don't take this at its face value', they can amount to a polite and face-saving way of saying something like 'pretty awful': …
>
> 　　A: How did you like the film?
>
> 　　B: It wasn't ↗BAD　(it was all ↗RIGHT).　　注：まあまあだ
>
> 　　　　Knowles (1987: 211)

e.　「知らない」を意味する idiom

　・A: Why does he want to drive such a big car?

　　B: ꞌ*Beats* ↘↗ *me!*　(I don't know.)

　・A: What's he shouting about?

　　B: ꞌ*Beats* ↘↗ *me!*

この idiom の音調に関して Wells の解説がある。

> ꞌ*Beats* ∨*me!*…[is] an English intonational idiom, in that it cannot be said with any other tone than a fall-rise.　Wells (Blog 2009.1.26)

参考：Lewis によれば、ꞌ*Beats* ∨*me!* は対比用法であり、下降調もあり得る。

> [T]here is nothing specially idiomatic about using a fall-rise tone in such a type of semantic context, here contrasting one person with some other or others… Finally, of course any phrase can be given an pressively neutral citational intonation which will be… high level plus low fall, i.e. ꞌ*Beats* ＼*me*. This intonation could also be used to suggest… a bored, indifferent, dismissive comment.
>
> 　　　　(Blog 155:2009.1.26)

課題 58   So he is. / So be it.

学習参考書には、So is he. の意味は「彼もそうだ」、一方、So he is. は「確かに彼はそうだ」（賛同）という趣旨のことが書いてある。

    A: I'm a student at this university.

    B: ⁻*So is* ↘ *he*.

    X: I hear he is a student at this university.

    Y: ⁻*So he* ↘ *is*.

        注：⁻So 中の横バー記号は、ピッチが高いことを示す（high prehead）。

しかし、*So he is*. は、単に相手の発言に賛同する言い方ではない。「（そう言えば）そうだったね」とか「（驚いて）あっ、本当だ！」の意味である。辞書定義では、used to show that you agree with something that has just been mentioned, especially something you had not noticed or had forgotten.

    'Look, she's wearing a hat just like yours.'

    'So she is.'   *Longman Dictionary of Contemporary English*

文献中の解説を紹介しよう。

    ・We very commonly agree with some remark, but are surprised that it is true. This element of the unexpected is expressed by using a response beginning with a high unstressed "so + pronoun" device.

            Allen (1954: 139)

    ・In replies, the construction So + S + op expresses surprised confirmation of what the previous speaker has asserted:

    A: It's past midnight.   注：op（<operator）は be 動詞や助動詞のこと

    B: [looks at the watch] ⁻So it ìs!

            Greenbaum & Quirk (1990: 254)

類例を示そう。

a. A: Excuse me. You've dropped your glove.

    B: ⁻*So I* ↘ *have*. Thank you.

b. A: Look! It's snowing!

    B: ⁻*So it* ↘ *is*.

課題 58　So he is. / So be it.

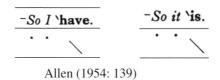

Allen (1954: 139)

c.　A: You've spilled coffee on your dress.

　　B: Oh dear, ⁻*so I* ↘ *have*.

d.　A: Waiter, there's a fly in my soup.

　　B: ⁻*So there* ↘ *is*. I'm sorry.

e.　A: Oh! We've forgotten to thank him.

　　B: ⁻*So we* ↘ *have*.

　ただし、以下では、短縮構文は返答ではない。驚きの気持ちはない。

　　You asked me to leave at once, and ⁻so I ↘ did. [= Indeed I did.]

　　I told him to come back at once and ⁻so he ↘ did.

(ii) 映画を見ていると、時々、¦So be ↘ it. というセリフを耳にする。この場合の so は、So we have. とか So it is. と同じで、「そのとおり」の意味である。この慣用句は、「それならそれでよい、それはそのままでよい、好きにするがよい、そういうことなら勝手にすれば」という不承不承の受諾を意味する。他に、Let it be so. とも言える。辞書の定義では、

・(*formal*) *used to show that you accept something and will not try to change it or cannot change it*. --- *Oxford Advanced Leaner's Dictionary*

・*used to show you do not like or agree with something, but you will accept it* --- *Longman Dictionary of Contemporary English*

a.　If he doesn't want to be involved, then ¦*so be* ↘ *it*.

b.　He'll never speak to me again. ¦*So be* ↘ *it*.

c.　If something happens, ¦*so be* ↘ *it*.

d.　If you really want to throw your career away for some idealistic principle, ¦*so be* ↘ *it*.

参考：キリスト教で祈りの終りに唱える言葉 Amen. は、言い換えると So be it.（かくあらせたまえ）を意味するが、日常的な意味とニュアンスが異なる。Amen to that!（それに賛成）

課題 59　Nelson 提督の信号文

(i) 1805 年 10 月 21 日、ネルソン（Nelson）提督は、ナポレオン軍とのトラファルガー海戦の前に信号文を送った。

England expects every man to do his duty.
この文は、イギリス国民に影響を与えた言葉として、現代でもよく用いられているようだ。

　この文を滑らに言うのは容易ではない。まず、*England* (onset) と *duty* (focus) には重要な文アクセントがあることは明らかである。他の内容語 *every, man, do* も重要であると見なして、文アクセントを置いて言うべきか。しかし、すべての内容語に文アクセントを置くとリズムに乗れない。音調単位は、通例、1 つ、または、2 つの文アクセントから成り立つ。それ故に、この文を適切な音調単位に分けなければならない。

　Bolinger (1986: 51-2) は、この文の発音の仕方について解説している。その一部を紹介しよう。以下は、ぎこちない言い方を示している。

$$\text{The} \quad \overset{\text{ná}}{\text{tion}} \ \text{ex}\overset{\text{pé}}{\text{cts}} \ \overset{\text{év'}}{\text{ry}} \ \text{mán to} \ \overset{\text{dó}}{\text{his}} \ \overset{\text{dú}}{\underset{\text{ty.}}{}}$$

One would not ordinarily get this many accents in a single utterance… And since accenting so many words is rather difficult to do in fluent speech, the speaker readily adopts strategies that will excuse him from accenting any more than he has to do.

敷衍すると、上記の模式図にあるような言い方は、普通ではない。発話の流れに乗れない。では、どうすればよいか。発話のリズムを確保するために情報上で重要な内容語の強勢を抑制することになる。Bolinger は続けて言う。

A more usual form of the… example would be

$$\text{The} \quad \overset{\text{ná}}{\text{tion}} \ \text{expects} \ \overset{\text{év'ry man to do his}}{} \ \overset{\text{dú}}{\underset{\text{ty.}}{}}$$

in which only *nation*, *every*, and *duty* are accented… Duties are done, so there is no need to accent *do*; and both *expect* and *man* are highly predictable (hence unnewsworthy) in any context in which this sort of

188

sentence is apt to be uttered.

　　Even when some of the content words are quite informative, the speaker is free to suppress accents if doing so fits the overall strategy of the utterance.

ここで初出の名詞主語 *nation* が下降音調になっていることに注目されたい。これは、*The nation* が独立した音調単位を形成していることを意味している。もし nation（の概念）が文脈に存在しているならば、次のようになるだろう。

```
                         év'ry man to do his dú
   The nátion expects
                                              ty.        （伊達が改変）
```

(ii) 他の文における名詞主語のステータスを検討してみよう。

a.　A: Everything OK after the operation?

　　B: Don't talk to me about it! *The butcher charged me a thousand bucks!*

この場合、*butcher* は初出の語であるが外科医の蔑称である。文脈から判断して、*butcher* は predictable であり既知情報である。では、①と②のうち、どちらが適切なイントネーションか。

```
①            butch                  thousand  bu
      The          er charged me a
                                            cks.
```

```
②            butcher charged me a  thousand  bu
      The                                   cks.         Ladd (1980: 65)
```

b.　He wasn't a damned valet and he wasn't a damned bodyguard…He took care of money, airplane reservations, getting the band to where they were supposed to go. *The cat worked his ass off.*　　　注：cat　（俗語）男、奴

```
①      cat              ass
    The      worked his
                          off.
```

```
②      cat worked his  ass
    The
                      off          (ibid.: 65-6)
```

ここで、cat——俗語で guy の意味——は初出語であるが、文脈から既知内容である。各ペアーとも、②が適切である。

課題 60　**It's not nice, getting old.**

(i) 標題の文は、後半部が前半部の概念を補強している。「下降調＋上昇調」という複合音調で言われる。

It's ⌐not ↘nice, ｜ getting ↗old.

これは、口語英語によく見られる現象である。真主語が後置されている。そう言えば、日本語でも相手のネクタイに目をやって「どなたの好み、このタイは？」という倒置表現があるが、イントネーションは重要ではない。

> There is also a spoken construction involving the displacement of the subject to the end of a statement. Here, too, we usually find a fall-plus-rise tone pattern…The displaced subject, in a separate IP, has a dependent rise (or less commonly fall-rise). 　　　　　Wells (2006: 81-2)

以下で類似例を示そう。

a.　They're ⌐all the ↘same, ｜ ⌐these poli↗ticians.

b.　It's a ⌐real ↘nuisance, ｜ ⌐that ↗dog.

c.　It ⌐(¹)can be ↘dangerous, ｜ ↗skiing.

d.　They're ⌐all over the ↘kitchen, ｜ ⌐those ↗cockroaches.

e.　It's ↘beautiful, ｜ ⌐this part of the ↗country.

f.　It's so ↘boring, ｜ ⌐being at home a↗lone all day.

g.　When he lost Tommy in the car accident, he just couldn't live with that. I didn't blame him. It's ⌐not ↘right, ｜ ⌐losing your ↗children.

h.　A: McKenzie? Is he dead?

　　B: Yes, sir.

　　A: ⌐Good ↘man, ｜ Mc↗Kenzie.

i.　I ⌐can't ↘stand it, ｜ ⌐cigarette ↗smoke.

j.　We ⌐have ↘everything in the world, ｜ you and ↗I.

k.　He ↘died, ｜ a ⌐happy ↗man.　（あの幸せだった男は生涯を終えた）

　　ところで、k とは違う構文として、以下がある。

　　He ⌐died a ⌐happy ↘man.　（彼は、幸せに生涯を終えた；He ⌐died ↘happily.）

文献からの解説を紹介しよう。

　　① He died a happy <u>man</u>.　（subjective complement 主格補語）

　　② He <u>died</u>, ｜ a happy <u>man</u>.　（apposition, implying 'he'd always been a happy man' he と happy man は同格）　　Tench (1996: 44)

また、Bolinger (1989: 73) には、以下のような模式図がある。

```
        great ma
He's a            po              （ナポレオンは偉大な男だった）
        n, Na  leon.
```

主格補語であるか、それとも、その同格であるかを決定するのは、文脈である。

In the village he lived in, he only had Sue and Sally Baker to choose from and them he wouldn't look twice at. *So he* ⌐*died a* ↘*bachelor*.

注：not look twice at... を見向きもしない（関心がない）

これは、So he remained single all his life. の意味だから、前者のケースである。

(ii) かつて、映画 *My Fair Lady* を観ているときに、気になるイントネーションを聞いた。それは、Eliza が、Higgins から自分の素性を疑われて抗議したときのことばである。以下のように言っている。

l.　I'm a ⌐good ↘girl, | ↗I am.

この文では、《主語＋ be 動詞》の反復が見られ、前者は下降調で、後者は上昇調で言われる。

Another type of tail, also with a rising tone, repeats the *subject+verb* in order to reinforce what we have just said. It is similar to a *tag*, and is used mainly in very informal speech.

A:　Maybe you could borrow the money from your brother?

B:　No, he's incredibly MEAN ↘, HE is ↗.

　　　Hewings (2007: 86)

m.　He is a ↘genius, | ↗John is.

n.　It ⌐went on ⌐far too ↘long, | his ↗lecture did.

o.　He ↘drinks now and then, | my ↗father does.

以下では、語順が逆になっている。　（注：イギリス英語用法）

p.　She's a ⌐lovely ↘girl, | is ↗Ann.

q.　They're ⌐good ↘sports, | are your ↗brothers.

r.　He ⌐speaks good ↘English, | does ↗Carlos.

課題 61　尻上がり口調 uptalk

　まず最初に、uptalk とは、「尻上がり口調」のことである。別称として、upspeak とか high rising terminal (HRT) とも言われる。

A:　Where did you get your degree?

B:　Corⁿell[1]　　　　Ladd (1980: 63)

話者 B の uptalk は、あたかも "Have you heard of it?" or "Is that good enough?" と言っているかのように聞こえ、相手に伺いを立てているというか、遠慮がちな印象を与える。

この uptalk に関しては、決まってオーストラリア英語が話題になる。

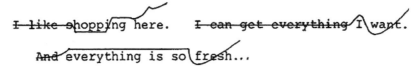

I like shopping here.　　I can get everything I want.

And everything is so fresh...

Platt & Platt (1975: 68)

かつて、NHK「ラジオ英語会話」の現地収録番組で以下のやりとりがあった。

A:　Hi, is this your first time to climb Ayers Rock?

B:　No, *it's the* ↗*second time*.

A:　How's the second time around?

B:　So far, better. |*Better pre* ↗*pared*.

A:　So you plan to make it to the top?

B:　Hopefully. ↗*Yes*.

A:　Where're you from?

B:　*From* ↗*Sydney,* | *Aus* ↗*tralia*.

　オーストラリア英語に見られる uptalk は、かつて、本国イギリスに対する劣等感と関係があるという論評があった。つまり、自分の発言に対する自信の欠如が背景にあるとされた（Do you approve of what I say?）。しかし、今日では、彼らの uptalk は、一方的に喋るのではなく、聞き手からの相づちを期待したり、two-way communication を図ろうという気配り——Are you with me?——の表れであると考えられている。

　Because the attitudinal function of rising tunes in English generally is to signal uncertainty, the HRT is sometimes confused with lack of confidence.

However, research has shown that the HRT has an important discourse function by involving the listener in the creation of the dialogue. It is used more frequently when delivering new information and is considered a mechanism for checking that the discourse partner is following the complex new information being presented.　　　　　　Cox (2012: 86)

さて、uptalk は、オーストラリア社会で、どのような人びとの間に広まっているのか。ある調査によると、age, gender, social class 別の probability は、

Age: 11-14 yrs 64%, 15-19 yrs 67%, 20-39 yrs 51%, 40+ yrs 21 %

Gender: Male 41%, Female 59%

Social Class: Middle 40%, Upper working 51%, Lower working 59%
　　　Collins & Blair (1989: 29-30)

これは 30 年以上も前のデータであるが、今日でも通説になっていることは、uptalk の頻度は、若年層ほど高く、また、男性よりも女性のほうが高く、中流階層よりも労働者階層のほうが高い。

今日 uptalk は、イギリスやアメリカでも日常的な現象である。

・Since about 1980 a new use of a rising tone on statements has started to be heard in English. It is used under circumstances in which a fall would have been used by an earlier generation (and a fall is still felt to be more appropriate by most speakers of English).　　　Wells (2006: 37)

・Use of uptalk is widespread across the English-speaking world today. It's perhaps most common in Australia, but is also heavily used in America and by many in Britain, though not typically by older British speakers.
　　　Lindsey (2019: 108)

では、uptalk の社会的評価はどのようなものだろうか。uptalk は、会話を進めていく上で必要な comfortable interaction や turn-taking を促進するのに有効な機能を果たしている。長い話になると Are you with me so far? と同等の働きをしている。しかし、uptalk は諸刃の剣であり、状況次第では、insecure, unconfident の印象を与えるので、unprofessional である。

Many people are annoyed by uptalk, and make judgements of speakers who use it, just like they do with regional accents. It's even been suggested that it can have a negative effect on your job prospects. A survey of 700 UK company bosses published in 2014 found that they were prejudiced against uptalk in job interviews. This is because, in the bosses' opinion, it makes the interviewee sound uncertain, insecure, and emotionally weak. The author of the report…concluded, 'If you know what you're talking about and want to be respected, then you need to sound like you know it.'

Setter (2019: 79)

この件について、友人 Judy Gilbert からメールが届いた。

When one of my daughters became a lawyer, I commented that perhaps she shouldn't use that final rise so much (she wants everybody to like her). She brushed off this remark until she read a verbatim record of her first deposition (a legal interrogation) and realized she was quite frequently ending a sentence with "OK?" It did not convey the confidence appropriate to her position as an attorney.

参考：尻上がり口調について

本文では、uptalk は、TPO 次第では、自信の欠如を示唆するというマイナスイメージが述べられていたが、私が知る限りでは、これは friendliness や politeness の表れのこともある。初対面の対話者どうしでは uptalk がよく聞かれる。

A: So where're you from?

B: ➚ *Plymouth*.

A: Are you? I'm from there, too.

B: Small world!

A: I tend bar in a pub nearby. What do you do?

B: |Wait ➚tables in a restaurant…

このような状況では、下降調よりも、上昇調のほうが社交的潤滑油（social lubricant）として相応しい話し方である感じがする。

課題 62　**Spiel: a case of poor prosody**

最初に、spiel とは、(軽蔑的に)「口上」のことである。辞書定義では、a long speech that somebody has used many times, that is intended to persuade you to believe something or buy something--- *Oxford Advanced Learner's Dictionary* 動詞では、talk a lot or talk quickly の意味である。また、prosody は、話しことばのアクセント、リズム、イントネーション、ポーズ（休止）の総称である。

　私は、旅行で英語圏の国に到着しホテルにチェックインしたら、まず最初にする主な行動は、観光用の市内巡回バス（hop-on-and-off bus，1 周約 50 分）に乗ることである。バスには 2 種類あって、ドライバーが一人二役で commentator を兼ねるものと、ガイド（commentator）が乗車しているものがある。後者の場合、写真にあるように、ガイドは、進行方向の先頭部分に立ち、乗客に向かってマイクを使って解説をする。もし open-air upper-deck の後方席に座っていたら、ear phone なしには街の騒音と風の音のために解説が聞き取れない。私は、出来る限りガイドの前に座ることにしている。解説の合間にガイドと会話ができる。

さて、commentaries の件であるが、未熟なガイドは、実に聴き取りにくい。とかく早口で、commentaries というよりも一本調子の **spiel** である。単に暗唱した内容を機械的にペラペラと（volubly）言っている印象を与える。外国人の乗客が多くいるのに、それにはお構いなしにまくしたてる。そんな場合、私はバスが最終 stop に着いても下車せずに、もう一周、同じガイドの「お付き合い」をする。お陰で、再出発前の待機時間中に少し彼／女と親しくなれる特典がある。また、同じ commentaries を 2 回聴くと少し理解度が増す。

　2017 年に第 104 代カンタベリー大主教 Rowan William（当時 Master of Magdalene College, Cambridge University）を訪問するために Cambridge に行ったときも、例によって、自由時間に Good Friday bus に乗った。ガイド

は、新米で、20 歳代後半の学生でアルバイトらしかった。観光シーズンでは
なく、乗客が少なかったので、多分、実地研修中であったのだろう。解説の合
間に乗客に背を向けて、頻繁に「台本」に目を通していた。彼は、地名や人
名、歴史的出来事を、抑揚乏しく、まくしたてたので、聴き取りが困難であっ
た。しかも、北部訛り（注1）があるよう

だった。そのことを Williams 師に話すと
同情してもらった。Cambridge 大学の学
生は、地方出身者が多く、3 年間の在学
中には regional accent を完全には払拭で
きない学生がいるとのことであった。そ
の上、今日では Oxbridge accent 以外の
accents も寛容に見られているので（注2）、学生の中には prestige accent を必
死で身に付けようという incentive が弱くなっている者が少なからずいるとの
ことであった。

　　参考：Williams 師訪問の理由は、著書 *Tokens of Trust* の翻訳書を教文館（銀座）か
　　　　ら出版したからである。お会いしたいという申し出があった。学寮長の公邸で
　　　　お会いした。

　帰国後、Cambridge のガイドの **spiel** のことを SUPRAS にメールし愚痴る
と、いろいろなコメントが一斉配信された。以下は、その一部である。

　・Anybody saying a **spiel** many times begins to slur it.
　・When I flew from Dallas to San Antonio, Texas, for TESOL this past
　　spring, the flight attendant went into a **spiel**. It was clearly English (I've
　　heard it enough times to pick up words) but it was almost completely
　　incomprehensible, far more so than usual. To me, her prosody was
　　affected, and this seemed to have the greatest effect on my ability to
　　understand her. I just wish I had had my recorder with me.
　・I once flew from Chicago to Warsaw on LOT airlines, and had
　　comprehension problems with the flight attendants' English. Those
　　who could not speak English fluently were easy to understand, but one
　　purportedly "fluent" attendant was the one who gave us a **spiel** over the
　　PA, and I honestly could never tell when she was speaking Polish and
　　when English.　　注：PA (public address system)

- My own story: I was touring the 18th century British ship, the Victory, and was baffled by the speech of the young sailor who was giving us the **spiel**. Then a young British lady behind me said to her companion. "What's he saying?"

- I suppose that if the crew were bored out of their minds, and they managed to convey the **spiel** through their intonation choices, they don't seem to be interested in engaging in communication with their customers. What they are doing is 'saying the words' out presumably because international and company guidelines require them to do so.

　一方、長距離観光バス（coach）のドライバーは、中年以上の年齢で経験豊かなプロフェッショナルである。運転しながらでも commentaries は明瞭である。長い乗車時間であるが、乗客を上手に entertain してくれる。絶えず、ミラー越しに乗客と eye contact を心がけ、乗客の反応を確かめているようだ。何しろ、朝に発車してからから夕方まで、運転席から commentaries をする

話術は大したものであった。それは、spiel とは対極にあった。アイルランドを訪問したときも、素晴らしい driver/commentator に恵まれた。西海岸にある Galway から Connemara 地方に向かっている道中、*The Quiet Man*（John Ford 監督、John Wayne & Maureen O'Hara 主演、1952 年作品）の撮影舞台となった Cong 村に近づいた時、ドライバーが、名調子で映画の解説をしてくれた。若い頃、何度も観た映画であり、よく理解できた。ただ、彼が、解説の前に乗客（30 名程度）に「この映画を見たことがある人？」と問いかけたら挙手したのは、私を含めて年配らしきの 3, 4 名の男性だけだった。若い男女は、名前すら聞いたこともないと言っていた。ロンドンのテムズ川クルーズ船に乗ったとき、PA を通しての spiel は、雑音まじりだったこともあって、よく理解できなかった。私は、操舵室の横のデッキまで行き、開いた窓越しに commentaries を聞いたが、やっぱり理解が難しかった。

　ここで私が言いたいことは、どんな話題であれ、あらかじめ聞き手のほうに地名と人名などについて予備知識がないと聴き取りに苦労するということである。私は、課題 4 の冒頭で次のように述べている。

「談話（discourse）において、話し手が留意することは、聞き手に対する配慮である。通常、話し手は、相手が全く知らないことを述べるのではなく、聞き手がある程度の予備知識をもっていることを前提として、または、両者の間に共通の認識があることを前提にして、それに新しい事柄、情報を付け加える」。

先ほど、非難した学生アルバイトのガイドの commentaries が聞き取り困難であったのは、明らかに私の予備知識不足のせいでもある。その証拠として、同じ commentaries を再度聴くと理解度が向上した。

　一般に、話し手と聞き手の知識または認識範囲は、下図を用いて表すことができる。それは、knowledge and view of the world のことである。当然、それらは互いに異なっているが、重なり合っている部分（斜線部分）もある。そのような部分には、相手が既に了解または推定しているであろうと、話し手が想定する内容も含まれている。そして、共有される領域（common ground）は動的であり、会話が進むにつれて増大していく。同じことが、上記の述べたガイド（話し手）と乗客の私（聞き手）についても言える。彼の commentaries を再度聴くと、共有領域が増えたので、私の理解が深まった。一方、イギリス人乗客とガイドの関係では、当初から共有領域はもっと広いので、commentaries の理解度がもっと高い。

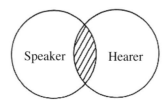

注1：
 ・北部訛りとすぐ分かるのは母音 /a/ である（*as in bath, dance, path,* etc.）
 ・母音 /ʌ/ に代わって /ʊ/、または、比較的若い世代の人びとの間では /ə/ が用いられる（as in: *bus, butter, cup,* etc.）。但し、London の発音は、/ˈlɔndən/、また、one と none, won では /ɔ/ である。
 ・rain や stay の母音は /e:/、また、road や home の母音は /o:/ となる。
注2：今日では、BBC では地方訛りのアナウンサーやレポーターが採用されている。

第二章　序論

　多くの英語教員は、授業で英語のリズムやイントネーションの指導をする余裕がないと言う。確かにそうかもしれないが、実際には、これらの指導に長い時間をかける必要はなく、教材の朗読の練習中に、ほんのわずかな時間を割くだけでよい。つまり、教科書の lesson 中の文脈と関連させてリズムやイントネーションを指導するほうが効果的である。最初のうちは毎回少しずつ数分かけて生徒の意識をそちらのほうへ向けていく。できれば、クイズやエピソードを提示して生徒の興味を高めるのも得策である。実際の場面や文脈とは関係のないイントネーションに指導は、無味乾燥である。一番手っ取り早い方法は、授業で生徒を指名してレッスンの一部を朗読させたあと、「声が大きくてよかった」とか「はきはきとした読み方でした」などの曖昧なコメントをしないで、褒めた後は、イントネーションについて改善点を指摘することである。抽象的／印象的コメントではなく建設的批評（constructive criticism）を心がけたい。その際、<u>必ず核強勢を置くべき語に言及する</u>。英語の文では、必ず1カ所が、他よりも目立って発音される特徴があることを、その都度、言及する。中高レベルの教材では、文中で核強勢のある語を見つけるのは比較的容易である。この点を軽視したイントネーション練習はまったく意味がない。個々の単語の発音では、地域、世代、教育レベルなどによって微小な違いがあるけれども、核強勢配置の理念は共通している。ただし、同じ文でも解釈の違いによって、イントネーションに個人差がある。

　以下は、英語教員として必要な心構えに関する文章である、

　イントネーションを練習するには、モデルリーディングを聴くのはいい方法であるが、基本的な規則が身についていないと、その場限りの練習になり、応用力が養えない。私が勧める方法は、モデルリーディングを聴く前に、自分でイントネーションを予想し、自分の予想したものとモデルリーディングとの間のズレを研究するものであり、このほうがはるかに主体的な練習となる。その際、留意するべきことは、特定の場面の場合、複数のネーテイブスピーカーが読めば、個人差があることである。The earth is round. や It snows in winter. などは誰が言っても同じイントネーションであろう。一方、具体的な状況のある場合、読み手によって違いがある。自分の予想が、実際の朗読と違っていても、その予想が間違いであったとは言えない。文中の内容についての解

釈の仕方が違うだけのこともある。従って、1人のネーテイブスピーカーの読み方を金科玉条のように思うのは間違いである。

　文は、機械的な読み方をしない限り、読み手によって韻律の付け方やイントネーションに個人差がある。複数のモデルリーディングを聴くことによって、比較対照することができ、理解度が深まる。しかし、個人差があると言っても、ネーテイブスピーカーの発音は、音声学上の規則を踏まえているので、読み方がてんでばらばらになることはない。彼らは、（無意識であるが）一定の法則を共有している。但し、文の解釈が互いに異なることもある。

　以下の表は、私が関係した英語暗唱大会（大阪府内女子中学生）で5名の審査員が評価した点数を示している。このコンテスト（今年で65年の歴史がある）では、大阪府知事賞、大阪府教育委員会賞、朝日新聞社賞、主催団体賞が授与されるので、ハイレベルな発表が聞かれる。審査委員長の私以外は、アメリカ、イギリス、カナダ出身の英語教育関係者である。集計表では、Aの評価が厳しい。British Council Osaka（今は撤退）の館長（女性）である。翌年のコンテストでは、新しく赴任した館長（課題14）が審査員を務めたが、やはり、他の審査員の評価と比べて辛口の評価点である。これは、発表者の発音が、どちらかと言えば、アメリカ英語よりであったからであろう。とは言え、音声ルールを踏まえての審査結果であるので、かなりのコンセンサスが見られる。

集　計　表

登壇順	A	Date	B	C	D	備考	成績順位
47	86	90	100	94	93		1
51	85	80	92	91	93		2
37	80	95	82	93	85		3
49	70	85	94	90	87		4
18	72	90	88	91	82		5
34	77	95	66	88	85		6
33	86	90	78	77	80		6
5	74	90	88	70	82		6
50	73	80	90	65	85		6
46	67	80	94	69	83		6
48	69	80	90	66	85		11
43	71	80	84	76	78		12
35	68	80	76	71	82		13
31	70	85	76	66	80		13
52	80	70	72	65	88		15
19	52	70	94	70	78		16
1	55	80	72	72	77		17
12	54	75	82	75	70		17
15	65	70	72	66	78		19
45	80	60	64	66	80		20

　第二章では、伊達（2019）と同じように、発音練習用資料として5題を提示している。朗読は、Bill Rockenbach 教授と Warren Wilson 司祭による。また、各課の最後には、韻律分析——発音上の留意事項——をつけている。

朗読資料の韻律分析（Ⅰ）

Eden Project

A: Planning to go away this year?

B: We've been away. We had a week in Cornwall.

A: And how was it?

B: Oh, we had a marvelous time. The only trouble was the weather.

Unfortunately, it rained most of the time.

A: So what did you do during all this rain?

B: Well, the best thing we did was to go to the Eden Project.

A: What was that?

B: It was a kind of museum of ecology. I found it utterly fascinating.

It's more like a theme park, really. There's a lot to do, and the children

loved it, too.　　　　　　　　(adapted from Wells (2006: 256))

韻律分析：

1. ˈPlanning to go a ↗way this year?
this year は、末尾にあってピッチが最も高いので、核強勢を受けると勘違いするかもしれない。しかし、-way でピッチの目立った上昇が起こるので、そこに核強勢が来る。

2. We've ↘been away.

3. Oh, we had a ↘marvelous time.
これは、名詞節の強勢配置の規則に違反しているが、have a great/splendid time も同じ強勢配置になる。一方、have a ˈgood ↘time となる。

4. Un ↗fortunately, | it rained…　または、Un ↘↗fortunately, | it rained…
文副詞は、文頭では上昇調または下降上昇調になる。

5. it ↘rained most of the time. では、文末の「時の副詞（句）」most of the time は、文アクセントを受けない。ただし、一般に、「時の副詞（句）」は、a certain degree of importance を付与される場合は、（低）上昇調になる。

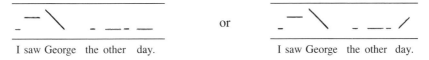

I saw George the other day.　　　　or　　　　I saw George the other day.

6. during all this rain は、既知情報であるので文アクセントを受けない。但し、5 の場合と同じように低上昇で言われることもある。

7. 音調単位の区切りは、the best thing we did ｜ was to go to the Eden Project または、the best thing we did was ｜ to go to the Eden Project

8. It's ｜more like a ↘theme park, ｜ ↗really.　文末の「副詞相当語／句」 (adverbial) は、通例、（低）上昇調になる。

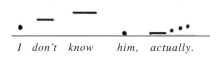

I don't know　him, actually.

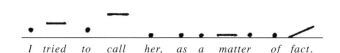

I tried to call her, as a matter of fact.

主文に追随する他の副詞を紹介しよう。

a. A: Don't you like him?

B: I ↘*don't*, ｜ ↗*frankly*.

b. A: Whose fault is it?

B: ↘*Mine*, ｜ ↗*actually*.

c. A: You're leaving soon, aren't you?

B: To ↘*morrow*, ｜ *as a matter of* ↗*fact*.

d. A: Should we tell John?

B: *He already* ↘*knows*, ｜ *ap* ↗*parently*.

9. The ↘children loved it, ｜ ↘too.

注：Eden Project: イギリスの南西部 Cornwall 州にある近未来的庭園。世界最大級の温室がある。

朗読資料の韻律分析（Ⅱ）

Revenge

A doctor had trouble with his plumbing. The pipes in his bathroom began to leak. The leak became bigger and bigger.

Even though it was 2 a.m., the doctor decided to phone his plumber. Naturally the plumber got sore being awakened at that hour of the morning. "For Pete's sake, Doc," he wailed. "This is some time to wake up a guy!"

"Well," the doctor answered testily. "You've never hesitated to call me in the middle of the night with a medical problem. Now it just happens I've got a plumbing emergency."

There was a moment's silence. Then the plumber spoke up. "Right you are, Doc," he agreed. "Tell me what's wrong."

The doctor explained about the leak in the bathroom.

"I'll tell you what to do," the plumber offered. "Take two aspirins every four hours, drop them down the pipe. If the leak hasn't cleared up by the morning, phone me at the office."

韻律分析：

1. A ↘doctor ǀ had ˈtrouble with his ↘plumbing. （水回り、排水）
   初出の名詞や名詞句は、独自の音調単位になる。

2. ↗Naturally the plumber got sore…　または↘↗Naturally the plumber got sore…

3. the ˈplumber got ↘↗sore ǀ being a ↘wakened at that hour of the morning. この場合、at that hour of the morning は、既に文脈にある内容であるので尾部となる。尾部は、-wak- を起点として起こる下降調の終結部を引き継ぎ、低いピッチで言われる。ただし、hour と morn(ing) にはリズム強勢（拍、beat）がある。

4. For ˈPete's ↘↗sake は間投詞である。一方、「ピートの利益のために」（for Pete's benefit)」という意味では、for ↘↗Pete's sake となり、sake は「虚辞」になる。

5. ˈThis is ↘↗some time ǀ to ˈwake ↘up a guy! では、some は、「たいへんな、普通ではない」の意味である。類例として、ˈThat was ↘some

203

party!（この場合、party は既に文脈にあるという前提である。）

6. 初出名詞 guy は、虚辞 person と同義であるので文アクセントを受けない。類例として、I'm ˈgoing to ↘see a guy.

7. ˈYou've ˈnever ˈhesitated to call ↘↗me ǀ in the ˈmiddle of the ↘↗night ǀ with a ↘↗medical problem. では、me は対比用法として強勢を受ける。また、domestic/legal/mechanical problem という組み合わせでは、problem は虚辞の扱いになる。人生には諸々の問題がつきものであるという発想があるからである。課題 54 参照。

8. ↗Now ǀ it just ↘↗happens ǀ … または ↘↗Now となる。

9. ˈplumbing eˌmergency は複合語である。

10. ↘↗Then ǀ the ˈplumber spoke ↘↗up,…

11. ↘Right you are, または ↘Right you ǀ ↘↗are,

12. ˈevery four ↗hours では、four は三連規則により強勢を受けない。
参考：He was here for ˈfour ↘hours.

13. If the ˈleak ˈhasn't cleared ˈup by the ↘↗morning でも、cleared は三連規則により強勢を受けない。

14. drop them down the pipe において、
pipe は厳密には wind（pipe 気管）のことであるが、ここでは「喉」の意味である。言い換えると、drop the aspirins down the throat である。参考までに、何かを口に入れて、むせたとき、It went down the wrong pipe/ way と言う。

朗読資料の韻律分析（Ⅲ）

Coffee Shop Confusion

The customer(A) can't hear very well, which makes the waiter(B) impatient.

A: Let's see. What can I have to start with?

B: Soup or salad?

A: What's super salad?

B: What do you mean, super salad?

A: Didn't you say you have a super salad?

B: No, we don't have anything like that. Just plain green salad.

Or you can start with tomato soup.

A: OK. Well, what do you have for dessert?

B: We have ice cream, pie and apples.

A: I don't care much for pineapples.

B: Are you making a joke or what? We have ice cream, pie, and apples.

A: OK. OK. Just give me the soup and a piece of apple pie.

B: Sorry, the only pie we have is berry.

A: Very what?

B: Excuse me?

A: You said the pie was very something. Very good?

B: I said the pie was berry — blackberry! And if you will wait just a moment,
I'm going to get another waiter to serve you.

韻律分析：

1. ˈcan't ↘hear well では、well は文アクセントを受けない。" ↘Eat well,
↘live well!" という TV コマーシャルがある。他に、sleep well とか
speak English well などでも well は文アクセントを受けない。

2. ˈWhat can I ↘have │ to ↗start with? では、to start with は独立不定詞で
あり、at first と同義である。これは、文末の副詞相当句（final adverbial）
であるので、通例、（低）上昇調で言われるが、時には、単に尾部となる
こともある。

3. Soup or salad? は、原則的には、上昇調＋下降調で言われるが、早いテン
ポでは、平板調＋下降調になることもある。課題 56 参照。

Model:

Would you prefer ⌍coffee | or ⌌tea?

   → Would you prefer ⌐coffee | or ⌌tea?   Wells (2006: 225)

この場合、Soup or salad? は、Super salad? のように聞こえる。

4. No, | we ˈdon't have ˈanything ⌌like that. しかし、話者の感情移入が あって「そんなもの」という意味では、…ˈanything like ⌌that となる。

5. Just ˈplain green ⌌salad では、三連規則により green の強勢が弱まる。

6. toˌmato ˈsoup は複合語だが、最初の要素 tomato が「材料」に相当する ので、名詞句と同じ強勢配置パターンになる。ˌapple ˈpie, ˌpaper ˈbag, etc.

7. I ˈdon't ⌌care much for pineapples.　または I ˈdon't ⌌care much | for ⌍pineapples.

8. Are you ˈmaking a ⌍joke | or ⌌what?

9. Ex⌍cuse me?　ここは、相手の言ったことを聞き洩らしたのではなく、 当惑の気持ちが込められている。

朗読資料の韻律分析（Ⅳ）

A Very Special Passenger

The big bus pulled over to the bus stop. Mr. Smith got on the bus. He looked around and laughed. "I see there's a seat for me today," he said to the bus driver. The driver laughed, too. Mr. Smith was the only passenger on the bus.

"We'll have another passenger soon,"said the driver. "We'll pick him up at West Street."

"How do you know?" asked Mr. Smith.

"Oh, I pick him up at West Street almost every day," the driver said with a smile. "He's a very special passenger."

"Is that so?" said Mr. Smith. "What's so special about him?"

"He doesn't have to pay to ride on my bus," the driver told him.

"That is special!" Mr. Smith said in surprise. "Why is that?"

"He saved a little girl who fell in the river. The father of the little girl is a bus driver. So now he is a very special passenger to all bus drivers."

"Do you stop for him whenever you see him?" asked Mr. Smith.

"No," said the driver. "If he wants to ride, he stands at a bus stop like anyone else. When he gets on, he goes right to his seat in the back."

Mr. Smith was surprised. "Doesn't he like to sit and talk to you?"

The driver shook his head. "He isn't much of a talker," he said.

The bus turned into West Street.

"There he is!" said the bus driver.

Mr. Smith looked around. He didn't see anyone at the bus stop. The bus stopped. The door opened. Into the bus came a big brown dog. The dog walked right to the back of the bus. He got right down on the back seat.

"There he is," said the driver, laughing. "He is my very special passenger."

韻律分析：

1. The ˈbig ↘bus │ │pulled ˈover to the ↘bus stop.

   初出の名詞（句）が主語の時、独自の音調単位を形成する。句動詞 pull over では、副詞が動詞よりも強い強勢を受ける。pull over to は「停車する」の意味。馬車時代に、御者が手綱を引いて馬を道路脇に寄せたことが

語源である。

2. Mr. ↘Smith | was the ˈonly ↘passenger on the bus.　名詞（句）が主語である場合、しばしば独立した音調単位を形成する。

3. We'll ˈhave aˈnother ↘passenger soon，または、We'll ˈhave aˈnother ↘passenger | ↗soon,　(two tone units)

4. ˈHow do you ↘know?
日本人学習者は、間違って how に核強勢を置く傾向がある。

5. I ˈpick him up at ˈWest Street… では、句動詞中の副詞 up は三連規則により、強勢を失うこともある。（optional）

6. Is ˈthat ↘so?　これは単なる相づちである。もし上昇調で言うと、疑いをもっている印象を与える。

7. ˈWhat's so ˈspecial a↘bout him?　むしろ special に核強勢が来るのではないかと思うだろう。それも可能であるが、通例は、慣用的に about に核強勢を置く。類例として
　ˈTell me ˈall a↘bout him.
　There's no ˈdoubt a↘bout it.
　There's no ˈquestion a↘bout it.
なお、他の option として ˈWhat's so ˈspecial about ↘him? もあり得る。その場合、「そんな乗客に」という強意用法である。

8. He doesn't ˈhave to ↘pay | to ˈride on ↘my bus…
この場合、pay と my を共に major information であると見なしている。
または He ˈdoesn't have to ↘↗pay | to ˈride on my ↘bus…

9. ˈThat ↘is special!　(=That certainly is special.)　be 動詞に強勢を置くのは、文全体を強調する手段である。類例として、
A: Do you think that he is capable of doing the job?
B: Sure, | he ↘is capable.

10. So ↘↗now | he is a ˈvery special ↘passenger | to ↘all bus drivers.
この場合、very special passenger に再焦点が置かれる。

11. like ˈanyone ↘else　なお、else は核強勢を受けることが多い。類例として、
ˈWhat ↘else did you see?
ˈWho ↘else came here?
ˈIs anyone ↗else coming?

There's ˈsomething ↘else ǀ I'd like to discuss with you.

12. ˈWhen he ˈgets ↗on, he ˈgoes right to his ˈseat in the ↘back.

    right は後続の句を強調する副詞だが、三連規則により強勢を失う。

13. He ˈisn't much of a ↘talker. （寡黙である）　much は、三連規則により強勢を失う。類例として

    He isn't much of a singer. （歌があまり上手くない）

    I'm not much of a public speaker.

    She is something of a singer. （少し歌が上手い）

14. ↘There he is!　または、↘There ǀ he ↘is!

    ↘Here you are.　または↘Here you ǀ ↗are.

    ↘There you go.　または↘There ǀ you ↗go.

15. The ˈbus ↘stopped. The ˈdoor ↘opened.

    文構造を見て、この短い 2 文は「出来事文（event sentence）」だと思いがちだが、決して突発的な出来事を伝えている文はなく、予定通りの動きを言っているに過ぎない。

16. ˈInto the ↘↗bus ǀ ˈcame a ˈbig ˈbrown ↘dog. または、ˈbig brown ↘dog.

    (faster tempo)

17. He ˈgot right ˈdown on the back ↘seat.

18. He is my ˈvery special ↘passenger.　(default pattern)

    他に、以下も可能である。

    ↘He is my very special passenger.　または

    ↘He ǀ is my ˈvery special ↘passenger. も可能である。

    前者では、very special passenger. の概念は既に文脈に存在している——話し手と聞き手との間の共通認識事項——という解釈である。その際、is から以降は尾部である。尾部では独自のピッチ変化が起こらない。ただし、very, special, passenger にはリズム強勢がある。

    後者では、ˈvery special ↘passenger. が再焦点を受けている。その概念を導入してから、しばらく時間が経過しているからである。

朗読資料の韻律分析（V）

Daffodils (1804)

I wandered lonely as a cloud
That floats on high o'er vales and hills,
When all at once I saw a crowd,
A host, of golden daffodils;
Beside the lake, beneath the trees,
Fluttering and dancing in the breeze.

Continuous as the stars that shine
And twinkle on the Milky Way,
They stretched in never-ending line
Along the margin of a bay:
Ten thousand saw I at a glance,
Tossing their heads in sprightly dance.

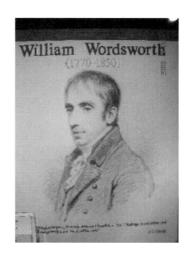

これは、イングランドのロマン派詩人 William Wordsworth（1770-1850）の代表作 Daffodils（『水仙』）である。彼は、イングランド北部の Lake District（湖水地方）出身で、湖畔に群生する黄金色の水仙を見て、その様子を4連からなる詩で謳った。水仙が風に揺れている光景を dancing という言葉で表現している。孤独な気持ちで湖畔を散策しているとき、突然現れた水仙の群れを見て、心が浮き立つような気分になった。ここでは、その一部を紹介する。

　詩には、reduced syllables と stressed syllables の「かたまり」が見られ、*cloud* と *crowd*, *hills* と *daffodils*, *trees* と *breeze* がそれぞれ脚韻（rhyme）を踏んでいる。また、1行目と6行目では、リズムに乗せるために機能語 *as* と *in* にも強勢が置かれる。　　　（朗読は Rockenbach 教授のみ）

引用文献

安倍、I. (1962)『英語イントネーションの研究』東京：研究社

Allen, W. S. (1954) *Living English Speech*. London: Longman.

Arnold, G.F. & Tooley, O.M. (1971) *Say it with Rhythm*. London: Longman

Bolinger, D. (1965) *Forms of English: Accent, Morpheme, Order* (I. Abe & T. Kanekiyo, eds.) Cambridge: Harvard University Press

(1968) *Aspects of Language*. New York: Hartcourt Brace Jovanovich

(1972a) *Intonation: Selected Readings*. Harmondsworth: Penguin

(1972b) "Accent is predictable (If you're a mind-reader)" in *Language 48*

(1986) *Intonation and Its Parts*. Stanford: Stanford Univ. Press

(1987) "Two views of accent" in Gussenhoven, Bolinger & Keijsper (eds.) *On Accent*. Bloomimgton: Indiana Univ. Linguistic Club

(1989) *Intonation and Its Uses*. Stanford: Stanford Univ. Press

(1998) "Intonation in American English" in Hirst, D & Cristo, D. (eds.) *Intonation Systems: A Survey of Twenty Languages*. London: CUP

Bolinger, D. & Sears, D. A. (1981) *Aspects of Language* 3rd edition. California: Harcourt College Pub

Bradford, B. (1988) *Intonation in Context*. Cambridge: CUP

Brazil, D. (1994) *Pronunciation for Advanced Learners of English. Student's Book*. Cambridge: CUP

Celce-Murcia, M., Brinton, D. & Goodwin, J. (2010) *Teaching Pronunciation* 2nd edition. Cambridge: CUP

Christophersen, P. (1956) *An English Phonetics Course*. New Jersey: Prentice Hall Press

Collins, P. & Blair, D. (1989) *Australian English: The Language of a New Society*. St. Lucia: Univ. of Queensland Press

Couper-Kuhlen. E. (1986) *An Introduction to English Prosody*. London: Edward Arnold

Cox, F. (2012) *Australian English: Pronunciation and Transcrption*. Cambridge: CUP

Cruttenden, A. (1984) "The relevance of intonational misfits" in Gibbon, D. & Richter,

H. (eds.) *Intonation, Accent and Rhythm*. Berlin: Walter de Gruyter

(1997) *Intonation*. Cambridge: CUP

(2014) *Gimson's Pronunciation of English*. London: Routledge

Crystal, D. (1969) *Prosodic Systems and Intonation in English* 8th edition. Cambridge: CUP

伊達，T. (2019)『教室の音声学読本』大阪：大阪教育図書

English Language Services, INC. (1967) *Stress and Intonation* Part 2. New York: Collier MacMillan International

Fuchs, A. (1984) "'Deaccenting' and 'default accent'" in Gibbon, D. & Richter, H.(eds.) *Intonation, Accent and Rhythm*. Berlin: Walter de Gruyter

Glenn, M. M. (1977) *Pragmatic Functions of Intonation* (Ph. D. Dissertation. Georgetown Univ.)

Greenbaum, S. & Quirk, R. (1990) *A Student's Grammar of the English Language*. London: Longman.

Gussenhoven, C. (1987) "Focus, mode and the nucleus" in Gussenhoven, Bolinger & Keijsper (eds.) *On Accent*. Bloomimgton: Indiana Univ. Linguistic Club

Halliday, M.A.K. & Greaves,W. (2008) *Intonation in the Grammar of English*. London: Equinox

Hewings, M. (1993) *Pronunciation* Tasks. Cambridge: CUP

(2007) *English Pronunciation in Use, Advanced*. Cambridge: CUP

Hirst, D. (1977) *Intonative Features*. The Hague: Mouton

(1998) "Intonation in British English" in Hirst, D. & Cristo, D. (eds.) *Intonation Systems: A Survey of Twenty Languages*. London: CUP

Jones, D. (1956) *The Pronunciation of English*. London: CUP

Kingdon, R. (1958) *The Groundwork of English Intonation*. London: Longman.

Knowles, G. (1984) "Variable strategies in intonation" in Gibbon, D. & Richter, H. (eds.)*Intonation, Accent and Rhythm*. Berlin: Walter de Gruyter

(1987) *Patterns of Spoken English*. London: Longman.

郡、S. (2020)『日本語のイントネーション』東京：大修館

引用文献

Ladd, R. (1980) *The Structure of Intonational Meaning*. Bloomington: Indiana Univ. Press

      (1996) *Intonational Phonology*. Cambridge: CUP

      (2008) *Intonational Phonology* 2nd edition. Cambridge: CUP

Ladefoged, P. (2001) *Vowels and Consonants*. Oxford: OUP

Lane, L. (2012) *Focus on Pronunciation*. New Jersey: Pearson Education

Leech, G & Svartvik, J. (1994) *A Communicative Grammar of English*. London: Longman.

Lewis, J. W. (不詳) "Accentuation: 'global' versus analytical stresses" carried in one of his PhonetiBlogs

Lindsey, G. (2019) *English After RP*. London: Palgrave Macmillan

Marks, J. (2007) *English Pronunciation in Use* (Elementary). Cambridge: CUP

McArthur, T. (1989) "The long-neglected phrasal verb" in *English Today* (Volume 5, Issue 2)

Oakeshott-Taylor, J. (1984) "Factuality and intonation" in *Journal of Linguistics* 20

O'Connor, J.D. & Arnold, G.F. (1973) *Intonation of Colloquial English*. London: Longman.

ピーターセン, M. (2013)『実践 日本人の英語』東京：岩波新書 1420

Platt, J. T & Platt, H. K. (1975) *The Social Significance of Speech*. Amsterdam: North-Holland Publishing Company

Prator, C. H & Robinett, B. W. (1972) *Manual of American English Pronunciation* (3rd ed.) 大浦幸男＆鴫原真一（訳）『アメリカ英語発音教本』（英潮社、昭和 63 年）

Roach, P. (2009) *English Phonetics and Phonology*. Cambridge: CUP

Rogerson, P. & Gilbert, J. B. (1990) *Speaking Clearly*. Cambridge: CUP

Schmerling, S. (1976) *Aspects of English Sentence Stress*. Austin: University of Texas Press

Schubiger, M. (1935) *The Role of Intonation in Spoken English*. Cambridge: St. Gall Fehr'sche Buchhandlung

      (1958) *English Intonation: Its Form and Function*. Tübingen: Niemeyer

Setter, J. (2019) *Your Voice Speaks Volumes*. Oxford: OUP

鈴木、T. (1996)『教養として言語学』岩波新書 460

ターニー、A. (1988)『英語のしくみが見えてくる』東京：光文社

Tench, P. (1990) *The Roles of Intonation in English Discourse*. Frankfurt am Main: Peter Lang

    (1996) *The Intonation Systems of English*. London: Cassel

Thompson, I. (1981) *Intonation Practice*. Oxford: OUP

Ward, N. (2019) *Prosodic Features in English Conversation*. Cambridge: CUP

渡辺、K. (1994a)『英語イントネーション論』東京：研究社

    (1994b)『英語のリズム・イントネーションの指導』東京：大修館書店

Wells, J. C. (2006) *English Intonation*. Cambridge: CUP

    (2014) *Sounds Interesting*. Cambridge: CUP

Woods, H. B. (1992) *Rhythm and Unstress*. Quebec: Canadian Government Publishing

Listening Practice (pp.13-4) の Answer keys

1. ˈGood ˈbye. ˈThank you for a deˈliciousˈdinner.
   詳細は、伊達（2019）pp.22-3 を参照。

2. I ˈusually get ˈup around ˈsix o'ˈclock.　詳細は、同上。

3. ˈWhat're you ˈlooking at?　（at は前置詞）

4. ˈWhat're you ˈlooking ˈup?　（up は副詞、句動詞の一部）

5. ˈAfter graduˈation, ｜ ˈwhat do you ˈwant to be?　（be は full verb）

6. ˈDuring the ˈgame, ｜ I ˈfell and ˈhurt myself.

7. ˈHearing the ˈstory, ｜ he ˈcouldn't ˈhelp himself ｜ and ˈburst out ˈcrying.
   再帰／不定／相互代名詞は、目的語用法の場合、文アクセントを受けない。

8. ˈSorry ｜ I ˈmade such a ˈfool of myself the other night. I ˈmust have been ˈdrunk.
   the other night が（低）上昇。伊達（2019）の課題 7 と 46 を参照。次頁に注がある。

9. The ˈplayers are ˈrivals ｜ but resˈpect each other.　（相互代名詞に注意）

10. They're in ˈconstant ˈcontact with one another.　（同上）

11. Have you ˈdone the ˈhomework yet?　*yet* について伊達（2019）課題 33 を参照。

12. Helˈlo? Is ˈanyone ˈhome?

13. He was ˈwith someone then.　（不定代名詞に注意）

14. She's ˈbusy at ˈwork, ｜ so she ˈcan't be here today.　または so she ˈcan't ˈbe
    here today.　*be* について伊達（2019）の課題 50 を参照。

15. ˈKen's such ˈfun to be with. または ˈKen's such ˈfun to ˈbe with.

16. ˈKeiko is a tour guide, so she ˈtravels a lot.　伊達（2019）の課題 6 を参照。

17. He's ˈnot himˈself recently.

18. I was ˈvery ˈtired, ｜ so I ˈslept most of the day.
    または so I ˈslept ｜ most of the ˈday.　(non-default pattern)

19. I ˈcan't ˈkeep it ˈquiet any longer. I've ˈjust got to ˈtell somebody.
    または I've ˈjust got to ˈtell ˈsomebody.　(non-default pattern)

20. ˈWatch what you ˈhave for ˈdinner. You ˈare what you ˈeat, you know.
    伊達（2019）の課題 9 を参照。

21. Sheˈthought to herself, "ˈSomething's wrong with me recently."

22. What you ˈneed ˈnow ｜ is self-confidence. You should ˈtrust yourself.

23. ˈPut it on the <u>ta</u>ble, ˈnot be<u>ˈside</u> it.　または ˈPut it ˈon the table, ˈnot be<u>ˈside</u> it.

    この場合、table は既知内容。

24. She ˈhad a ˈworried ˈ<u>look</u> on her face.　伊達（2019）の課題 8 を参照。

25. [What's your job?] I ˈhaven't ˈ<u>got</u> a job. I'm beˈ<u>tween</u> jobs.

参考：Answer key #8 では、↘Sorry ｜ I made… と表記しているが、聴覚印象では、中途
　　半端な、または部分的な下降に聞こえる。下降が声域の底部まで届かない。他の箇所でも、
　　下降調は、そのように聞こえる。渡辺（1994a: 151）と（1994b: 134）によれば、部分
　　音調は、アメリカ英語の非文末位置でかなり用いられている。

Track 番号リスト表

1 - Track 1
2 - Track 2
3 - Track 4-1
4 - Track 4-2
5 - Track 4-3
6 - Track 4-4
7 - Track 5-1
8 - Track 5-2
9 - Track 5-3
10 - Track 5-4
11 - Track 6
12 - Track 7-1
13 - Track 7-2
14 - Track 7-3
15 - Track 8 (2 key sentences)
16 - Track 8 (4 more key sentences)
17 - Track 8 (i) 第1文型
18 - Track 8 (ii) 第2文型
19 - Track 9

第2章 Wilson 牧師の朗読

20 - 1. Eden Project
21 - 2. Revenge
22 - 3. Coffee Shop Confusion
23 - 4.A Very Special Passenger

第2章 Rockenbach 教授の朗読

24 - Track 1 Eden Project
25 - Track 2 Revenge
26 - Track 3 Coffee Shop Confusion
27 - Track 4 A Very Special Passenger
28 - Track 5 Daffodils

著者　伊達 民和

大阪市立大学文学部卒業、関西外国語大学大学院修了（英語学修士）。キャンベラ大学教育学部に国費留学（2 期）。大阪府立高校教諭及び大阪府教育委員会指導主事を経て、プール学院大学教授を定年退職。名誉教授。現在、日本実践英語音声学会顧問。日本英語教育音声学会副会長。芦屋聖マルコ教会（兵庫県）会員。

主な著書：『英語のリズム・イントネーションのトレーニング法——理論から実践へ——』（青山社、1998）、『映画・ドラマから学ぶ英語音法読本』（青山社、2001）、*English in Singapore — Phonetic Research on a Corpus*（共著、McGraw-Hill、2005）、『現代音声学・音韻論の視点』（共著、金星堂、2012）、『教室の音声学読本——英語のイントネーションの理解に向けて』（大阪教育図書、2019）、『英語音声学・音韻論』（共著、長瀬慶來教授古希記念出版刊行委員会代表、大阪教育図書、2022）。

監修・執筆：『実践的な英語の学び方・教え方——通訳修業、GDM 教授法、イントネーションの視点から』（大阪教育図書、2021）、『GDM で英語の授業が変わる』（大阪教育図書、2021）。

監訳・翻訳書：ローマカトリック教会ドミニコ会元総長 Timothy Radcliffe 著『なぜ教会に行くの』*Why Go to Church?: The Drama of the Eucharist*（聖公会出版、2013）及び『なぜクリスチャンになるの』*What is the Point of Being a Christian?*（教文館、2016）、第 104 代カンタベリー大主教 Rowan Williams 著『信仰のしるし』*Tokens of Trust*（教文館、2017）。

英語教師のための Intonation in Context 読本

2023 年 2 月 20 日　初版第 1 刷発行

著　者　伊達 民和
校　閲　Bill Rockenbach・牧 晋也
朗　読　Bill Rockenbach・Warren Wilson
発行者　横山 哲彌
印刷・製本　株式会社 共和印刷

発行所　大阪教育図書株式会社
〒 530-0055　大阪市北区野崎町 1-25
TEL 06-6361-5936　　FAX 06-6361-5819
振替 00940-1-115500

ISBN978-4-271-41029-4 C3082　　　落丁・乱丁本はお取り替え致します。